Warren Buffett's
Ground Rules

Warren Buffett's

Ground

Rules

Words of Wisdom from the Partnership
Letters of the World's Greatest Investor

JEREMY MILLER

P

PROFILE BOOKS

First published in Great Britain in 2016 by
PROFILE BOOKS LTD
3 Holford Yard
Bevin Way
London
WC1X 9HD
www.profilebooks.com

1 3 5 7 9 10 8 6 4 2

Printed and bound in Great Britain by
Clays, St Ives plc

A CIP catalogue record for this book is available from the
British Library.

ISBN 978 1 78125 563 6
eISBN 978 1 78283 214 0

||||||||||||||||||||||||||||||||||||||||||||||||||||||||||||||||||||||||||||||||||||||||||||||||||||||||||||||||||||||||||||||||||||||||||||||||||||

Dedicated to the memory of my dear friend and
colleague, Peter Sauer (1976–2012). Peter, you left us all too
early. While you were here, your many great achievements
were equaled only by your humbleness.

||||||||||||||||||||||||||||||||||||||||||||||||||||||||||||||||||||||||||||||||||||||||||||||||||||||||||||||||||||||||||||||||||||||||||||||||||||

The excerpts from Warren Buffett's Partnership Letters are being used with his permission.

Mr. Buffett has had no other connection with this book whatsoever. In other words, while all the wisdom is his, all the errors are mine.

To maintain the narrative flow of the excerpts, omissions are not always indicated.[1]

CONTENTS

‖‖‖

INTRODUCTION

||||||||||||||||||||||||||||||||||||||||||||||||||||||||||||||||||||||||||||||||||||

"If I was running $1 million, or $10 million for that matter,
I'd be fully invested. The highest rates of return I've ever
achieved were in the 1950's. I killed the Dow. You ought to
see the numbers. But I was investing peanuts back then. It's
a huge structural advantage not to have a lot of money. I
think I could make you 50% a year on $1 million. No, I know
I could. I guarantee that."[1]

—WARREN BUFFETT, *BUSINESSWEEK*, 1999

In 1956, Warren Buffett was working in New York with his
mentor, value investing's founder, Benjamin Graham. When
Graham decided to retire, he offered his best student a stake
in his partnership, Graham-Newman, but the twenty-five-year-
old Buffett opted to return home instead. Not long after, at the
bequest of four family members and three friends, a new investment
partnership—Buffett Associates, Ltd.—was formed. Before agree-
ing to accept their checks, however, he asked them to meet him for
dinner at the Omaha Club. Everyone went Dutch.[2]

That night, Buffett handed each of them a few pages of legal documents containing the formal partnership agreement and suggested
they not worry too much about what was in them; he assured them
there would be no surprises. The gathering was intended to discuss
something he considered much more important: the Ground Rules.
He had made carbons of this short list of precepts and carefully
went through each point. Buffett insisted on complete autonomy.
He was not going to talk about what the Partnership was actually

doing; he gave very little detail on his actual holdings. He told them, "These ground rules are the philosophy. If you are in tune with me, then let's go. If you aren't, I understand."[3]

The Ground Rules

1. In no sense is any rate of return guaranteed to partners. Partners who withdraw one-half of 1% monthly are doing just that—withdrawing. If we earn more than 6% per annum over a period of years, the withdrawals will be covered by earnings and the principal will increase. If we don't earn 6%, the monthly payments are partially or wholly a return of capital.

2. Any year in which we fail to achieve at least a plus 6% performance will be followed by a year when partners receiving monthly payments will find those payments lowered.

3. Whenever we talk of yearly gains or losses, we are talking about market values; that is, how we stand with assets valued at market at yearend against how we stood on the same basis at the beginning of the year. This may bear very little relationship to the realized results for tax purposes in a given year.

4. Whether we do a good job or a poor job is not to be measured by whether we are plus or minus for the year. It is instead to be measured against the general experience in securities as measured by the Dow-Jones Industrial Average, leading investment companies, etc. If our record is better than that of these yardsticks, we consider it a good year whether we are plus or minus. If we do poorer, we deserve the tomatoes.

5. While I much prefer a five-year test, I feel three years is an absolute minimum for judging performance. It is a certainty that we will have years when the partnership performance is poorer, perhaps substantially so, than the Dow. If any three-year or longer period produces poor results, we all should start looking around for other places to have our money. An exception to the latter statement would be three years covering a speculative explosion in a bull market.

6. I am not in the business of predicting general stock market or business fluctuations. If you think I can do this, or think it is essential to an investment program, you should not be in the partnership.

7. I cannot promise results to partners. What I can and do promise is that:

    a. Our investments will be chosen on the basis of value, not popularity;
    b. That we will attempt to bring risk of permanent capital loss (not short-term quotational loss) to an absolute minimum by obtaining a wide margin of safety in each commitment and a diversity of commitments; and
    c. my wife, children and I will have virtually our entire net worth invested in the partnership.[4]

Everyone invited to the Omaha Club that night signed on and Buffett took their checks. As new partners joined, they were each carefully taken through the ground rules. Then, every partner was sent an updated copy annually.

Over the years that followed, Buffett communicated his performance and described his activities through a series of letters to this small but growing band of followers. He used them as a teaching tool to reinforce and expand upon the concepts behind the ground rules, discuss his expectations for future performance, and make comments about the market environment. At first these were annual updates but when enough partners griped that "a year was a long time between drinks," he began writing at least semi-annually.

These "Partnership Letters" chronicle his thoughts, approaches, and reflections in the period immediately prior to his better-known tenure at Berkshire Hathaway; it was a period that delivered an unprecedented record of investing success, even when compared to his track record at Berkshire. While he expected to have good years and bad, he thought that a 10% advantage to the Dow was achievable over most 3–5 year periods and that's what he set to do.

He did far better. He consistently beat the market and never had a down year. For the entire period, he compounded partners' capital at nearly a 24% annual rate, after fees. This earlier period produced many of the best performance years of his career.

The lessons that come out of this commentary offer timeless guidance for every type of investor—from beginners and amateurs to sophisticated pros. They lay forth a consistent and highly effective set of principles and methods that avoid the trendy and technical temptations abundant in today's (or any day's) market. While they do contain the type of sophisticated analysis that should appeal to seasoned professionals, the letters also are Buffett's take on Investing 101—they provide a basic, commonsense approach that should resonate with everyone.

The Partnership Letters and their wisdom have been compiled comprehensively and accessibly for the first time in this book and include such bedrock principles as his contrarian diversification strategy, his almost religious celebration of compounding interest, and his conservative (as opposed to conventional) decision-making process. They also include his methods for investing in Generals, Workouts, and Controls, his three principal "methods of operation," which evolved in interesting and important ways over time, ways that we'll explore.

Essentially, the letters have tremendous value because they describe the mindset of a successful young investor working initially with very modest sums—a mindset that investors can adopt and use to achieve long-term success as they venture into the market themselves. They make a powerful argument for a long-term value-oriented strategy, one that is especially viable in turbulent times such as our own, when people are vulnerable to a speculative, oftentimes leveraged, short-term focus that is rarely effective in the long run.

They provide timeless principles of conservatism and discipline that have been the cornerstone of Buffett's success.

If a young Buffett were starting his Partnership today, there is little doubt he would achieve the same tremendous results. In fact, he's in print "guaranteeing" that he could earn 50% annual returns on just a few million dollars today. This high rate of return (on a small sum) would be just as feasible now as it was years ago because market inefficiencies remain, especially in smaller, less-followed businesses and because he's a brilliant investor; however, as long as stocks continue to have short memories, oscillating in value because of fear and greed, opportunities for terrific returns will always exist for all enterprising investors who can adopt the proper mindset.

As much as ever, many today lack the steadfastness to stay true to the discipline that value investing requires. In letter after letter, Buffett returns to the unchanging nature of his principles. It's an attitude-over-IQ approach—staying true to one's process without getting drawn in by the trends is one of the hardest things for even the most seasoned investors. Everyone can learn from Buffett's mastery of his own investment emotions.

Each chapter in this book is organized around a single idea or theme from the letters and follows the same basic format, starting with a summary essay intended to provide some of the backstory. Hopefully this will add historical context and allow for a fuller appreciation of the relevance of the content in our time.

Then all the critical excerpts from the letters on each topic are presented in full. This not only allows for "long drinks" from the well of Buffett's own writing but should also allow the book to be a useful reference tool for sourcing his work from this period. Aggregating all the commentary on a given topic in its own chapter is often revealing. We can see various patterns emerge over multiple letters where he's revisiting certain ideas and track the progression of his thinking, something that can be more difficult to pick up on when the letters are read chronologically.

Buffett has never published a textbook on investing, at least in the traditional sense of the word. What we do have, in addition to the articles he's written and the notes that have been taken from his talks and speeches, are his letters. In effect these represent a correspondence course that has continued from 1957 to this day, the entire length of his career. The Partnership Letters represent the first section in that course, and I'm delighted to be sharing them with you. I hope you enjoy reading them as much as I have enjoyed putting them together.

I am grateful to Mr. Buffett for entrusting me in the use of his letters in this book and note once again that he wasn't otherwise involved in this project. I've aimed to present his material in a manner that I hope he approves of and in a way that makes his teaching accessible to emerging investors and seasoned professionals alike.

Part I

CHAPTER 1

ORIENTATION

||||||||||||||||||||||||||||||||||||||||||||||||||||||||||||||||||||||||||||||||

"The availability of a quotation for your business interest
(stock) should always be an asset to be utilized if desired. If
it gets silly enough in either direction, you take advantage
of it."[1]

—JULY 12, 1966

Picture yourself in Omaha, Nebraska: It is early one evening in the fall of 1956. Elvis just debuted on *The Ed Sullivan Show* and Eisenhower is in the White House. Tonight, you and twenty other adults are filing into a classroom at the University of Nebraska Omaha for the first lecture in a course called "Investment Principles." Your teacher will be a twentysomething named Warren Buffett. As it turns out, you've chosen the seat next to Buffett's Aunt Alice, one of the original seven investors in his first partnership.

I like to think of this book, in its own way, as a re-creation of that early "Investing Principles" class, drawing on the lessons he taught in the Partnership Letters that were written during the very time this course was offered. It's your annotated guide to the basics of intelligent investing, as told through the key excerpts from almost forty of these early letters. These were the pre-Berkshire years, 1956 to 1970, a time when his capital was modest and his opportunity set was unbounded. It was a time, especially in the early days of the Partnership, when he was most like you and me in that he was able to invest in nearly everything, when no companies were too small for him to be interested.

Buffett, while investing during the day, really did teach an evening class throughout the late 1950s and 1960s and his Aunt Alice, along with a few other eventual partners, really did attend his class. After completing Dale Carnegie's course to overcome his discomfort with public speaking, Buffett taught as a way to keep up his skills. Not only that, but he was following the example of his mentor, Ben Graham, who in addition to writing letters to his investors also taught a course on securities analysis at Columbia Business School, while running Graham-Newman, his investment company.

The Bedrock Principles of Benjamin Graham

There is no better place to start a book on basic intelligent investing than with the foundational tenet of Buffett's general thinking, one that's universally shared by Graham's disciples: The market can and will at times be completely deranged and irrational in the *short term*, but over the *long term* it will price securities in line with their underlying intrinsic values.

Buffett uses his mentor's somewhat paradoxical idea as a teaching tool throughout the letters because it so effectively distinguishes what we're actually after as investors: consistently sound, rational business analysis based on logic and good reasoning that leads to the selection of securities offering the highest potential return with the lowest possible amount of corresponding risk. That's the long-term investor's approach, and it's a very different approach from trying to generate gains by speculating on what other investors will or will not do or by making guesses around short-term changes in macro variables like oil prices or interest rates. Investors, as we'll come to define the term, buy businesses; speculators "play" markets.

Investors learn to see short-term gyrations in stock prices as basically random squiggles and believe they can be largely ignored; then, because they are seen as random, no attempt is made to systematically predict them. This is simply not our game.

Over the long term, however, markets do tend to get it right and ultimately reflect the economic experience of a business into the price of its stock. Knowing this, investors therefore focus on solid long-term business analysis and conservative reasoning—that's what we believe leads to above-average results over time.

This big, foundational principle comes directly from Ben Graham, Buffett's teacher, former employer, hero, and the man who practically invented securities analysis. Known as the Dean of Wall Street, Ben Graham was a revolutionary, the first to turn what had formerly been somewhat of a "dark art" into a real profession. Buffett was consumed by Graham's ideas from the moment he encountered them—so much so that he even named his son, who is in line to become the next nonexecutive chairman of Berkshire Hathaway, Howard *Graham* Buffett. Grasping Buffett's investing principles, the part that's remained constant from the Partnership years all the way through to the present day, requires a firm understanding of several of Graham's foundational ideas and influences. Here's how it all began:

Buffett graduated a year early from the University of Nebraska–Lincoln in 1950 at the age of nineteen. He then applied to Harvard Business School but was told he would have a better chance if he re-applied in a few years. Getting turned down by Harvard was one of the luckiest things that ever happened to him. As he began looking at other business schools, he came across Columbia's catalog. In it, he discovered that the author of his favorite book, *The Intelligent Investor*, was not only alive but also teaching there. Buffett immediately applied. Several weeks later (he applied in August) he was enrolled at Columbia and not too long after that he was sitting in Graham's classroom as the star pupil. One can only imagine the intensity of the intellectual dynamic between these two men. Graham was laying Buffett's intellectual foundation and Buffett, the only student to get an A-plus, was picking up on everything Graham was putting down.[2]

After graduation, Buffett was absolutely desperate to work for Graham's investment company, but, as he later joked, he was turned down for being "overvalued" despite an offer to work for free.[3] The real reason he didn't get the job was probably more linked to Graham-Newman being one of only a few Jewish-owned investment companies; Buffett could get a good job elsewhere but other highly qualified Jews, if turned down by Graham, might be otherwise shut out.[4]

Disappointed, he returned to Omaha to join his dad in the securities brokerage business, where he continued pursuing the idea of working with Graham. A three-year steady stream of letters and stock ideas was all it took; his mentor finally relented and invited him back to New York in 1954.[5] Buffett didn't get much time at Graham-Newman, though—a year after he joined, Graham decided to retire.

Once again, now at the age of twenty-five, Buffett returned to Omaha, although this time, he didn't return to brokering stocks with his dad. This time, against the advice of both Graham and his father, he started an investing partnership of his own. He structured it in the image of what Graham had set up, and operated it mostly according to his principles. Graham and Buffett remained very close all the way through Graham's passing in 1976.

Mr. Market

Graham's most valuable explanation of exactly how short-term market inefficiency works was crystallized in his concept of "Mr. Market." The idea is that a securities market can be thought of like a moody, manic-depressive fellow who stands ready to buy or sell you a half stake in his business every day. His behavior can be wild, and irrational, and is difficult to predict. Sometimes he's euphoric and thinks highly of his prospects. Here he'll offer to sell you his stake only at the highest of prices. At other times he's depressed and doesn't think much of himself or his business. Here he offers to sell you the same stake in the same business at a much lower, bargain price. Oftentimes he's neutral. While you can never be sure what mood you will find him in, you can be sure that regardless of whether you trade with him today, Mr. Market will be back again with a new set of prices tomorrow.

Viewing the market through the lens of Graham's allegory reveals why the market price on any given day should not inform our view of a security's underlying intrinsic value. We must arrive at that figure independently and then only act when Mr. Market's mood is in our favor. That is what Buffett is driving home in his letters when he teaches, "a market quote's availability should never be turned into a liability whereby its periodic aberrations in turn formulate your judgments."[6] If you rely on the market's price to value a business, you're apt to miss opportunities to buy at times when he's depressed and sell when he's manic. You can't let the market do your thinking for you. Investors know they have to do their own work.

When You Own a Stock You Own a Business

The "work," of course, is the appraisal of business value. While short-term prices may be at the mercy of Mr. Market's mood, over the long term a stock is going to approximately track the underlying intrinsic value of the business. Or as Graham put it: "In the short term, the market is like a voting machine, but in the long term, it's more like a weighing machine." This is true because a stock, by definition, is a fractional ownership claim on an entire company. If we can value the business, we can value the stock.

It's a mathematical certainty that a company's shares, in aggregate and over the entire span of the corporation's lifetime, must produce a return exactly in line with the results of the company's business. Yes, some shareholders will do better than others in the interim depending on the timing of their purchases and sales, but in aggregate and in the end, the results of all the savvy or lucky outperformers will be matched dollar for dollar by an equal amount of underperformance from those who are naive or unlucky. Therefore, investors who through sound analysis are able to surmise the long-term future returns of a business will likely get those same long-term future returns through the ownership of its shares, as long as they are careful not to overpay.

That is why investors play for the long term. We learn through Buffett's teaching to focus our efforts on the business, not the short-term timing of when sound investments are likely to pay off. As Buffett wrote, "The course of the stock market will determine, to a great degree, when we will be right, but the accuracy of our analysis of the company will largely determine whether we will be right. In other words, we tend to concentrate on what should happen, not when it should happen."[7]

This idea is consistently stressed throughout the letters so I'll stress it again here: Stocks are not just pieces of paper to be traded back and forth, they are claims on a business, many of which can be analyzed and evaluated. If market prices of businesses (stocks) move below intrinsic values for any extended period of time, market forces will eventually act to correct the undervaluation because in the long term, the market is efficient.

"When" is not the relevant question because it's dependent on "Mr. Market," who is not reliable. It's hard to know at the time of purchase what's going to get him to wake up to the value you might see as being plainly there. However, companies often buy back their stock when they recognize it's cheap. Larger companies and private equity firms often look to acquire undervalued companies in their entirety. Market participants, aware of the potential for all of the above, often hunt for and buy such bargains, which in and of itself helps remove the discount. Buffett teaches investors to trust that the market will get it right eventually; he focuses us on finding the right businesses at the right prices, largely ignoring the timing of when to buy or when to expect the investment to work out.

Market Guessing

Another lesson Buffett stresses is that the market's mood swings can be random, making them, *by definition*, often unpredictable. Trying to figure out what's going to happen in the short term is simply too hard and so his views on macro variables (general view on stocks, rates, FX, commodities, GDP) play no part in his investing decisions. Criticisms of those who use short-term predictions to make buy or sell decisions in stocks are peppered throughout the letters. He enjoys quoting Graham: "Speculation is neither illegal, immoral nor fattening (financially)."[8]

To this day, Buffett has remained true to this idea. There are just too many variables at play. Nonetheless, many Wall Street professionals continue to make these types of predictions. One need only turn on the television to see these market pundits, all seemingly following Lord Keynes's derisive advice: "If you can't forecast well, forecast often."

As investors, we understand that the right answer to questions about what stocks, bonds, interest rates, commodities, etc., are going to do over the next day, month, quarter, year, or even several years is "I don't have the first clue." Through Buffett's insights, we learn not to fall victim to the siren songs of these "expert" opinions and churn our portfolios, jumping from guesstimate to guesstimate and allowing what could otherwise be a decent result to be consumed by taxes, commissions, and random chance. According to Buffett, predictions often tell you more about the forecaster than they do about the future.

Some advice naturally follows: Give yourself permission to embrace the "I don't have the first clue" mode of thinking. It will free you from wasting valuable time and effort and allow you to focus on thinking from the vantage point of the owner or prospective owner of an entire business you might understand and come to find as attractive. Who would sell a farm because they thought there was at least a 65% chance the Fed was going to raise rates next year?

Also, be skeptical of anyone who claims to have a clear view into the future. Here again we are reminded that you really can't out-source your thinking—you have to do it yourself. Your paid advisors, whether they do it willingly or not, will likely only steer you in the direction of doing what's good for *them*. It's just human nature. A good deal of Buffett's astonishing success during the Partnership years and beyond has come from never pretending to know things that were either unknowable or unknown. His teaching encourages other investors to embrace a similar agnostic attitude and to think for themselves.

Predictable Pullbacks

Inclusive in the list of unknowables is when a big drop in the market is going to come. This is yet another key orienting principle that Buffett drew from Graham and Mr. Market. The market is inevitably going to slump into truly dour moods from time to time—very little can typically be done to avoid getting caught in the downdrafts. Buffett reminds investors that during such periods even a portfolio of extremely cheap stocks is likely to decline with the general market. He stresses this as an inevitable part of owning securities and that if a 50% decline in the value of your securities portfolio is going to cause you hardship, you need to reduce your exposure to the market.

The good news is that the occasional market drop is of little consequence to long-term investors. Preparing yourself to shrug off the next downturn is an important element of the method Buffett lays out. While no one knows what the market is going to do from year to year, odds are we will have at least a few 20–30% drops over the next decade or two. Exactly when these occur is of no great significance. What matters is where you start and where you end up—shuffle around the order of the plus and minus years and you still come to the same ultimate result in the end. Since the general trend is up, as long as a severe 25–40% drop isn't going to somehow cause you to sell out at the low prices, you're apt to do pretty well in stocks over the long run. You can allow the market pops and drops to come and go, as they inevitably will.

Unfortunately, those who lack this mindset often fall victim to their emotion and sell out of fear after markets have already declined. According to one study done by Fidelity, the best performing of all their account holders were those who literally forgot about their portfolios.[9] While most investors were selling when the market outlook became worrisome or even cloudy, those who ignored market sell-offs (or forgot they were invested at all) did vastly better. This is a great example: To be a successful investor, you need to separate your emotional reaction to a plunge from your cognitive ability as a rational appraiser of long-term business value. You can never let the market quote turn from an asset to a liability.

Graham described this brilliantly in *The Intelligent Investor*:

> *The true investor scarcely ever is* forced to sell *his shares, and at all other times he is free to disregard the current price quotation. He need pay attention to it and act upon it only to the extent that it suits his book, and no more. Thus the investor who permits himself to be stampeded or unduly worried by unjustified market declines in his holdings is perversely transforming his basic advantage into a basic disadvantage. That man would be better off if his stocks had no market quotation at all, for he would then be spared the mental anguish caused him by* other persons' *mistakes of judgment*.[10]

From the Partnership Letters: Speculation, Market Guessing, and Pullbacks

JANUARY 18, 1965

. . . my own investment philosophy has developed around the theory that prophecy reveals far more of the frailties of the prophet than it reveals of the future.

JULY 12, 1966

I am not in the business of predicting general stock market or business fluctuations. If you think I can do this, or think it is essential to an investment program, you should not be in the partnership.

Of course, this rule can be attacked as fuzzy, complex, ambiguous, vague, etc. Nevertheless, I think the point is well understood by the great majority of our partners. We don't buy and sell stocks based upon what other people think the stock market is going to do (I never have an opinion) but rather upon what we think the company is going to do. The course of the stock market will determine, to a great degree, when we will be right, but the accuracy of our analysis of the company will largely determine whether we will be right. In other words, we tend to concentrate on what should happen, not when it should happen.

In our department store business I can say with considerable assurance that December will be better than July. (Notice how sophisticated I have already become about retailing.) What really counts is whether December is better than last December by a margin greater than our competitors' and what we are doing to set the stage for future Decembers. However, in our partnership business I not only can't say whether December will be better than July, but I can't even say that December won't produce a very large loss. It sometimes does. Our investments are simply not aware that it takes 365 days for the earth to make it around the sun. Even worse, they are not aware that your celestial orientation (and that of the IRS) requires that I report to you upon the conclusion of each orbit (the earth's—not ours). Therefore, we have to use a standard other than the calendar to measure our progress. This yardstick is obviously the general experience in securities as measured by the Dow. We have a strong feeling that this competitor will do quite decently over a period of years (Christmas will come even if it's in July) and if we keep beating our competitor we will have to do something better than "quite decently." It's something like a retailer measuring his sales gains and profit margins against Sears'—beat them every year and somehow you'll see daylight.

I resurrect this "market-guessing" section only because after the Dow declined from 995 at the peak in February to about 865 in May, I received a few calls from partners suggesting that they thought stocks were going a lot lower. This always raises two questions in my mind: (1) if they knew in February that the Dow was going to 865 in May, why didn't they let me in on it then; and, (2) if they didn't know what was going to happen during the ensuing three months back in February, how do they know in May? There is also a voice or two after any hundred point or so decline suggesting we sell and wait until the future is clearer. Let me again suggest two points: (1) the future has never been clear to me (give us a call when the next few months are obvious to you—or, for that matter the next few hours); and, (2) no one ever seems to call after the market has gone up one hundred points to focus my attention on how unclear everything is, even though the view back in February doesn't look so clear in retrospect.

If we start deciding, based on guesses or emotions, whether we will or won't participate in a business where we should have some long run edge, we're in trouble. We will not sell our interests in businesses (stocks) when they are attractively priced just because some astrologer thinks the quotations may go lower even though such forecasts are obviously going to be right some of the time. Similarly, we will not buy fully priced securities because "experts" think prices are going higher. Who would think of buying or selling a private business because of someone's guess on the stock market? The availability of a quotation for your business interest (stock) should always be an asset to be utilized if desired. If it gets silly enough in either direction, you take advantage of it. Its availability should never be turned into a liability whereby its periodic aberrations in turn formulate your judgments. A marvelous articulation of this idea is contained in chapter two[11] (The Investor and Stock Market Fluctuations) of Benjamin Graham's "The Intelligent Investor." In my opinion, this chapter has more investment importance than anything else that has been written.

‖‖

JANUARY 24, 1968

My mentor, Ben Graham, used to say, "Speculation is neither illegal, immoral nor fattening (financially)." During the past year, it was possible to become fiscally flabby through a steady diet of speculative bonbons. We continue to eat oatmeal but if indigestion should set in generally, it is unrealistic to expect that we won't have some discomfort.

‖‖

JANUARY 24, 1962

I think you can be quite sure that over the next ten years there are going to be a few years when the general market is plus 20% or 25%, a few when it is minus on the same order, and a majority when it is in between. I haven't any notion as to the sequence in which these will occur, nor do I think it is of any great importance for the long-term investor.

||||||||||||||||||||||||||||||||||||||||||||||||||||||||||||||||||||||||||||||||||||||||||||||||||||||||||||||||||||||||||||||||||||||||||||||

JANUARY 18, 1965

If a 20% or 30% drop in the market value of your equity hold-ings (such as BPL) is going to produce emotional or financial distress, you should simply avoid common stock type invest-ments. In the words of the poet—Harry Truman—"If you can't stand the heat, stay out of the kitchen." It is preferable, of course, to consider the problem before you enter the "kitchen."

||||||||||||||||||||||||||||||||||||||||||||||||||||||||||||||||||||||||||||||||||||||||||||||||||||||||||||||||||||||||||||||||||||||||||||||

Wisdom Compounded

Through Buffett's commentary and Ben Graham's Mr. Market allegory, we can absorb these principles and integrate them into our foundational thinking about how markets work and how we should behave in them. Thinking of ourselves now as investors, we come to understand short-term fluctuations in securities prices are often driven by swings in market psychology, but over multi-year periods investing results will be determined by the underlying fundamental results of the businesses we own and the prices we paid. Market swoons are inevitable, and since we can't predict their timing we accept them as our price of admission as investors.

The swoons do not bother us much because we understand that the availability of a market quote is an advantage to be utilized, al-lowing us to be buyers at times when others are fearful. It provides the mental construct for the fortitude during swoons in the market that keeps us from selling out at low prices.

Even investors who live below their means and consistently look to invest the difference in the broad market without attempting to pick stocks or value businesses should do far better than average if they possess the emotional fortitude to follow these principles. In fact, investors who are able to adhere to these core ideas throughout an investing lifetime will have a hard time *not* becoming comfort-ably wealthy, in large part due to the power of compound interest, the subject of our next chapter.

CHAPTER 2

COMPOUNDING

||||||||||||||||||||||||||||||||||||||||||||||||||||||||||||||||||||||||||||||||||||

"Such fanciful geometric progressions illustrate the value of either living a long time, or compounding your money at a decent rate. I have nothing particularly helpful to say on the former point."[1]

—JANUARY 18, 1963

Einstein is said to have called compound interest the eighth wonder of the world and said that "those who understand it, *earn* it, and those who don't, *pay* it."[2] Using humorous stories throughout the letters, Buffett teaches investors that the power of compounded interest is unmatched by any other factor in the production of wealth through investment. Compounding over a life-long investment program is your best strategy, bar none.

At its very root, an investment program is first and foremost a compounding program. It is the process of continuously reinvesting gains such that each subsequent addition begins earning a return itself. These gains on gains become an increasingly dominant component of an investment program's total returns over time. The two determining factors of the ultimate result are (1) the annual average rate of gain and (2) time.

Compounding derives its power from its parabolic nature; the longer it goes, the more impactful it becomes. However, it does take significant amounts of time to build sufficient scale to become an obvious driver within an investment program and so many under-appreciate its importance. If you latch on early to these ideas and give it time, you won't need much else to be a successful investor. Unfortunately, many are shortsighted or impatient and fail to take full advantage of what they offer.

Take for example a $100,000 account earning 10% a year. The total return will be about 7% higher when the gains are reinvested rather than harvested after a 5-year period. Not that impressive. However, after 10 years, the account that reinvests its gains (let's call this account the *Compounder*) will produce 30% more than one that doesn't reinvest. Then the "pulse quickening"[3] results start to get going by year 15. Now the Compounder is doing roughly 70% better. Compounding is exponential, it builds momentum as it goes; after 20 years, the advantage widens to 125%. There is nothing more powerful. Spending away your gains will diminish your total return significantly; as investors, we allow our gains to pile up upon them-selves as the primary driver of our wealth creation. We do it patiently.

Compounding's importance is hard to overstate. It explains why Charlie Munger, Buffett's friend in the Partnership years and current vice chairman of Berkshire, once said Buffett viewed a $10 haircut like it was actually costing him $300,000. Turns out he was only modestly conservative; a $10 haircut skipped by Buffett in 1956 and instead invested in the Partnership would be worth more than $1 million today ($10 compounded at 22% for 58 years). Viewed through Buffett's compound interest lens, it's not hard to see why he has lived such a frugal life. His haircuts really are expensive!

Buffett was convinced by his mid-twenties that the power of com-pound interest was going to make him rich. Returning to Omaha with a little over $100,000 before starting the partnerships, he already considered himself to be essentially retired. He figured he would read a lot and perhaps attend some university classes. He was so sure of what compound interest would do that he literally began worrying about the potentially adverse effect all this coming wealth might have on his family; he didn't want spoiled kids and wanted a strategy to keep them grounded. While avoiding spoiled children is an understandable concern in and of itself, keep in mind he was in his twenties at the time and working out of his bedroom investing very modest sums.[4]

Some advice naturally follows from all of this: If you can manage to underspend your income while achieving even a modestly better than average return, you are likely to be just fine financially. Patience, however, is critical. You can't force compounding; you have to let it season over time. Consider the case of Ronald Read, a gas station attendant from Vermont who amassed an $8 million net worth by consistently investing a small portion of his salary into high-quality dividend-paying stocks over a lifetime.[5]

Buffett has resided in the same house for decades. His approach to life and investing is pragmatic and fulfilling. His patience and frugality have allowed him to keep the maximum amount of funds invested and compounding. This, in combination with the high rates of return he's been able to generate, has led to an ability to give all his Berkshire stock to the Gates Foundation, the largest philanthropic gift in the history of the world. Not only that, he's one of the happiest guys I can think of, having done exactly what he wanted with the majority of each and every day of his adult life.

The Joys of Compounding

When talking to partners about the power of compound interest, Buffett included the following table showing the gains from compounding $100,000 for 10–30 years at a rate between 4% and 16%:

	4%	8%	12%	16%
10 Years	$ 48,024	$ 115,892	$ 210,584	$ 341,143
20 Years	$ 119,111	$ 366,094	$ 864,627	$ 1,846,060
30 Years	$ 224,337	$ 906,260	$ 2,895,970	$ 8,484,940

Take a minute to absorb these numbers. Scan the figures in the upper left and work your way down to the bottom right. Notice the *huge* advantage financially from a long investment life and the *huge* advantage that comes with a high rate of return. If you can combine the two factors, the results are eye-popping: $100,000 compounded at 16% will be worth more than $8.5 million in 30 years!

Buffett relates three amusing stories in the letters—of Columbus, *Mona Lisa*, and the Manhattan Indians—which are reproduced in full at the end of the chapter, to emphasize these points for us: (1) Compounding is equally sensitive to changes in time as it is to changes in rate, and (2) seemingly insignificant changes in rate really add up when viewed through the lens of a long-term investment program.

The story of Christopher Columbus emphasizes his point that, when it comes to compound interest, time is definitely on your side. As you'll see, had Queen Isabella not spent the $30,000 to finance Columbus's voyage and had instead invested in anything that was compounding at just 4% annually, it would have grown to be worth $2 trillion by 1963 ($7.3 trillion today). As Buffett joked, "Without attempting to evaluate the psychic income derived from finding a new hemisphere, it must be pointed out that even had squatter's rights prevailed, the whole deal was not exactly another IBM."[6] With the benefit of long periods of time, even modest amounts of initial capital invested at modest rates pile up into staggering sums.

Take a moment to look again at the table of compound interest, this time with a focus on the 8% return column. Ten years of compounded interest produces a $115,892 gain. Double the length of time and the gain triples. Triple the length of compounding (to 30 years from 10) and the gain increases almost ninefold.

In the second story, Buffett tells the tale of King Francis I of France, who paid $20,000 for the *Mona Lisa*. Here Buffett illustrates how a high rate of return *and* a long period of time produce an absurdity if extrapolated out too far. If that same $20,000 were to somehow have compounded instead at 6% annually, it would have grown to $1 quadrillion by 1964, nearly 3,000 times the national debt at the time. Buffett may have been speaking directly to his wife, a lover of art and a gallery owner for a time, when he said, "I trust this will end all discussion in our household about any purchase of paintings qualifying as an investment."[7]

There is no question that a long time period and a high rate of growth combine to produce nonsensical projections when allowed to go too far. This is why Buffett was always trying to keep partners from extrapolating his results too far into the future. As an example, in 1963 he said:

> *Some of you may be downcast because I have not included in the above table the rate of 22.3%. . . . This rate, of course, is before income taxes which are paid directly by you—not the Partnership. Even excluding this factor, such a calculation would only prove the absurdity of the idea of compounding at very high rates—even with initially modest sums. . . .*[8]

To give you a more modern example, under Buffett's stewardship, Berkshire has been able to compound its per share value by 21.6% annually for the last 50 years. The stock, which traded for around $18 in 1965, is worth a staggering $218,000 *per share* as of this writing (2015). The total market value of the company today is $359 billion. If Berkshire's stock manages to compound annually at the same rate, the *per share* value will be $3.8 billion by 2065 and the market value will be over $6 quadrillion, far more than the value of all the public companies on the planet combined.

As you can see, continued high rates of growth become impossible to sustain. The larger an investment program becomes, the harder it is to grow. This is the law of large numbers at work and Buffett, from the Partnership Letters to today, has always been very candid in this regard. Today Berkshire is simply too big to grow a lot faster than the general economy.

What's at Stake for Today's Investors

Buffett estimated the overall market would compound somewhere between 5% and 8% per year on average and over a long period of time. Looking back, the S&P 500 has actually delivered a little more than a 7% compound annual growth rate (CAGR) since 1950 and the average of all the 10-year periods since has been 6.8%. With untaxed dividends added back, it's been closer to 10%. These better-than-expected results come in large part from the unexpected drop in interest rates (the lower the government bond yield, the more valuable stocks will be, all else equal). Today, with bond yields not too far from zero, a 5–6% per annum result over the next 20 to 30 years seems like a reasonable assumption. If we get those kinds of results, the power of compound interest will be just as important, but it will take longer for the effects to gain momentum.

My 5–6% figure is just a guesstimate; you can make your own. Buffett offered his most detailed description of how he was thinking it through in a letter written in October 1969, just as he was winding up the Partnership. This was part of a letter to help partners, who would soon be on their own as investors, think about what proportion of their capital should be in stocks and what the returns might look like:

> *The ten year expectation for corporate stocks as a group is probably not better than 9% overall, say 3% dividends and 6% gain in value. I would doubt that Gross National Product grows more than 6% per annum—I don't believe corporate profits are likely to grow significantly as a percentage of GNP—and if earnings multipliers don't change (and with these assumptions and present interest rates they shouldn't) the aggregate valuation of American corporate enterprise should not grow at a long-term compounded rate above 6% per annum. This typical experience in stocks might produce (for the taxpayer described earlier*) 1¾% after tax from divi-*

---

* Assumes a 40% margin tax rate.

dends and 4¾% after tax from capital gain, for a total after-tax return of about 6½%. The pre-tax mix between dividends and capital gains might be more like 4% and 5%, giving a slightly lower after tax result. This is not far from historical experience and overall, I believe future tax rules on capital gains are likely to be stiffer than in the past.[9]

Whatever outcome the stock market is going to deliver to you over your investment lifetime, Buffett's final story in his compounding trilogy serves to really hammer home how even minor decrements down—small fractional changes in the compound rate—produce hugely different outcomes over long periods. In an amusing story, Buffett figures the $24 paid to the Indians for the island of Manhattan was worth about $12.5 billion in 1965, working out to about a 6.12% compounded gain. But he was making a point:

To the novice, perhaps this sounds like a decent deal. However, the Indians have only had to achieve a 6½% return (The tribal mutual fund representative would have promised them this.) to obtain the last laugh on Minuit. At 6½%, $24 becomes $42,105,772,800 ($42 billion) in 338 years, and if they just managed to squeeze out an extra half point to get to 7%, the present value becomes $205 billion.[10]

This story serves us a powerful reminder: Fees, taxes, and other forms of slippage can add up to have an enormous cumulative impact. While 1–2% a year in such costs seems minor when isolated to a given year (and you can be sure that's how financial products are sold), the power of compounding turns something that looks minor into something that in reality is actually colossal. Consider the huge swing in outcomes that exists for a middle-aged investor saving in a 401(k) retirement account for the next 20–30 years at 5% versus 7%: The effect of missing out on 2% per year for 30 years results in an account that is worth half as much. Buffett's story of the Manhattan Indians makes it all so plainly obvious—every percentage point in the rate of compounding really matters!

Fees and taxes (not to mention underperformance) have been crushing the long-term investment results of most Americans. In fact, the actual average result of individual investors in this country in the 20 years ending 2011 has been closer to 2%. In real dollars (after inflation) purchasing power has been lost! It's a scandalous state of affairs relative to the 7.8% delivered by the market index.[11] Buffett and others have been sounding this alarm for decades, but these practices continue.

Investors take the long view and think of stocks as fractional ownership claims on businesses. They don't get spooked by the market swings and avoid fees and taxes to the fullest extent practical. They harness the parabolic nature of long-term compound interest, at the highest rate for the longest period of time possible—it's your primary tool as an investor.

From the Partnership Letters: The Joys of Compounding

JANUARY 18, 1963

Columbus

I have it from unreliable sources that the cost of the voyage Isabella originally underwrote for Columbus was approximately $30,000. This has been considered at least a moderately successful utilization of venture capital. Without attempting to evaluate the psychic income derived from finding a new hemisphere, it must be pointed out that even had squatter's rights prevailed, the whole deal was not exactly another IBM. Figured very roughly, the $30,000 invested at 4% compounded annually would have amounted to something like $2,000,000,000,000,000 (that's $2 trillion for those of you who are not government statisticians) by 1962. Historical apologists for the Indians of Manhattan may find refuge in similar calculations. Such fanciful geometric progressions illustrate the value of either living a long time, or compounding your money at a decent rate. I have nothing particularly helpful to say on the former point.

. . . It is always startling to see how relatively small differences in rates add up to very significant sums over a period of years. That is why, even though we are shooting for more, we feel that a few percentage points advantage over the Dow is a very worthwhile achievement. It can mean a lot of dollars over a decade or two.

||||||||||||||||||||||||||||||||||||||||||||||||||||||||||||||||||||||||||||||||||||||||||||||||||||||||||||||||||||||||||||||||||||||||||

JANUARY 18, 1964

Mona Lisa

Now to the pulse-quickening portion of our essay. Last year, in order to drive home the point on compounding, I took a pot shot at Queen Isabella and her financial advisors. You will remember they were euchred into such an obviously low-compound situation as the discovery of a new hemisphere.

Since the whole subject of compounding has such a crass ring to it, I will attempt to introduce a little class into this discussion by turning to the art world. Francis I of France paid 4,000 ecus in 1540 for Leonardo da Vinci's Mona Lisa. On the off chance that a few of you have not kept track of the fluctuations of the ecu, 4,000 converted out to about $20,000.

If Francis had kept his feet on the ground and he (and his trustees) had been able to find a 6% after-tax investment, the estate now would be worth something over $1,000,000,000,000,000.00. That's $1 quadrillion or over 3,000 times the present national debt, all from 6%. I trust this will end all discussion in our household about any purchase or paintings qualifying as an investment.

However, as I pointed out last year, there are other morals to be drawn here. One is the wisdom of living a long time. The other impressive factor is the swing produced by relatively small changes in the rate of compound.

Below are shown the gains from $100,000 compounded at various rates:

	4%	8%	12%	16%
10 Years	$ 48,024	$ 115,892	$ 210,584	$ 341,143
20 Years	$ 119,111	$ 366,094	$ 864,627	$ 1,846,060
30 Years	$ 224,337	$ 906,260	$ 2,895,970	$ 8,484,940

It is obvious that a variation of merely a few percentage points has an enormous effect on the success of a compounding (investment) program. It is also obvious that this effect mushrooms as the period lengthens. If, over a meaningful period of time, Buffett Partnership can achieve an edge of even a modest number of percentage points over the major investment media, its function will be fulfilled.

ııı

JANUARY 18, 1965

Manhattan Indians

Readers of our early annual letters registered discontent at a mere recital of contemporary investment experience, but instead hungered for the intellectual stimulation that only could be provided by a depth study of investment strategy spanning the centuries. Hence, this section.

Our last two excursions into the mythology of financial expertise have revealed that purportedly shrewd investments by Isabella (backing the voyage of Columbus) and Francis I (original purchase of Mona Lisa) bordered on fiscal lunacy. Apologists for these parties have presented an array of sentimental trivia. Through it all, our compounding tables have not been dented by attack.

Nevertheless, one criticism has stung a bit. The charge has

been made that this column has acquired a negative tone with only the financial incompetents of history receiving comment. We have been challenged to record on these pages a story of financial perspicacity which will be a benchmark of brilliance down through the ages.

One story stands out. This, of course, is the saga of trading acumen etched into history by the Manhattan Indians when they unloaded their island to that notorious spendthrift, Peter Minuit in 1626. My understanding is that they received $24 net. For this, Minuit received 22.3 square miles, which works out to about 621,688,320 square feet. While on the basis of comparable sales, it is difficult to arrive at a precise appraisal, a $20 per square foot estimate seems reasonable giving a current land value for the island of $12,433,766,400 ($12.5 billion). To the novice, perhaps this sounds like a decent deal. However, the Indians have only had to achieve a 6.5% return (The tribal mutual fund representative would have promised them this.) to obtain the last laugh on Minuit. At 6.5%, $24 becomes $42,105,772,800 ($42 billion) in 338 years, and if they just managed to squeeze out an extra half point to get to 7%, the present value becomes $205 billion.

So much for that.

Some of you may view your investment policies on a shorter term basis. For your convenience, we include our usual table indicating the gains from compounding $100,000 at various rates:

	4%	8%	12%	16%
10 Years	$ 48,024	$ 115,892	$ 210,584	$ 341,143
20 Years	$ 119,111	$ 366,094	$ 864,627	$ 1,846,060
30 Years	$ 224,337	$ 906,260	$ 2,895,970	$ 8,484,940

This table indicates the financial advantages of:

1. A long life (in the erudite vocabulary of the financial sophisticate this is referred to as the Methuselah Technique)

2. A high compound rate

3. A combination of both (especially recommended by this author)

To be observed are the enormous benefits produced by relatively small gains in the annual earnings rate. This explains our attitude which while hopeful of achieving a striking margin of superiority over average investment results, nevertheless, regards every percentage point of investment return above average as having real meaning.[12]

Wisdom Compounded

Buffett understands the power of compound interest as well as anyone. His stories offer, in his humorous and folksy way, invaluable examples of the costs and benefits derived from minor changes in the average rate of gains or the length of the compounding program. In addition to Graham's lesson—that stocks are businesses and the market is there to serve, not inform—we now have another mantra: "Investment decisions should be made on the basis of the most probable compounding of after-tax net worth with minimum risk."[13] Everyone has the ability to think and invest this way and those who do gain a significant competitive edge over many other investors operating under a win-now mentality.

The big question from here, which we'll explore next, is: Given your interest and capabilities, should you try to pick stocks and follow Buffett's lead as a stock picker, or should you simply dollar-cost-average your way to prosperity by increasing your share of American business through a low-cost index over a lifetime? Doing nothing else but indexing is a highly attractive option—relative to the little time or effort required, the results, compounded over many years, can actually be remarkably good. For most people, this will be the best choice.

CHAPTER 3

MARKET INDEXING: THE DO-NOTHING RATIONALE

||||||||||||||||||||||||||||||||||||||||||||||||||||||||||||||||||||||||||||||||||||||

"The Dow as an investment competitor is no pushover and the great bulk of investment funds in the country are going to have difficulty in bettering, or perhaps even matching, its performance."[1]

—JANUARY 24, 1962

As detailed in the last chapter, Buffett told partners he expected the market to compound at around a 5–7% per year rate, on average and over the very long run (20–30 years). At the high end of his range, that meant the market would roughly double ever 10 years or so. Such is the power of American business and compound interest. Today, investors can harness this power by simply owning the entire market through a low-cost index fund. This is one of the best strategies going. It's the "do-nothing" approach. Its main benefit, aside from working so well, is that it's cheap and easy to implement on your own. You certainly don't need to pay anyone a big fee to tell you to just buy the market, sit back, and latch on to the power of compounding.

John Bogle founded the Vanguard 500 Index Fund in 1975 and created the first security that itself owned a slice of every company in S&P 500 index. However, index investing wasn't around in the Buffett Partnership Ltd. (BPL) era. Had partners not been invested with Buffett, they most likely would have been invested in a trust or mutual fund. For this reason, each of Buffett's year-end letters included a comparison table of BPL's performance, the market's performance, *and* the results of a handful of the leading investment companies. Here is the reason he gave partners.

> *In outlining the results of investment companies, I do so not because we operate in a manner comparable to them or because our investments are similar to theirs. It is done because such funds represent a public batting average of professional, highly paid investment management handling a very significant $20 billion of securities. Such management, I believe, is typical of management handling even larger sums. As an alternative to an interest in the partnership, I believe it reasonable to assume that many partners would have investments managed similarly.*[2]

Buffett carefully points out that the broad market average is likely to be the tougher competitor and that the majority of actively managed funds will tend to underperform the Dow.

Higher Standards for Today's Mutual Funds

With no other alternative available, its no surprise that Buffett excused this underperformance at the time:

> *The collective record of such investment media is necessarily tied to the record of corporate America. Their merits, except*

in the unusual case, do not lie in superior results or greater re-
sistance to decline in value. Rather, I feel they earn their keep
by the ease of handling, the freedom from decision making
and the automatic diversification they provide, plus, perhaps
most important, the insulation afforded from temptation to
practice patently inferior techniques which seem to entice so
many would-be investors.[3]

The simple truth is that John Bogle, through the advent of the low-cost index fund, significantly raised the bar for mutual funds and all the other products that had previously existed to provide investors "ease of handling" and "broad diversification." Index funds do that better. Today, all active investors, both professional and individual, have to outperform to justify their action. Most don't. Many funds, especially the ones investing in hundreds of stocks at a time (Buffett calls these the Noah's Ark school of investing—two of everything), appear to be clinging to a business model whose extinction seems almost inevitable. Vanguard and the other index products like it have steadily taken share from active managers since they became available forty years ago.

To what extent is the mutual fund industry a "buggy whip" business as a result of this new competitor? It is a question that has loomed larger in recent years given the huge majority of funds that have failed to do better than their lower-cost competitor. Who would want to pay a higher fee for a lower return?

Of course, any professional investor who outperforms over an extended period of time adds significant value and will always be in demand, whether their structure is mutual, partnership, hedge fund, or otherwise, no matter how many stocks they own. Even modestly better results produce tremendous financial advantages when compounded over time. However, the majority of those who invest on their own or through actively managed mutual funds underperform the market. The chance of doing better by investing actively as opposed to passively comes with a significant risk that results will actually be worse.

Buffett's last will and testament reflects his own view on the matter particularly well, which he outlined in his 2013 annual letter.

> ... *Both individuals and institutions will constantly be urged to be active by both those who profit from giving advice or effecting transactions. The resulting frictional costs can be huge and, for investors in aggregate, devoid of benefit. So ignore the chatter, keep your costs minimal, invest in stocks as you would a farm.*
>
> *My money, I should add, is where my mouth is: What I advise here is essentially identical to certain instructions I've laid out in my will. One bequest provides that cash will be delivered to a trustee for my wife's benefit. (I have to use cash for individual bequests, because all of my Berkshire shares will be fully distributed to certain philanthropic organizations over the ten years following the closing of my estate.) My advice to the trustee could not be more simple: Put 10% of the cash in short-term government bonds and 90% in a very low-cost S&P 500 index fund. (I suggest Vanguard's.) I believe the trust's long-term results from this policy will be superior to those attained by most investors—whether pension funds, institutions or individuals—who employ high-fee managers.*[4]

Buffett has been teaching investors for a very long time that you can't get much more from the market than what you put into it. If you're uninterested, unable, or unwilling to dedicate the time and effort to your investments, you should buy the index. The only reason to choose an active investment program is a belief that you, or the investment manager you've chosen, will outperform the "do-nothing" strategy.

Most Funds Fail to Flap Their Wings

Even in the absence of index funds in the 1960s, Buffett understood this idea intuitively. He saw the Dow as his main competitor and outperforming it was his principal objective. He saw *absolute* performance, the percentage gain or loss a fund achieves in any given year, as largely a matter of random luck. For investors, skill is measured through *relative* performance—how much better (or worse) one's returns are relative to the market. Here is how he put it:

> *The results of these [investment] companies in some ways resemble the activity of a duck sitting on a pond. When the water (the market) rises, the duck rises; when it falls, back goes the duck.... I think the duck can only take the credit (or blame) for his own activities. The rise and fall of the lake is hardly something for him to quack about. The water level has been of great importance to BPL's performance ... however, we have also occasionally flapped our wings."*[5]

While the term *index fund* was still a decade away, the term *behavioral finance* would take much longer to enter the lexicon. Remarkably, Buffett anticipated both of these related investing megatrends: the importance of the index as the primary yardstick and the psychological factors leading to the chronic underperformance of active managers.

Why do smart, well-staffed, well-resourced, well-connected, experienced investment managers so consistently fail to beat an unmanaged index? Writing in 1965, Buffett offered his own opinion:

> *This question is of enormous importance, and you would expect it to be the subject of considerable study by investment managers and substantial investors.... Curiously enough, there is practically nothing in the literature of Wall Street attracting this problem, and discussion of it is virtually absent*

at security analyst society meetings, conventions, seminars, etc. My opinion is that the first job of any investment management organization is to analyze its own techniques and results before pronouncing judgment on the managerial abilities and performance of the major corporate entities of the United States.

In the great majority of cases the lack of performance exceeding or even matching an unmanaged index in no way reflects lack of either intellectual capacity or integrity. I think it is much more the product of: (1) group decisions—my perhaps jaundiced view is that it is close to impossible for outstanding investment management to come from a group of any size with all parties really participating in decisions; (2) a desire to conform to the policies and (to an extent) the portfolios of other large well-regarded organizations; (3) an institutional framework whereby average is "safe" and the personal rewards for independent action are in no way commensurate with the general risk attached to such action; (4) an adherence to certain diversification practices which are irrational; and finally and importantly, (5) inertia.[6]

Classical economic theory assumes individuals always behave rationally. But "Prospect Theory," Daniel Kahneman and Amos Tversky's foundational paper uprooting this idea, showed how economic decisions are often not rational in the classic sense (Kahneman was awarded the Nobel Prize in 2002). It ushered in behavioral economics and a new way of thinking when it was published in 1979, but keep in mind that this was nearly fifteen years after Buffett's own critique.

The advice to investors is clear and straightforward: Seriously consider a low-cost, passive index fund as your best investment choice. While the benefits of compounding at an above-market rate are clear, most investors fail to do so. Picking stocks is hard. Investors who decide to follow Buffett down the road of active investment cannot say that Professor Buffett has not weighed in with ample warnings ahead of time, suggesting they take an alternate route.

|||||||||||||||||||||||||||||||||||||||||||||||||||||||||||||||||||||||||||||||||||||||||||||||||||||||||||||||||||||||||||||||||||||||||||||||||

From the Partnership Letters:
The Case for Passive Investing

NOTE: The performance table Buffett included in each year-end letter and referred to in the below excerpts can be found in Appendix A.

|||||||||||||||||||||||||||||||||||||||||||||||||||||||||||||||||||||||||||||||||||||||||||||||||||||||||||||||||||||||||||||||||||||||||||||||||

JANUARY 24, 1962

You may feel I have established an unduly short yardstick in that it perhaps appears quite simple to do better than an unmanaged index of 30 leading common stocks. Actually, this index has generally proven to be a reasonably tough competitor.

|||||||||||||||||||||||||||||||||||||||||||||||||||||||||||||||||||||||||||||||||||||||||||||||||||||||||||||||||||||||||||||||||||||||||||||||||

JULY 6, 1962

To the extent that funds are invested in common stocks, whether the manner of investment be through investment companies, investment counselors, bank trust departments, or do-it-yourself, our belief is that the overwhelming majority will achieve results roughly comparable to the Dow. Our opinion is that the deviations from the Dow are much more likely to be toward a poorer performance than a superior one.

|||||||||||||||||||||||||||||||||||||||||||||||||||||||||||||||||||||||||||||||||||||||||||||||||||||||||||||||||||||||||||||||||||||||||||||||||

JANUARY 24, 1962

My own record of investing such huge sums of money, with restrictions on the degree of activity I might take in companies where we had investments, would be no better, if as good. I present this data to indicate the Dow as an investment competitor is no pushover, and the great bulk of investment funds in the country are going to have difficulty in bettering, or perhaps even matching, its performance.

||||||||||||||||||||||||||||||||||||||||||||||||||||||||||||||||||||||||||||||||||||||||||||||||||||||||||||||||||||||||||||||||||||||||||||||

JANUARY 18, 1964

Within their institutional framework and handling the many billions of dollars involved, the results achieved are the only ones attainable. To behave unconventionally within this framework is extremely difficult. Therefore, the collective record of such investment media is necessarily tied to the record of corporate America. Their merits, except in the unusual case, do not lie in superior results or greater resistance to decline in value. Rather, I feel they earn their keep by the ease of handling, the freedom from decision making and the automatic diversification they provide, plus, perhaps most important, the insulation afforded from temptation to practice patently inferior techniques which seem to entice so many would-be investors.

||||||||||||||||||||||||||||||||||||||||||||||||||||||||||||||||||||||||||||||||||||||||||||||||||||||||||||||||||||||||||||||||||||||||||||||

JANUARY 18, 1965

The repetition of these tables has caused partners to ask: "Why in the world does this happen to very intelligent managements working with (1) bright, energetic staff people, (2) virtually unlimited resources, (3) the most extensive business contacts, and (4) literally centuries of aggregate investment experience?" (The latter qualification brings to mind the fellow who applied for a job and stated he had twenty years of experience—which was corrected by the former employer to read "one year's experience—twenty times.")

This question is of enormous importance, and you would expect it to be the subject of considerable study by investment managers and substantial investors. After all, each percentage point on $30 billion is $300 million per year. Curiously enough, there is practically nothing in the literature of Wall Street attracting this problem, and discussion of it is virtually absent at security analyst society meetings, conventions, seminars, etc. My opinion is that the first job of any investment management organization is to analyze its own techniques and results before pronouncing judgment on the managerial abilities and performance of the major corporate entities of the United States.

In the great majority of cases the lack of performance exceeding or even matching an unmanaged index in no way reflects lack of either intellectual capacity or integrity. I think it is much more the product of: (1) group decisions—my perhaps jaundiced view is that it is close to impossible for outstanding investment management to come from a group of any size with all parties really participating in decisions; (2) a desire to conform to the policies and (to an extent) the portfolios of other large well-regarded organizations; (3) an institutional framework whereby average is "safe" and the personal rewards for independent action are in no way commensurate with the general risk attached to such action; (4) an adherence to certain diversification practices which are irrational; and finally and importantly, (5) inertia.

Perhaps the above comments are unjust. Perhaps even our statistical comparisons are unjust. Both our portfolio and method of operation differ substantially from the investment companies in the table. However, I believe both our partners and their stockholders feel their managements are seeking the same goal—the maximum long-term average return on capital obtainable with the minimum risk of permanent loss consistent with a program of continuous investment in equities. Since we should have common goals, and most partners, as an alternative to their interest in BPL, would probably have their funds invested in media producing results comparable with these investment companies, I feel their performance record is meaningful in judging our own results.

There is no question that an important service is provided to investors by investment companies, investment advisors, trust departments, etc. This service revolves around the attainment of adequate diversification, the preservation of a long-term outlook, the ease of handling investment decisions and mechanics, and most importantly, the avoidance of the patently inferior investment techniques which seem to entice some individuals. All but a few of the organizations do not specifically promise to deliver superior investment performance although it is perhaps not unreasonable for the public to draw such an inference from their advertised emphasis on professional management.

One thing I pledge to you as partners—just as I consider the previously stated performance comparison to be meaningful now, so will I in future years, no matter what tale unfolds. Correspondingly, I ask that you, if you do not feel such a standard to be relevant, register such disagreement now and suggest other standards which can be applied prospectively rather than retrospectively.

One additional thought—I have not included a column in my table for the most widely-used investment advisor in the world—Bell management. People who watch their weight, golf scores, and fuel bills seem to shun quantitative evaluation of their investment management skills although it involves the most important client in the world—themselves. While it may be of academic interest to evaluate the management accomplishments of Massachusetts Investors Trust or Lehman Corporation, it is of enormous dollars-and-cents importance to evaluate objectively the accomplishments of the fellow who is actually handling your money—even if it's you.

|||||||||||||||||||||||||||||||||||||||||||||||||||||||||||||||||||||||||||||||||||||||||||||||||||||||||||||||||||||||||||||||||||||||||||

JULY 9, 1965

Of course, the beauty of the American economic scene has been that random results have been pretty darned good results. The water level has been rising. In our opinion, the probabilities are that over a long period of time, it will continue to rise, though, certainly not without important interruptions. It will be our policy, however, to endeavor to swim strongly, with or against the tide. If our performance declines to a level you can achieve by floating on your back, we will turn in our suits.

Wisdom Compounded

The advent of the low-cost index fund was a game changer for the traditional mutual fund industry. Their primary role of providing "ease of handling" and keeping individuals from picking stocks themselves was replaced by a superior, lower-cost product. Indexing, or passive investing, has been growing in popularity at a largely uninterrupted pace since the products were introduced in the late 1970s. Buffett himself, in providing for his wife in his will, chose an index fund over an actively managed one. That fact alone should give every investor pause.

Fees, taxes, and psychology are all working against the active manager, and the results you're likely to get as an index investor are not only pretty good, but they also require little to no thought or effort. You can design an investment program using low-cost index funds in well under an hour, then "set-it-and-forget-it" for the decades that follow.

All that being said, the financial benefits from sustained outperformance are equally compelling if you can find a way to do it. Clearly, not everyone can be above average. Given what's at stake, if you decide the active route is the path for you, you'll need an objective system to test your results, whether they are yours or the results of a professional manager.

So far, Buffett's lessons from the letters have revolved around six key ideas for all investors: Think of stocks (1) as fractional claims on entire businesses, (2) that swing somewhat erratically in the short term but (3) behave more in line with their gains in intrinsic business value over the longer term, which, when (4) viewed through the lens of a long-term compounding program (5) tend to produce pretty good results, which, with (6) an index product, can be captured efficiently in a low-cost, easy-to-implement way. From here we're going to turn to Buffett as an active investor, starting with his ideas on what exactly he's setting out to achieve and how he intends to measure it.

CHAPTER 4

MEASURING UP: THE DO-NOTHINGS VERSUS THE DO-SOMETHINGS

|||||||||||||||||||||||||||||||||||||||||||||||||||||||||||||||||||||||||||||||||||

"If our performance declines to a level you can achieve by floating on your back, we will turn in our suits."[1]

—JULY 9, 1965

The proper measurement of active investment performance is so critical to Buffett that he dedicated two of the original eight Ground Rules to it. Poor measurement, in Buffett's view, is a dangerous investment sin. He sets two fundamental rules to (a) establish the measurement "how," which is based on a relative-to-market-performance test, and then (b) establish the measurement "how long," which sets forth the minimum span over which an investment operation can be judged.

The outstanding item of importance in my selection of partners, as well as in my subsequent relations with them, has been the determination that we use the same yardstick.

If my performance is poor, I expect partners to withdraw, and indeed, I should look for a new source of investment for my own funds. If performance is good, I am assured of doing splendidly, a state of affairs to which I am sure I can adjust.[2]

As we learned earlier, the power of compound interest means that even a modest amount of outperformance can produce huge incremental increases in your ultimate results over time. If your methods are underperforming the broad market on a 3- or 5-year basis, however, it makes sense to stop and seriously consider "throwing in the towel" (Buffett's words) and buying the index. As an investor, the only way to know how you are doing is to develop and apply a properly formulated test. Buffett gives us the tools to do exactly that:

1.   Ground Rule #4: "Whether we do a good job or a poor job is not to be measured by whether we are plus or minus for the year. It is instead to be measured against the general experience in securities as measured by the Dow Jones Industrial Average, leading investment companies, etc. If our record is better than that of these yardsticks, we consider it a good year whether we are plus or minus. If we do poorer, we deserve the tomatoes."[3]

2.   Ground Rule #5: "While I much prefer a five-year test, I feel three years is an absolute minimum for judging performance. It is a certainty that we will have years when the partnership performance is poorer, perhaps substantially so, than the Dow. If any three-year or longer period produces poor results, we all should start looking around for other places to have our money. An exception to the latter statement would be three years covering a speculative explosion in a bull market."[4]

These two simple measures still work perfectly well for investors today. The first test measures each year's results *relative* to the market's performance—we simply don't care if we are up or down in any given year. Instead, we focus on whether the year has been better or worse than the market average. Because the general trend is up, if you can manage to be down a little less in down markets and up a little more in up markets, your performance will likely be stellar. Investors simply want to beat the averages on a relative basis cumulatively and as often as possible, letting the plus and minus years fall where they may in absolute terms.

The second test Buffett gives investors establishes that relative performance should be measured on at least a 3-year trailing basis to be relevant and that a 5-year test is even better. Again, those that chronically fail to outperform over a 3–5 year period for any reason should consider finding something else to do with their funds. After all, why bother expending all that effort for a poorer result?

Buffett insisted that all his partners were in agreement with this approach; everyone had to be in tune with his relative-versus-the-market yardstick and his 3-year test before the first dollar was put to work. He made a consistent effort to educate each subsequent new partner about these standards, which he often repeated in the letters.

It's not that he insisted his standards were the best, or that others weren't equally valid, but these were *his* standards, and he made it clear that only those who agreed with them should be in the Partnership. If he achieved what he set out to do, he wanted to receive the proper "hosannas." If not, he expected partners to withdraw. The takeaway for the rest of us is to establish and ensure the yardsticks are in place ahead of time in order to avoid any misunderstanding about what you should be cheering for, because, as Buffett puts it, you don't want soft fruit thrown when the expectation is for vigorous applause.

If all the professional money managers adhered to his standards, we'd witness a record number of early retirements on Wall Street. Buffett continues to hold himself to a 5-year "yardstick" of relative performance today at Berkshire Hathaway.[5] It was, and continues to be, a very high bar. All investors need a yardstick. If you can devise a better test, great, but be sure to establish it in advance.

Ambitious Goals

Buffett's own performance goals for the Partnership would not be achieved easily. After first establishing what he was trying to avoid (3–5 year rolling relative underperformance), he laid out his aim to beat the Dow by an average margin of 10 points per year. This was the maximum amount of advantage he thought one could achieve and he aimed to capture it. So, if the Dow was –5% on the year, he hoped to be +5%. Investors might ask what the origin of this 10% figure was, and to be honest, I'm not sure. However, it's not a question I have spent much time thinking about—we should be more than satisfied if we can manage to do even marginally better than the market over time. Inquiring about the ceiling of our potential outperformance is putting the cart in front of the horse.

While he had no idea what any given year would bring in the overall market, you'll recall he figures 5–7% will be the average. The additional 10% advantage meant he was aiming for 15–17% average annual returns. One hundred thousand dollars compounded at 15% for 10 years grows to $405,000 and after 20 years to $1.6 million. This result would be staggeringly good.

Virtually every comment he makes regarding performance is made on a relative basis. At one point, he explains his thinking as if he were talking to a golfing buddy:

> I would consider a year in which we declined 15% and the Average 30% to be much superior to a year when both we and the Average advanced 20%. Over a period of time there are going to be good and bad years; there is nothing to be gained by getting enthused or depressed about the sequence in which they occur. The important thing is to be beating par; a four on

*a par three hole is not as good as a five on a par five hole and
it is unrealistic to assume we are not going to have our share
of both par three's and par five's.*[6]

Investors are taught to think about performance in one way: If
the market is down and you are down less, you've had a good year,
and vice versa. As long as your performance is even slightly better
than the market average, whether the outperformance comes in up
or in down markets, the results will likely be excellent.

While the Partnership never had a down year or even a year that
underperformed the market, Buffett trained investors to expect
both.

His skill as an investor, the advantage of working with relatively
smaller sums, a market that was right for his style, and luck were
all factors that helped the Partnership achieve such consistently outstanding results, but since then Berkshire has had a handful of underperforming years and a couple that were down, albeit modestly.

The Best Test Is a Long Test

Investors should not expect too much consistency from any style of
investing. Everything will have its seasons. With the understanding that his own relative performance would likely vary, Buffett
warned he could very well lag the market by as much as 10% in the
bad years and thought he could be up as much as 25% when "everything clicks."[7] Because of the wide expected amplitude between
any two given years, he felt it essential that investors should measure their results over a multiyear period and thought three years
was the absolute minimum; he much preferred five. The best test
would be conducted over a flat market period. That way, changes
in the speculative fervor of the overall market would be removed
as a factor. He taught and reminded investors that even a given
year's relative performance was largely a matter of luck. It relies on
the "voting machine" nature of short-term market movements. As

you stretch out your evaluation horizon, the test becomes more and more like a "weighing machine."

Buffett also teaches investors that there is one important caveat to the multiyear test: Underperformance in the late stages of a speculative bull market is highly likely. It's a caveat that he repeats to this day.

We saw this effect in the final few years of the Partnership, when a few "performance funds" were trouncing BPL during the "Go-Go" era leading up to the devastating market crash in the early 1970s, and then again more recently when Buffett and Berkshire Hathaway were seen as "out of step" just before the bursting of the Internet bubble in the 2000s. Market manias, in their full speculative ferment, cause stocks to become divorced from the business fundamentals. Those who view the market as a "voting machine" thrive in these environments, while Buffett and other investors, who consider themselves members of the "weighing machine" school, will appear to be out of step.

Because of the conservative nature of his value-oriented investment style, Buffett teaches us to generally expect better relative performance in down markets. Again, he was perfectly fine with being down in such periods, but he expected to be down less than the market as a whole. Investors following these principles today should share in this expectation. Because of the methods deployed and the types of securities purchased, down markets tend to show the best performance. As Buffett told partners in 1962,

> *a declining Dow gives us our chance to shine and pile up the percentage advantages which, coupled with only an average performance during advancing markets, will give us quite satisfactory long-term results. Our target is an approximately ½% decline for each 1% decline in the Dow and if achieved, means we have a considerably more conservative vehicle for investment in stocks than practically any alternative.*[8]

Buffett reminds investors that principles, including those that measure performance, don't change. He insisted on a minimum 3-year test for active managers versus the market when the industry wasn't really measuring at all. By the end of the 1960s, the industry had gone from not measuring up at all to measuring up way too frequently. He was still advocating a minimum 3-year test when these folks were measuring by the minute, which was just as bad as not measuring at all.

We learn from Buffett to think about performance measurement in a way that's internally consistent with the other core tenets. If we set out as our first principle that the stock market is not very efficient, it would be inconsistent to think our own short-term performance is something to pay attention to. The squiggles, as it were, are "for giggles." We should only care about trailing 3-year figures (at a minimum) because that is the threshold where markets can be expected to become efficient. Five years is better. A full market cycle is the best period over which to evaluate an active manager (market low to market low, or market high to market high).

||||||||||||||||||||||||||||||||||||||||||||||||||||||||||||||||||||||||||||||||||||||||||||||||||||||||||||||||||||||||||||

From the Partnership Letters:
Measuring Up

||||||||||||||||||||||||||||||||||||||||||||||||||||||||||||||||||||||||||||||||||||||||||||||||||||||||||||||||||||||||||||

JANUARY 24, 1962

A Word About Par

The outstanding item of importance in my selection of partners, as well as in my subsequent relations with them, has been the determination that we use the same yardstick. If my performance is poor, I expect partners to withdraw, and indeed, I should look for a new source of investment for my own funds. If performance is good, I am assured of doing splendidly, a state of affairs to which I am sure I can adjust.

The rub, then, is in being sure that we all have the same ideas of what is good and what is poor. I believe in establishing yardsticks prior to the act; retrospectively, almost anything can be made to look good in relation to something or other.

I have continuously used the Dow-Jones Industrial Average as our measure of par. It is my feeling that three years is a very minimal test of performance, and the best test consists of a period at least that long where the terminal level of the Dow is reasonably close to the initial level.

While the Dow is not perfect (nor is anything else) as a measure of performance, it has the advantage of being widely known, has a long period of continuity, and reflects with reasonable accuracy the experience of investors generally with the market. I have no objection to any other method of measurement of general market performance being used, such as other stock market averages, leading diversified mutual stock funds, bank common trust funds, etc.

||||||||||||||||||||||||||||||||||||||||||||||||||||||||||||||||||||||||||||||||||||||||||||||||||||||||||||||||||||||||||||||||||||||||||||

JULY 8, 1964

We will regularly follow this policy wherever it may lead. It is perhaps too obvious to say that our policy of measuring performance in no way guarantees good results—it merely guarantees objective evaluation. I want to stress the points mentioned in the "Ground Rules" regarding application of the standard—namely that it should be applied on at least a three-year basis because of the nature of our operation and also that during a speculative boom we may lag the field. However, one thing I can promise you. We started out with a 36-inch yardstick and we'll keep it that way. If we don't measure up, we won't change yardsticks. In my opinion, the entire field of investment management, involving hundreds of billions of dollars, would be more satisfactorily conducted if everyone had a good yardstick for measurement of ability and sensibly applied it. This is regularly done by most people in the conduct of their own business when evaluating markets, people, machines, methods, etc., and money management is the largest business in the world.

||||||||||||||||||||||||||||||||||||||||||||||||||||||||||||||||||||||||||||||||||||||||||||||||||||||||||||||||||||||||||||||||||||||||||||||||||||||||||||||||||||||||||

JANUARY 20, 1966

I certainly do not believe the standards I utilize (and wish my partners to utilize) in measuring my performance are the applicable ones for all money managers. But I certainly do believe anyone engaged in the management of money should have a standard of measurement, and that both he and the party whose money is managed should have a clear understanding why it is the appropriate standard, what time period should be utilized, etc.

Frank Block put it very well in the November–December 1965 issue of the *Financial Analysts Journal*. Speaking of measurement of investment performance he said, " . . . However, the fact is that literature suffers a yawning hiatus in this subject. If investment management organizations sought always the best performance, there would be nothing unique in careful measurement of investment results. It does not matter that the customer has failed to ask for a formal presentation of the results. Pride alone should be sufficient to demand that each of us determine objectively the quality of his recommendations. This can hardly be done without precise knowledge of the outcome. Once this knowledge is in hand, it should be possible to extend the analysis to some point at which patterns of weakness and strength begin to assert themselves. We criticize a corporate management for failure to use the best of tools to keep it aware of the progress of a complicated industrial organization. We can hardly be excused for failure to provide ourselves with equal tools to show the efficiency of our own efforts to handle other people's money. . . . Thus, it is our dreary duty to report that systems of performance measurement are not automatically included in the data processing programs of most investment management organizations. The sad fact is that some seem to prefer not to know how well or poorly they are doing.

||||||||||||||||||||||||||||||||||||||||||||||||||||||||||||||||||||||||||||||||||||||||||||||||||||||||||||||||||||||||||||||||||||||||||||||||||||||||||||||

JANUARY 20, 1966

Frankly, I have several selfish reasons for insisting that we apply a yardstick and that we both utilize the same yardstick. Naturally, I get a kick out of beating par—in the lyrical words of Casey Stengel, "Show me a good loser, and I'll show you a loser." More importantly, I insure that I will not get blamed for the wrong reason (having losing years) but only for the right reason (doing poorer than the Dow). Knowing partners will grade me on the right basis helps me do a better job. Finally, setting up the relevant yardsticks ahead of time insures that we will all get out of this business if the results become mediocre (or worse). It means that past successes cannot cloud judgment of current results. It should reduce the chance of ingenious rationalizations of inept performance. (Bad lighting has been bothering me at the bridge table lately.) While this masochistic approach to measurement may not sound like much of an advantage, I can assure you from my observations of business entities that such evaluation would have accomplished a great deal in many investment and industrial organizations.

So if you are evaluating others (or yourself!) in the investment field, think out some standards—apply them—interpret them. If you do not feel our standard (a minimum of a three-year test versus the Dow) is an applicable one, you should not be in the Partnership. If you do feel it is applicable, you should be able to take the minus years with equanimity in the visceral regions as well as the cerebral regions—as long as we are surpassing the results of the Dow.

|||||||||||||||||||||||||||||||||||||||||||||||||||||||||||||||||||||||||||||||||||||||||||||||||||||||||||||||||||||||||||||||||||||||||||

JANUARY 24, 1962

Over any long period of years, I think it likely that the Dow will probably produce something like 5% to 7% per year compounded from a combination of dividends and market value gain. Despite the experience of recent years, anyone expecting substantially better than that from the general market probably faces disappointment.

Our job is to pile up yearly advantages over the performance of the Dow without worrying too much about whether the absolute results in a given year are a plus or a minus. I would consider a year in which we were down 15% and the Dow declined 25% to be much superior to a year when both the partnership and the Dow advanced 20%. I have stressed this point in talking with partners and have watched them nod their heads with varying degrees of enthusiasm. It is most important to me that you fully understand my reasoning in this regard and agree with me not only in your cerebral regions, but also down in the pit of your stomach.

For the reasons outlined in my method of operation, our best years relative to the Dow are likely to be in declining or static markets. Therefore, the advantage we seek will probably come in sharply varying amounts. There are bound to be years when we are surpassed by the Dow, but if over a long period we can average ten percentage points per year better than it, I will feel the results have been satisfactory.

Specifically, if the market should be down 35% or 40% in a year (and I feel this has a high probability of occurring one year in the next ten—no one knows which one), we should be down only 15% or 20%. If it is more or less unchanged during the year, we would hope to be up about ten percentage points. If it is up 20% or more, we would struggle to be up as much. The consequence of performance such as this over a period of years would mean that if the Dow produces a 5% to 7% per year overall gain compounded, I would hope our results might be 15% to 17% per year.

The above expectations may sound somewhat rash, and there is no question but that they may appear very much so when viewed from the vantage point of 1965 or 1970. It may turn out that I am completely wrong. However, I feel the partners are certainly entitled to know what I am thinking in this regard even though the nature of the business is such as to introduce a high probability of error in such expectations. In any one year, the variations may be quite substantial. This happened in 1961, but fortunately the variation was on the pleasant side. They won't all be!

||||||||||||||||||||||||||||||||||||||||||||||||||||||||||||||||||||||||||||||||||||||||||||||||||||||||||||||||||||||||||||||||||||

JULY 8, 1964

When the water (the market) rises, the duck rises; when it falls, back goes the duck. SPCA or no SPCA, I think the duck can only take the credit (or blame) for his own activities. The rise and fall of the lake is hardly something for him to quack about. The water level has been of great importance to B.P.L.'s performance. . . . However, we have also occasionally flapped our wings.

||||||||||||||||||||||||||||||||||||||||||||||||||||||||||||||||||||||||||||||||||||||||||||||||||||||||||||||||||||||||||||||||||||

JANUARY 18, 1965

. . . I would like to emphasize that the above is conjecture, perhaps heavily influenced by self-interest, ego, etc. Anyone with a sense of financial history knows this sort of guesswork is subject to enormous error. It might better be left out of this letter, but it is a question frequently and legitimately asked by partners. Long-range expectable return is the primary consideration of all of us belonging to BPL, and it is reasonable that I should be put on record, foolish as that may later make me appear. My rather puritanical view is that any investment manager, whether operating as broker, investment counselor, trust department, Investment Company, etc., should be willing to

state unequivocally what he is going to attempt to accomplish
and how he proposes to measure the extent to which he gets
the job done.

IIIIIIIIIIIIIIIIIIIIIIIIIIIIIIIIIIIIIIIIIIIIIIIIIIIIIIIIIIIIIIIIIIIIIIIIIIIIIIIIIIIIIIIIIIIIIIIIIIIIIIIIIIIIIIIIIIIIIIIIIIIIIIIIIIIIIIIIIIIIIIIIIIIIIIIIII

Wisdom Compounded

No matter how others in the market were changing their yardsticks—no matter whether they were measuring too infrequently or too often—Buffett teaches us never to change ours. It is
the market that changes around the investor's fixed mindset; the
market never holds sway over us.

Speculative bull markets aside, Buffett thought he could beat the
market by a wide margin. He teaches us to establish clear, consistent measurements so that performance can be monitored and
judged fairly and accurately. He spells out ahead of time exactly
what we are setting out to do, and he encourages us to regularly test
ourselves against that yardstick.

Today, performance measurement in the field of equity investment has been largely corrupted and obfuscated with terms like
alpha, beta, sharp ratios, Treynor ratios, and so forth. It doesn't
have to be all that complicated. Investors who decide to go the active
route simply need to think it through ahead of time and commit to
sticking to a measurement plan. Whether actively investing on your
own or through a professional, monitor the 3- and 5-year trailing
results and when there is chronic underperformance, in the absence
of speculative bull market runs, strongly consider making a change.
The effect of long-term underperformance is just too costly.

This makes the selection of a potential new investment manager
very important and requires an understanding of the power of the
incentives in governing how a manager is likely to behave. By studying the way Buffett structured the Partnership, which we'll do next,
you'll see the areas of potential conflict between an investor and an
investment manager that should be minimized to the greatest extent
possible.

CHAPTER 5

THE PARTNERSHIP: AN ELEGANT STRUCTURE

IIIIIIIIIIIIIIIIIIIIIIIIIIIIIIIIIIIIIIIIIIIIIIIIIIIIIIIIIIIIIIIIIIIIIIIIIIIIIII

"The new partnership will represent my entire investment operation in marketable securities, so that my results will have to be directly proportional to yours, subject to the advantage I obtain if we do better than 6%."[1]

—JULY 22, 1961

Incentive dictates behavior. Whether we're talking about investment managers, business leaders, or politicians, more often than not, people will behave according to what they're being rewarded for.

By understanding how and why an investment manager gets paid, you can compare their expected behavior with your own best interest. While most people get the idea that you get what you reward for, the magnitude of this superpower's influence is often underestimated. As Charlie Munger has said, "I think I've been in the top 5% of my age cohort almost my entire adult life in understanding the power of incentives, and yet I've always underestimated that power. Never a year passes but I get some surprise that pushes a little further my appreciation of incentive superpower."

An example from FedEx is one of his favorite cases in point. As he explains, the integrity of the FedEx system relies heavily on the ability to unload and then quickly reload packages at one central location within an allotted time. Years ago, the company was having a terrible problem getting its workers to get all the boxes off and then back on the planes in time. They tried numerous different things that didn't work, until someone had the brilliant idea of paying the workers by the shift as opposed to by the hour. Poof, the problem was solved.[2]

FedEx's old pay-by-the-hour system rewarded those who took longer to get the job done. They were incentivized to take *longer*. By switching to pay-by-the-shift, workers were motivated to work faster and without error so they could go home, yet still earn the wages of a full shift. For the workers, finishing early amounted to a higher effective hourly wage. By aligning the business's interests with the worker's incentives, FedEx got the outcome it and its workers both desired.

The investment management business is no different. "If you want ants to come, you put sugar on the floor."[3] If you want your investment manager to behave with your best interests in mind, you have to ensure that your interests are aligned. Buffett was masterfully aligned with his investors.

The Buffett Partnership Basics

The Partnership was modeled from Newman-Graham, one of the earliest hedge funds in the country. Graham had pioneered the basic structure. It had a general partner, the *GP* (Buffett), who was responsible for the management and took a percentage of the profits. The limited partners, the *LPs* (like Aunt Alice), contributed capital but had no say in how funds were deployed.

Here is Buffett describing how the first Partnership came together when he returned to Omaha after Graham-Newman at the age of twenty-five:

I had no plans to start a partnership, or even have a job. I had no worries as long as I could operate on my own. I certainly did not want to sell securities to other people again. But by pure accident, seven people, including a few of my relatives, said to me, "You used to sell stocks, and we want you to tell us what to do with our money." I replied, "I'm not going to do that again, but I'll form a partnership like Ben and Jerry had, and if you want to join me, you can." My father-in-law, my college room-mate, his mother, my aunt Alice, my sister, my brother-in-law, and my lawyer all signed on. I also had my hundred dollars. That was the beginning—totally accidental.[4]

The first partnership was started with people he cared about deeply. There is no doubt that these feelings influenced the way he formulated the specifics of each partnership's fee structure. Ten more separate partnerships were formed between 1956 and 1961. As partnerships were added, Buffett offered different terms depending on the risk tolerance of each new group. He knew most of the joining partners personally. Many lived in Omaha.

In each case, Buffett took a percentage of the gains beyond a certain return threshold, which is called the *interest provision*. Generally, when he took more of the risk himself, he took a greater percentage of the overage. Across the eleven partnerships, the interest provisions ranged from 0% to 6%, after which the excess to the general partner kicked in. The earliest partnership had a loss sharing provision where Buffett agreed to personally absorb a percentage of any losses. He was consistently fair and accommodating to the needs and risk tolerance of the different partners. Those willing to take more risk were charged a lower fee. When he took on additional risk, he charged more.

One BPL

While he started with $105,100 and a single partnership, by 1960 assets had grown to $1,900,000 across seven distinct partnerships, and it was getting a bit unwieldy. He indicated his desire to merge the partnerships for the first time, acknowledging the issue of varying performance across partnerships:

> [T]he family is growing. There has been no partnership which has had a consistently superior or inferior record compared to our group average, but there has been some variance each year despite my efforts to keep all partnerships invested in the same securities and in about the same proportions. This variation, of course, could be eliminated by combining the present partnerships into one large partnership. Such a move would also eliminate much detail and a moderate amount of expense. Frankly, I am hopeful of doing something along this line in the next few years. The problem is that various partners have expressed preferences for varying partnership arrangements. Nothing will be done without unanimous consent of partners.[5]

The consolidation to one entity in 1962, Buffett Partnership, Ltd. (BPL), removed any potential for further performance variation among partners. The move was well timed because his total partnership assets had more than tripled in a single year to $7,178,500. Buffett's personal share accounted for 14.3% and when the collective interest of his family members was added, the Buffett family accounted for slightly more that 25%. This is a remarkably high percentage, more akin to a family office than a hedge fund or partnership. Buffett was now not just the general partner collecting fees; he and his family also had more at stake financially than any other limited partner.

BPL's Terms

When all partnerships were consolidated into BPL, all LPs were asked to migrate to the same, universal terms. The interest provision was set at 6% for everyone, beyond which Buffett would take 25% of the gains. Since he figured the market was going up 5–7% a year on average, the interest provision was set at a level so he earned nothing unless he was beating the market. He had a "high-water mark"—any cumulative deficiency below a 6% annual gain would have to be recouped before he would resume taking his fee.

Some partners relied on the Partnership for income and wanted to collect on their interest provision. Others wanted the maximum amount of capital to remain invested. In order to appease both groups, the 6% would be distributed, ½% each month, to those who wanted it. Those who wished to keep their funds fully invested could choose to forgo these payments, which would be reinvested back into the Partnership at year-end.

Let's now look at the ways Buffett's structure for the Partnership was a brilliant example of how to align manager incentives and investor objectives. The ability to design simple, easy-to-understand incentive structures has remained a key source of Buffett's success throughout the Partnership years and indeed throughout his entire career.

Ways Managers Get Paid When Investors Don't

Today's hedge funds and mutual funds typically charge a management fee, computed as a fixed percentage of the investor's assets under management. These can range from .25% to 2% or more, per year, and the fee is taken irrespective of performance.

Because the asset management business is highly scalable—an increase in assets usually requires few additional costs—the more funds under management, the more profitable the asset manager will be. While performance is certainly a key component of a fund's ability to grow, a great marketing effort can bring in new investors and has the ability to drive asset growth even faster. Most asset managers—particularly mutual fund companies—earn fees, and therefore are incentivized to maximize the size of their total assets.

Fees based on a fixed percent of assets under management make it hard for asset managers to say no to the incremental dollar of investor capital, even when it's clearly going to have a dampening effect on performance. When an investor's primary interest (annual percentage gains) is out of step with the primary interest of the manager (more assets, more fees), a potential conflict exists. Buffett charged no management fee. He got paid only on performance. His system was better because it removed a source of potential conflict between his interest and the interest of the LPs.

Underperformance Fee

In addition to not charging a management fee, Buffett thought he should get paid only for performance in excess of what a "do-nothing" investor would otherwise get; he only took a fee beyond a 6% return threshold, which was the midpoint of his 5–7% average return expectation for the market. In this way, he was further aligned with his partners' interests.

Today hedge funds tend to charge what's known as "2 and 20"; the 2% is the management fee, and then they charge an additional 20% of *all* profits, without a threshold minimum return. Managers can earn big fees even if they deliver nominally positive returns while failing to outperform the market. This has been the unpleasant state of affairs since the end of the financial crisis, where the hedge fund industry in aggregate has failed to outperform the broad market index each and every year (2008–2014). Like Buffett's duck analogy, these funds have failed to "flap their wings" but the investors in these products have still been asked to pay 20% of their "gains" in fees. Buffett's pay-for-performance structure lives up to his own ideas about treating people the way he would want to be treated if their positions were reversed.

Heads They Win, Tails We Lose

In many cases, fund managers' personal stakes are not a significant portion of the assets being managed or their personal net worth. This can result in a "heads they win, tails we lose" dynamic where the manager who does well gets paid spectacularly, but when they do very poorly, we also do poorly, but they simply close their fund. A manager who has a down 30% year but doesn't have a significant portion of his or her net worth in the fund will certainly miss out on a performance fee, but will take a smaller loss themselves relative to their investors. If the fund were to close, the investors not only lose 30% of their capital; they lose the value of the high-water mark, which gives them the ability to recoup their losses before they start paying performance fees again.

Buffett and his family were the largest partners of BPL. With the most capital at stake, he was aligned with all partners' interests in maximizing performance. He had to focus on risk, to protect his own capital, and reward, both to grow the capital he had in the Partnership and to generate fees. Buffett was like many of today's hedge funds in that he was certain to do splendidly well if his results were great, but where he was unique was that he also set it up so that if the Partnership's results were poor, his performance would be equally miserable.

Liquidity Provisions

Buffett set it up so that additions and redemptions could be made only once a year, which forced investors to look at their performance from a long-term perspective. However, partners could borrow as much as 20% of their capital or pre-fund year-end additions. For this privilege, Buffett charged or paid 6% interest respectively, giving LPs access to funds in the event that they really needed them and more than fairly compensating those who wished to add to their existing investment.

Here Buffett explained his *"un-Buffett-like"* 6% borrowing/lending feature:

> *Why then the willingness to pay 6% for advance payment money when we can borrow from commercial banks at substantially lower rates? For example, in the first half we obtained a substantial six-month bank loan at 4%. The answer is that we expect on a long-term basis to earn better than 6% (the general partner's allocation is zero unless we do although it is largely a matter of chance whether we achieve the 6% figure in any short period). Moreover, I can adopt a different attitude in the investment of money that can be expected to soon be a part of our equity capital than I can on short-term borrowed money. The advance payments have the added advantage to us of spreading the investment of new money over the year, rather than having it hit us all at once in January. On the other hand, 6% is more than can be obtained in short term dollar secure investments by our partners, so I consider it mutually profitable.*

Through the commentary and description of the Partnership's structure, Buffett gives investors several important lessons on how an investment manager's incentives can be aligned with investors' objectives. We can look to management fee, the performance fee, see how much skin they have in the game, and what the liquidity provisions are to make our own assessment and choose the manager who is most aligned with our objectives.

Moreover, observing the world through the lens of incentives is a valuable tool whenever you're trying to predict any outcome where people are involved. Incentives make the world go round. It's helpful to think it through backward and look for ways that others will do well when you won't, an obvious red flag.

If you're considering investing with an active manager today, you can be sure that most salespeople aren't going to highlight these for you—you're going to have to figure them out on your own. Here again we see the power of Munger's "incentive superpower" and the difficulty with "hiring your thinking done." As he said, in most cases it works terribly. However, all you can do is your best and if you're going to hire an outside manager, a comparison to Buffett's Partnership structure and the incentive biases it was structured to avoid is a good place to start.

‖‖‖

From the Partnership Letters:
Full 1960 Letter on BPL's Structure

‖‖‖

JULY 22, 1961

To My Partners:

In the past, partners have commented that a once-a-year letter was "a long time between drinks," and that a semi-annual letter would be a good idea. It really shouldn't be too difficult to find something to say twice a year; at least it isn't this year. Hence, this letter which will be continued in future years.

During the first half of 1961, the overall gain of the Dow-Jones Industrial Average was about 13%, including dividends. Although this is the type of period when we should have the most difficulty in exceeding this standard, all partnerships that operated throughout the six months did moderately better than the Average. Partnerships formed during 1961 either equaled or exceeded results of the Average from the time of formation, depending primarily on how long they were in operation.

Let me, however, emphasize two points. First, one year is far too short a period to form any kind of an opinion as to investment performance, and measurements based upon six months become even more unreliable. One factor that has caused some reluctance on my part to write semi-annual letters is the fear that partners may begin to think in terms of short-term performance which can be most misleading. My own thinking is much more geared to five year performance, preferably with tests of relative results in both strong and weak markets.

The second point I want everyone to understand is that if we continue in a market which advances at the pace of the first half of 1961, not only do I doubt that we will continue to exceed the results of the DJIA, but it is very likely that our performance will fall behind the Average.

Our holdings, which I always believe to be on the conservative side compared to general portfolios, tend to grow more conservative as the general market level rises. At all times, I attempt to have a portion of our portfolio in securities as least partially insulated from the behavior of the market, and this portion should increase as the market rises. However appetizing results for even the amateur cook (and perhaps particularly the amateur), we find that more of our portfolio is not on the stove.

We have also begun open market acquisition of a potentially major commitment which I, of course, hope does nothing marketwise for at least a year. Such a commitment may be a deterrent to short range performance, but it gives strong promise of superior results over a several year period combined with substantial defensive characteristics.

Progress has been made toward combining all partners at yearend. I have talked with all partners joining during this past year or so about this goal, and have also gone over the plans with representative partners of all earlier partnerships.

Some of the provisions will be:

A.   A merger of all partnerships, based on market value at yearend, with provisions for proper allocation among partners of future tax liability due to unrealized gains at yearend. The merger itself will be tax-free, and will result in no acceleration of realization of profits;

B.   A division of profits between the limited partners and general partner, with the first 6% per year to partners based upon beginning capital at market, and any excess divided one-fourth to the general partner and three-fourths to all partners proportional to their capital. Any deficiencies in earnings below the 6% would be carried forward against future earnings, but would not be carried back. Presently, there are three profit arrangements which have been optional to incoming partners:

	INTEREST PROVISION	EXCESS TO GEN. PARTNER	EXCESS TO LTD. PARTNERS
(1)	6%	1/3	2/3
(2)	4%	1/4	3/4
(3)	None	1/6	5/6

C.   In the event of profits, the new division will obviously have to be better for limited partners than the first two arrangements. Regarding the third, the new arrangement will be superior up to 18% per year; but above this rate the limited partners would do better under the present agreement. About 80% of total partnership assets have selected the first two arrangements, and I am hopeful, should we average better than 18% yearly, partners presently under the third arrangement will not feel short-changed under the new agreement;

D.   In the event of losses, there will be no carry back against amounts previously credited to me as general partner. Although there will be a carry-forward against future excess earnings. However, my wife and I will have the largest single investment in the new partnership, probably about one-sixth of total partnership assets, and thereby a greater dollar stake in losses than any other partner or family group. I am inserting a provision in the partnership agreement which will prohibit the purchase by me or my family of any marketable securities. In other words, the new partnership will represent my entire investment operation in marketable securities, so that my results will have to be directly proportional to yours, subject to the advantage I obtain if we do better than 6%;

E.   A provision for monthly payments at the rate of 6% yearly, based on beginning of the year capital valued at market. Partners not wishing to withdraw money currently can have this credited back to them automatically as an advance payment, drawing 6%, to purchase an additional equity interest in the partnership at yearend. This will solve one stumbling block that has heretofore existed in the path of consolidation, since many partners desire regular withdrawals and others wish to plow everything back;

F.   The right to borrow during the year, up to 20% of the value of your partnership interest, at 6%, such loans to be liquidated at yearend or earlier. This will add a degree of liquidity to an investment which can now only be disposed of at yearend. It is not intended that anything but relatively permanent funds be invested in the partnership, and we have no desire to turn it into a bank. Rather, I expect this to be a relatively unused provision, which is available when something unexpected turns up and a wait until yearend to liquidate part or all of a partner's interest would cause hardship;

G.   An arrangement whereby any relatively small tax adjustment, made in later years on the partnership's return will be assessed directly to me. This way, we will not be faced with the problem of asking eighty people, or more, to amend their earlier return over some small matter. As it stands now, a small change, such as a decision that a dividend received by the partnership has a 63% return of capital instead of 68%, could cause a multitude of paper work. To prevent this, any change amounting to less than $1,000 of tax will be charged directly to me.

We have submitted the proposed agreement to Washington for a ruling that the merger would be tax-free, and that the partnership would be treated as a partnership under the tax laws. While all of this is a lot of work, it will make things enormously easier in the future. You might save this letter as a reference to read in conjunction with the agreement which you will receive later in the year.

The minimum investment for new partners is currently $25,000, but, of course, this does not apply to present partners. Our method of operation will enable the partners to add or withdraw amounts of any size (in round $100) at yearend. Estimated total assets of the partnership will be in the neighborhood of $4 million, which enables us to consider investments such as the one mentioned earlier in this letter, which we would have had to pass several years ago.

This has turned out to be more of a production than my annual letter. If you have any questions, particularly regarding anything that isn't clear in my discussion of the new partnership agreement, be sure to let me know. If there are a large number of questions, I will write a supplemental letter to all partners giving the questions that arise and the answers to them.

Compounded Wisdom

Once you start viewing the world through the lens of incentives, many otherwise challenging decisions become easier to make. When we know what motivates people, we pretty much know how they will behave. The lessons from the Partnership structure therefore go well beyond how to avoid making mistakes in choosing your next investment manager, although they also help with that decision.

Where we really see incentives at work is when we start to evaluate businesses and particularly business managers. As business owners (shareholders) we want to understand the motivational drivers of those in charge of our assets. Here we're talking about securities analysis and stock picking. Our next section looks at the three principal types of stock picking Buffett did for the Partnership. He referred to these three categories as Generals, Workouts, and Controls.

Part II

CHAPTER 6

THE GENERALS

||||||||||||||||||||||||||||||||||||||||||||||||||||||||||||||||||||||||||||||||

"We like good management—we like a decent industry—we like a certain amount of 'ferment' in a previously dormant management or stockholder group. But, we demand value."[1]

—JANUARY 18, 1964

How do you define your investment style? Are you drawn to deep value situations? Do you like to hunt for the cheapest of the cheap, irrespective of the underlying business's quality or current fundamentals, with the view that you'll be protected by an attractive purchase price that harnesses the power of mean reversion in your favor? This was one of Graham's principal approaches and continues to define how many great investors operate today.

Or, perhaps you prefer to look for great, high-return, well-protected franchise businesses that can compound at above-average rates for long periods of time, companies in situations where competition is somehow being kept at bay. Another huge swath of modern value investors spend their time primarily in this field, looking for great companies at reasonable prices.

Maybe you're at your investing best when scouring the universe of micro-cap companies where institutional investors can't go, or then again, maybe you tend to find the most value in well-followed mid- and large-cap companies trading in plain sight. You might like to find the "undiscovered" opportunities yourself, or maybe you're more prone to wait for well-respected, well-informed investors to do the work first, then "coattail" their ideas. You might even be interested in influencing corporate management teams yourself by amassing a significant portion of a company's outstanding shares. With micro-cap companies, some individuals will have this additional option open to them.

Which of these can we say was Buffett's style in the Partnership years when he was working with relatively modest capital? The answer is he was all the above. You can be, too. There is absolutely no need to classify yourself into a particular style bucket. You will, however, need to figure out what is and isn't going to work for you. You may be capable or inclined to operate in some of the above fields and not in others. There are no right answers. No one approach is necessarily better than another, although some might be better *for you than others*. Once you understand yourself, you can simply go where the opportunities are.

By tracing the arc and diversity of Buffett's investing styles and understanding why he migrated his focus from Graham's deep value focus to a larger interest in quality, we can take and use the methods that will work best for us in our own investment endeavors. We start with the Generals, or generally undervalued securities, because these were, and remain, the bread-and-butter general equity investments that have always defined value investing.

For Buffett, the Generals were a highly secretive, highly concentrated portfolio of undervalued common stocks that produced the majority of the Partnership's overall gains. Buffett was the ultimate craftsman in the art of stock picking and this was the primary field in which he plied his trade. No General was ever named explicitly, with one exception, Commonwealth Trust Company, which Buffett disclosed only after the investment operation was complete and the stock was no longer a holding of the Partnership. He disclosed it in order to illustrate the type of stocks he was buying in this category. Individual investments were otherwise considered trade secrets.

Using the Moody's Manuals and other primary sources of statistical data, Buffett scoured the field to find stocks trading at rock-bottom valuations. Often these were tiny, obscure, and off-the-radar companies trading below their liquidation value. In the early years especially, the Partnership was small enough to be largely unconstrained, allowing for a go-anywhere, do-anything approach, similar to that of most individual investors today. As the Partnership grew, smaller companies became increasingly less investable; when BPL got too big, even if they could have acquired a significant amount of these companies' outstanding shares, the investment dollars at stake would just be too small to move the needle on the Partnership's overall results.

Regardless of size, all investors can follow Buffett's lead and load up when we find a really good idea that meets our requirements. Throughout the Partnership years, Buffett typically committed 5–10% of his total assets in five or six Generals with smaller positions in another 10–15%.[2] Concentrating on the best ideas was a key component of his success. We see him take this concept even further in 1965 when he amended the ground rules to allow as much as 40% of the portfolio in a single General.

You'll recall from lessons in Part I that the investor's primary focus is on getting the business analysis and the valuation right, not the timing of when they will work out. Many of the Generals remained in the portfolio for years. As the Partnership grew and additional capital was received, Buffett would add to existing positions that remained attractively priced. Buffett trusted his method to the point that he wasn't affected by the day-to-day vagaries of the market; he believed that sooner or later, the market would reward his analysis and valuation efforts.

With a portfolio of value stocks, investors should expect that some will be "working"—rising in price faster than the overall market—while others will be lying fallow or even declining. Irving Kahn, a Buffett contemporary and former teaching assistant to

Graham, had the best analogy for this. He taught that an investment portfolio is like an orchard of fruit trees. You cannot expect fruit every year from each species of tree. Each will ripen according to its own, typically unknowable schedule.[3] In aggregate, though, a portfolio of properly selected Generals should do better than the market over time. For the Partnership, Buffett expected his would do about 10% better.

> *Sometimes these work out very fast; many times they take years. It is difficult at the time of purchase to know any specific reason why they should appreciate in price. However, because of this lack of glamour or anything pending which might create immediate favorable market action, they are available at very cheap prices. A lot of value can be obtained for the price paid. This substantial excess of value creates a comfortable margin of safety in each transaction. This individual margin of safety, coupled with a diversity of commitments creates a most attractive package of safety and appreciation potential. Over the years our timing of purchases has been considerably better than our timing of sales. We do not go into these generals with the idea of getting the last nickel, but are usually quite content selling out at some intermediate level between our purchase price and what we regard as fair value to a private owner.[4]*

Many of the Generals were acquired at steep discounts to their appraised intrinsic value using the private owner method—what a well-informed private buyer would pay for the entire company. These tended to be much smaller companies where, if the stock remained dormant in price for long enough, Buffett would come to gain a large enough stake to have a say over how it was being run. He was, in effect, willing to become the "well-informed private buyer" himself. Through this process, several companies that started out as Generals became controlled investments of the Partnership, and thus a wholly separate category of investments that we'll explore later in this section.

Occasionally, other private owners—third parties, not Buffett—would buy the Partnership out of its stake in a General to obtain control for themselves. This made the private owner method a less risky investment method because the stocks would either appreciate on their own, or Buffett (or some other third party) would acquire enough stock to at least influence and sometimes take full control of the companies. This typically led companies to take the necessary steps to realize the value inherent in their business. As long as he was right in his analysis and the value was really there, the chance of a permanent loss in these types of investments was minimal.

Later, Buffett expanded beyond this private owner method for selecting Generals and began acquiring the stocks of companies that he deemed too large for a single private owner to acquire but that were still undervalued relative to where peer companies were trading. To distinguish this group he subdivided Generals. The Generals we've been discussing up to this point were now called "Generals–Private Owner" and the new category was called "Generals–Relatively Undervalued."

This new investment method was somewhat riskier because there was no potential for the Buffett partnership or any other private owner to acquire control in these companies; Buffett mitigated some of that risk by hedging them, meaning when he bought one he would sell short* the more expensive peer company. For example, by buying a stock trading at 10 times earnings and simultaneously shorting a similar company trading at 20 times earnings, Buffett reduced the risk of overpaying for the company he liked because if it declined to, say, 8 times, one would expect the stock of the company he sold short (at 20 times) to decline further.

Both categories of Generals are more sensitive to the market's cycle than Workouts and Controls. As Buffett put it:

Just because something is cheap does not mean it is not going to go down. During abrupt downward movements in the

---

* A position that benefits from a decline in price.

> market, this segment may very well go down percentage-wise
> just as much as the Dow. Over a period of years, I believe
> the generals will outperform the Dow, and during sharply ad-
> vancing years . . . this is the section of our portfolio that turns
> in the best results. It is, of course, also the most vulnerable in
> a declining market.[5]

Because the market trends higher over time, this isn't much of a drawback longer term but it can impact performance figures from year to year. If the Partnership had only invested in Generals, its year-to-year record would not have been nearly as stable as it was.

The essential methods involved in investing in Generals come down to doing good valuation work and doing it consistently. Intrinsic value can be estimated a number of different ways. Most are a derivation of an appraisal of either the value of a company's (1) assets or (2) earnings power. Each method, asset based or earnings based, can be useful at different times and indeed they are linked; the value of any asset will always be linked to the earnings it is capable of producing. However, one approach is typically more practical depending on the situation.

The current level of profit in relation to the assets of any business can help steer you to the appropriate choice; often both an earnings and an asset-based approach can be used to cross-check one against the other. The letters provide examples of Buffett using both.

In some situations, Buffett was buying companies that were not very profitable but owned valuable assets. When a company is doing a poor job generating sufficient earnings in relation to the value of its assets, a liquidation value approach, which estimates the realizable resale or auction value of the assets, can be the best choice. Graham is best known for this approach. He got excited when he came upon the ultra-cheap companies that had liquid current assets (here we're talking about cash in the bank, unsold inventories, or receivables) that in aggregate, even after subtracting all the liabilities of the business, were worth more than the market value of the company. We see Buffett using this approach as well, especially in the early years.

In other cases where companies had earnings that were healthy, we see Buffett using an earnings-based valuation. This can be the way to go when the business is expected to continue largely "as is." It is a simple estimation of the present value of all future expected earnings.

As mentioned, Commonwealth Trust of Union City, New Jersey, was the first and only General described in the letters and offers a glimpse into his methods. Buffett evaluated the company's value based on an earnings approach. Commonwealth had earnings of about $10 per share, which he saw as resilient and growing. As he described it, he figured the intrinsic value of such an earnings stream was $125 per share* and he expected that value to build over time. It should be no surprise then, that when the stock became available at $50, he put 10–20% of the various 1957 partnerships into the stock. In 1958 he sold at $80 in order to move on to another stock he liked even more.

You can gain great insights about investing from a careful study of Buffett's Generals. He was constantly appraising the value of as many stocks as he could find, looking for the ones where he felt he had a reasonable ability to understand the business and come up with an estimate for its worth. With a prodigious memory and many years of intense study, he built up an expansive memory bank full of these appraisals and opinions on a huge number of companies. Then, when Mr. Market offered one at a sufficiently attractive discount to its appraised value, he bought it; he often concentrated heavily in a handful of the most attractive ones. Good valuation work and proper temperament have always been the two keys pillars of his success as an investor.

Buffett was a highly disciplined buyer, especially in the early years. In many cases, a stock that he was involved in appreciated before he could buy the full amount he wanted. He took several opportunities to lament those lost opportunities, noting that while

---

* While Buffett never explicitly laid out his math, the value of $10 in annual earnings growing at 2% is $125 when discounted back to present value at a 10% rate.

partners may have been satisfied with the near-term performance figures these "stub" positions produced, he recognized that had those stocks not appreciated so quickly he would have been able to acquire more and the ultimate results for the Partnership would have been better. This happened in 1966:

> *While any gains looked particularly good in the market environment that intimately developed in 1966, you can be sure I don't delight in going round making molehills out of mountains. The molehill, of course, was reflected in 1966 results. However, we would have been much better off from a long range standpoint if 1966 results had been five percentage points worse and we were continuing to buy substantial quantities of the stock at the depressed prices that might have been expected to prevail in this year's market environment.*[6]

Why Generals Work

On May 17, 1984, the fiftieth anniversary of the first publication of *Securities Analysis*, Buffett laid out why value investing works, in one of his seminal speeches, titled "The Super Investors of Graham-and-Doddsville." The "Super Investors" he identified were a relatively small group of Graham students and disciples, himself and Charlie Munger included, who all had a long history of investing in Generals. To Buffett, the collective superior performance of this cohort proved the validity of the value investing method and demonstrated a great flaw in the efficient market hypothesis.

Buffett encouraged listeners to think of how unlikely it would be that ten finalists in a hypothetical national coin-flipping contest would all hail from the same town. If investing success was all luck and randomness (as the efficient market theory suggested)—just like coin flipping—how could the country's best all originate from the same town, Graham-and-Doddsville, USA, where everyone was using the same methods? The Super Investors of Graham and Doddsville's tremendous results represented a statistical absurdity under the efficient market framework, which would have predicted that the successful investors were randomly distributed throughout the country.

After introducing the stellar records of this anomalous group, Buffett laid out their unifying method, which should sound familiar:

> *While they differ greatly in style, these investors are, mentally,* always buying the business, not buying the stock *(emphasis Buffett). . . . Their attitude, whether buying all or a tiny piece of a business, is the same. Some of them hold portfolios with dozens of stocks; others concentrate on a handful. But all exploit the difference between the market price of a business and its intrinsic value.*

Value investors' methods are highly atypical in one important way. Usually when a new idea or rules-based trading system is introduced and shown to be effective, market participants copy it, and by doing so, the excess return from the new idea gets "arbitraged away." Simply buying cheap stocks, however, has remained a remarkably effective strategy, despite the fact that its efficacy has been well documented for decades. Buffett concludes his famous speech by addressing this anomaly:

> *I can only tell you that the secret has been out for 50 years, ever since Ben Graham and David Dodd wrote* Security Analysis, *yet I have seen no trend toward value investing in the last 35 years I've practiced it. There seems to be some perverse human characteristic that likes to make easy things difficult. The academic world, if anything, has actually backed away from the teaching of value investing over the last 30 years. It is likely to continue that way. Ships will sail around the world but the Flat Earth Society will continue to flourish. There will*

continue to be wide discrepancies between price and value in
the marketplace, and those who read their Graham & Dodd
will continue to prosper.

And the crowd goes wild . . . The full text of the speech is available on Columbia's website.

The Deep Value Method

Graham, in a 1946 Graham-Newman's investor letter that Buffett surely read, spoke about how his investment company largely focused on the purchase of "securities at prices less than their intrinsic value as determined by careful analysis, with particular emphasis on purchase of securities at less than their liquidating value."[7] The origin of this approach was grounded in the history of its creator.

Buffett's mentor had been wiped out in the stock market crash of 1929; Benjamin Graham's own mother was devastated by the crash before it. There is little surprise Graham focused on tangible net asset and liquidation values in order to ensure that a significant backstop of value existed to limit the risk of a permanent loss in an investment.

Because his primary focus was not to lose money, Graham liked to "look down before he looked up." He relished acquiring companies that could (if necessary) be shuttered, where all the assets could be sold off and all the debts and obligations extinguished, and yet still, once all this activity was complete, a residual amount would be remaining as a profit above the market price. These companies were literally worth more dead (in liquidation) than they were alive (as going concerns). It's not that the companies were actually liquidated all that often, although sometimes they were—the point was that there was value in the equity even in liquidation. Graham's system not only generated healthy returns, but also all but ensured that he would never go broke again.

Buffett was also purchasing these kinds of stocks for the Partnership, called "net-nets" for short. In these situations, he often found some combination of a large pile of cash, securities in the bank, trade receivables due, or salable inventory. The collective liquidation value of these assets alone was "netted" against all the company's liabilities—when what remained was still worth more than the market price of the company, he possessed a large margin of safety.

Buyers like Graham and Buffett (and the once-famous Ned "Net-Quick" Evans, whose name in his era was as well known as Buffett's is today) defined the times by investing in these types of situations. Whether they chose to wind up the business at a profit or allowed it to recover on its own, they were usually buying below the liquidation value, getting the value of the underlying business for free or even at a *negative* value.

Think about that. Take a simplified example of a company with a market value of $45 that has no debt, and cash and securities in the bank worth $65. The only way that market price can make sense is if the company's underlying business is expected to produce either a large amount or a long stream of losses in the future. How else could a business have a negative present value of $20? Should the business simply liquidate, the buyer at $45 stands to receive the full $65 value of the cash and securities, realizing a 45% gain ($20), before factoring in the other assets and the cost of winding it up.

Of course, if the business operates at a loss that is expected to continue indefinitely, it will eventually erode away any surpluses that may be present. In such cases, something has to be done to preserve the value, either through the action of a motivated management or through actions taken by the shareholders. After all, shareholders—the owners of the business—have the ultimate say. They elect the board of directors, who in turn hire the management and set the strategy.

As Buffett describes it, Generals that also offered the potential for a majority stake represented a " 'two strings to our bow' situation where we should either achieve appreciation of market prices from external factors or from the acquisition of a controlling position in a business at a bargain price. While the former happens in the overwhelming majority of cases, the latter represents an insurance policy most investment operations don't have."[8] In other words, Buffett was willing to take the action needed to realize the value in his net-nets if necessary. In the 1980s, this approach was called "corporate raiding," but is now more politely referred to as activism. Buffett was willing to take on management if that's what was necessary to create value.

Better yet was when he spotted others doing the work on behalf of all shareholders, and he could go along for the ride. Investing alongside them but not participating in the activism directly was called "coattail riding." Anyone can do that. Buying the securities right after an activist files a 13D, a formal Securities and Exchange Commission document signaling an investor's intent to attempt influence over corporate decisions, is a strategy that has meaningfully outperformed the market over time.[9]

Today Graham-inspired ultra-cheap Generals tend to emerge in smaller, obscure securities. They frequently trade off the major exchanges and their prices are often published only periodically, as opposed to the mainstream issues that are listed in the newspapers daily. Often these companies are not covered by Wall Street research houses. Buffett and his contemporaries had to hunt for them—and they loved the hunt.

This is fertile ground for small, enterprising investors. First, familiarize yourself with all the net-nets in the market. While Buffett thumbed through the Moody's Manual page by page, there are plenty of free stock screeners on the Web these days to help you get started. Then as you go along, cross the ones off the list when you find a disqualifier, such as a hidden liability or a lawsuit that causes the stock to screen as a net-net even when it isn't.

One warning: It's very unlikely that anyone is going to bring these investment opportunities to you; you have to find them yourself. Be particularly skeptical of stock promoters in this area of the market. If you find yourself being "pitched" a stock of this sort, first grab your wallet, then run!

One current example of a net-net is Nam Tai Property Inc.,[10] a closely held, small-cap U.S.-listed company (symbol NTP) that has shifted its business from the manufacturing of electronic components to the development of property in China. The total market value of the company is currently around $219 million, or $5.52 for each of the 39.62 million shares outstanding. With $250 million, or $6.15 per share of net cash in the bank, an investor today can purchase Nam Tai's dollar bills in the bank for 90 cents apiece and also get all the other assets of the company, mostly properties in China that I believe have substantial value, for free.

Nam Tai's ultra-cheap price is largely an anomaly but can be partially understood by several key facts: First, it's a very small company. With a total market cap of less than $250 million, most professional investors will deem it too small to do the work on. Second, it's in the process of shifting its business model from manufacturing to property development and so it's hard to say with any precision what level of earnings they will be capable of producing in the future. Third, there are no Wall Street analysts currently publishing research on the company. Lastly, their operations are all in China and China is currently out of favor.

The New Idea

Grahamite "Super Investors" were all originally taught to jump from cheap stock to cheap stock. The results were typically fabulous and the chance of loss was small. Again, most of these are not good businesses, but they are often mouthwateringly cheap, and good returns for buyers of a portfolio of these securities are almost a lock given the prices paid. Buffett, looking back twelve years into the Partnership, said, "over the years this has been our best category, measured by average return, and has also maintained by far the best percentage of profitable transactions. This approach was the way I was taught the business, and it formerly accounted for a large proportion of all our investment ideas. Our total individual profits in this category during the twelve-year BPL history are probably fifty times or more our total losses."

Buffett has since called the whole category of net-nets and other ultra-cheap stocks his "soggy cigar-butts." To this day he describes these often marginally profitable companies as mostly gross and disgusting from a business standpoint, but for a time he did very well investing in them because they offered a "free puff" (profit) with little risk of permanent loss. Today a partial interest in a situation like Nam Tai Property, even at $220 million for the whole company, would be of little interest to Buffett, who's looking for multibillion-dollar investments. Nam Tai simply can't move the needle for him, even if he could buy the whole company at the current price.

Throughout the Partnership, as his assets grew and his thinking evolved, Buffett continued to move toward a broader range in defining what "value" really meant and became increasingly willing to broaden the scope of what he would accept in the form of downside protection. He began looking more at the quality of the business to determine how sustainable and therefore valuable its earnings might be, moving progressively further away from the statistically cheap hard asset valuation approach used for the "cigar butt" net-nets.

For partners, Buffett provided his most explicit recognition of this evolutionary transition in his fall letter of 1967. As he said then,

> *The evaluation of securities and businesses for investment purposes has always involved a mixture of qualitative and quantitative factors. At the one extreme, the analyst exclusively oriented to qualitative factors would say, "Buy the right company (with the right prospects, inherent industry conditions, management, etc.) and the price will take care of itself." On the other hand, the quantitative spokesman would say, "Buy at the right price and the company (and stock) will take care of itself." As is so often the pleasant result in the securities world, money can be made with either approach. And, of course, any analyst combines the two to some extent—his classification in either school would depend on the relative*

weight he assigns to the various factors and not to his consideration of one group of factors to the exclusion of the other group.

Interestingly enough, although I consider myself to be primarily in the quantitative school (and as I write this no one has come back from recess—I may be the only one left in the class), the really sensational ideas I have had over the years have been heavily weighted toward the qualitative side where I have had a "high-probability insight." This is what causes the cash register to really sing. However, it is an infrequent occurrence, as insights usually are, and, of course, no insight is required on the quantitative side—the figures should hit you over the head with a baseball bat. So the really big money tends to be made by investors who are right on qualitative decisions but, at least in my opinion, the more sure money tends to be made on the obvious quantitative decisions.

As you read his comments, remember that while the net-nets and ultra-cheap stocks had largely vanished by 1967, and while he felt that when it came to his quantitative approach to investing, he "may be the only one left in class," this was only a temporary phenomenon. Quantifiable opportunities are often available, particularly at market cycle lows, and while the extreme cases of ultra-cheap net-nets have become more infrequent from cycle to cycle, value investors of the more quantitative bent, with marginally lower standards of what defines cheap, still manage to do very well with the bargains they find.

As he continued in the 1967 letter,

October 1967
Such statistical bargains have tended to disappear over the years. This may be due to the constant combing and recombing of investments that has occurred during the past twenty years, without an economic convulsion such as that of the '30s to create a negative bias toward equities and spawn hundreds

of new bargain securities. It may be due to the new grow-
ing social acceptance, and therefore usage (or maybe it's vice
versa—I'll let the behaviorists figure it out) of takeover bids
which have a natural tendency to focus on bargain issues. It
may be due to the exploding ranks of security analysts bring-
ing forth an intensified scrutiny of issues far beyond what ex-
isted some years ago. Whatever the cause, the result has been
the virtual disappearance of the bargain issue as determined
quantitatively—and thereby of our bread and butter. There
still may be a few from time to time. There will also be the oc-
casional security where I am really competent to make an im-
portant qualitative judgment. This will offer our best chance
for large profits. Such instances will, however, be rare. Much
of our good performance during the past three years has been
due to a single idea of this sort.[11]

Here we can see two distinct factors operating simultaneously. First, as the bull market was maturing, it was getting harder and harder to find cheap stocks—a phenomenon that is typical of every cycle. But second, and more interesting because it was independent of the market cycle, is Buffett's growing appreciation for the qualities that make a business "good" as opposed to just cheap. When he said that "much of our good performance during the past three years has been due to a single idea of this sort,"[12] he was talking about the huge position he had taken in American Express, a high-quality franchise business that was not statistically cheap in the Graham sense but had a tremendous amount of future earnings power. It was a franchise business. As he continued to gain assets he had no choice but to leave the cigar butt strategy behind; he outgrew it financially.

Let's fast-forward to Buffett's 2014 Berkshire letter, where he looked back on this time in his life and the merits of the early "cigar-butt" strategy:

My cigar-butt strategy worked very well while I was manag-
ing small sums. Indeed, the many dozens of free puffs I ob-

*tained in the 1950's made the decade by far the best of my life
for both relative and absolute performance. . . .*

*But a major weakness in this approach gradually became
apparent: Cigar-butt investing was scalable only to a point.
With large sums, it would never work well.*

*In addition, though marginal businesses purchased at cheap
prices may be attractive as short-term investments, they are
the wrong foundation on which to build a large and enduring
enterprise. Selecting a marriage partner clearly requires more
demanding criteria than does dating. (Berkshire, it should be
noted, would have been a highly satisfactory "date": If we had
taken [the tender offer presented], BPL's weighted annual return
on its Berkshire investment would have been about 40%.)*

The Quality Compounder Method

As you'll recall, Buffett's slow evolution away from statistical bargains, net-nets, and cigar butts toward better businesses caused
him to split the category to accommodate some of his new ideas.
The new subcategory of Generals was called "Generals–Relatively
Undervalued." Here Buffett was further breaking away from
Graham in some additional ways, largely as a result of Munger's influence. As Buffett continued in his look-back letter, "It took Charlie
Munger to break my cigar-butt habits and set the course for building
a business that could combine huge size with satisfactory profits. . . .
The blueprint he gave me was simple: Forget what you know about
buying fair businesses at wonderful prices; instead, buy wonderful
businesses at fair prices."

Munger also chimed in himself in that letter, looking back on
their evolved thinking and saying,

*having started out as Grahamites—which, by the way, worked
fine—we gradually got what I would call better insights. And*

we realized that some company that was selling at two or three
times book value could still be a hell of a bargain because of
the momentum implicit in its position, sometimes combined
with an unusual managerial skill plainly present in some indi-
vidual or other, or some system or other.

    And once we'd gotten over the hurdle of recognizing that
a thing could be based on quantitative measures that would
have horrified Graham, we started thinking about better busi-
nesses. . . . Buffett Partnership, for example, owned American
Express and Disney when they got pounded down.[13]

Buffett introduced this new category to partners in 1964, the
same year he bought the large stake in American Express. There
was a scandal at one of its subsidiaries that created a potentially
large liability and was perceived to threaten the reputation and
value of the brand—the stock had gotten pummeled. Once Buffett realized the issues were recoverable, and that America Express
could survive the scandal with its brand, reputation, and business
fundamentals still intact, Buffett loaded up. The beauty of American Express, like many others in the Generals–Relatively Undervalued category, was that it produced magnificent profits year in
and year out. He could potentially hold it for a very long time,
while most Generals–Private Owner investments, with their one
free puff, required a treadmill of work.

American Express would dominate the Partnership's portfolio
in its last several years. This was the stock that caused Buffett to
amend the Ground Rules so he could invest up to 40% of the fund
in the company. The $13 million he invested produced a whopping
$20 million in profits, more than any other investment BPL ever
produced in a single security.

Another major purchase for this new category of Generals was
the Walt Disney Company. After he and Munger dissected the business while touring the park on a family vacation, Buffett bought
5% of the company for $4 million in 1965.[14] Buffett figured he had
a softer, less tangible, but equally valuable backstop in the value of

the video library, which he estimated justified the stock price on its own with the parks and studio "thrown in for free." In a way, he was straddling the quality stocks versus cigar-butt hard asset. Today Buffett talks about buying great businesses at a fair price—these were great businesses at a great price. In keeping with his earlier dictate not to reveal the names of individual firms in which the Partnership had invested, Buffett never told his partners that they were such substantial owners of either company.

What Should You Do?

Let's return to the question we opened this chapter with: Assuming you are an investor operating with modest sums, should you follow an approach more like Graham and early Buffett, which emphasize statistical value, or should you emphasize quality, in line with how Buffett was investing toward the end of the Partnership? Should you focus on the surer things in balance-sheet-oriented bargains, or is it better to look for the great, enduring, high-quality businesses that have become the hallmark of Berkshire's acquisition strategy more or less since 1967? One can make a strong case for either method, just as many well-respected investors have done. Both can work, but what's right for you will depend on the size of funds you are working with, your personality, your own ability to do good valuation work, and your ability to define objectively the outer edges of your own competence.

Tobias Carlisle, with his 2014 book, *Deep Value*, comes out as a good example of a Graham purist. His research shows that the worse a cheap company's fundamentals, the better the stock is likely to do. With his deeply quantitative orientation, Tobias has developed something he calls the "Acquirer's Multiple"[15] to identify and systematically make good investment decisions. He seems to have found something that he understands and that works well for him. Note that he literally shuns quality in his approach to finding value.

Below-average returns in an industry tend to cause competitors to flee. Managements motivated to restore at least an adequate return on their time and money often change strategy, improve their process, or stop doing the business that is losing money. Buying stocks that are cheap when the companies are struggling gives the investor a chance to be rewarded twice: once through improved business results and then again through an improved market valuation in accordance with the better business results. Tobias's picks are available on his website.

While he's smart to have found something that works for him, he's even smarter to avoid what doesn't. O*f course* he'd prefer to buy a great business over a poor business *if* he could be sure that it could maintain its high returns well into the future. However, he hasn't yet found a way to identify the companies with the factors needed to protect those high returns from competition, at least systematically, so he avoids them.

In a free market system, high-return businesses naturally attract competitors seeking to get in on the action. In the absence of barriers to entry, these competitors will keep coming into an industry until all the outsize returns have been leveled. While this dynamic is the engine of our economic system and the reason behind decades of massive productivity gains for American corporations, it's also the reason returns on equity have consistently cycled around 12–14%. That was true in the 1950s and it's true today. Competition tends to drive good returns down with only a few exceptions. Those who choose to find value in highly profitable companies need to find the ones that are going to stay that way.

Tom Gayner, the longtime investment manager for the Markel Corporation, is a wonderful example of a modern investor with a deep-seated quality bias. He's willing to assess the ability for a high-quality company to endure. He looks for high-return, established businesses with strong track records of success through past business cycles, run by managers demonstrating equal measures of talent and integrity. He wants companies to reinvest earnings into high-incremental-return projects when they are available and return the remaining earnings to shareholders when they are not. Finally, he looks for a reasonable purchase price. He's found a way to out-perform the indexes for decades with his system.

Tom emphasizes that you have to get only a very small number of these right for this type of strategy to really pay off. The companies you get right will harness the power of compounding and grow to dwarf the mistakes. He argues that investors who make twenty or so sound purchases over a lifetime will come to see one or two grow to become a significant percentage of their net worth.

Tom has a great example of this phenomenon that also reminds us not to pigeonhole Ben Graham as purely a deep value investor. Graham paid up for quality when he bought the insurance company GEICO—he ended up making more profits from that single invest-ment than he did from all his other activities combined.[16]

Tom's strategy is almost the opposite of Tobias's but he under-stands it and it works for him. Neither one is "right" or "wrong"; each has developed a value system that works for him. What's right in investing is what works for the individual.

Other well-respected modern investors, also unconstrained by the size of their capital base, are able to invest using both categories. Professor Joel Greenblatt, a brilliant investment manager, has put together one of history's best track records by investing in special situations and misunderstood small-cap companies. He now uses a system that quantitatively identifies high-quality stocks trading at attractive valuations that he calls the magic formula, which has also worked exceedingly well.

As you can see, there are many ways modern investors are suc-cessfully utilizing the various methods used in the Partnership years, even the ones Buffett himself has long since moved on from. When they were available to him, he did wonderfully well with the net-nets and cigar butts that Tobias now favors. Some of his highest-return years were had when he was investing in the 1950s in the spe-cial situations that Greenblatt later did so well with. When his funds grew to a size that made these types of activities too small to move the performance needle, he moved on to investing in the style Tom

Gayner has largely picked up on. All work. The important question is, really, what will work for you.

Here again, as you can probably guess by now, we are talking about knowing yourself, what Buffett would later call the circle of competence. Remaining in the circle is a linchpin of Buffett's success. He has consistently shown that when he finds something he likes and can understand, whether it be a net-net or a compounder, he has pounced. He passes on anything seen as outside the circle.

In a 2007 talk to students, Buffett gave the following advice, which sums up the idea of how you should be investing in Generals with your circle of competence in mind:

> *I have three mailboxes in my office—IN, OUT, and TOO HARD. I was joking with the MIT students that I should have a TOO HARD bin and they made me one, so now I have it and I use it. I will only swing at pitches that I really like. If you do it 10 times in your life, you'll be rich. You should approach investing like you have a punch card with 20 punch-outs, one for each trade in your life.*[17]

As Buffett continued in his talk to students,

> *I think people would be better off if they only had 10 opportunities to buy stocks throughout their lifetime. You know what would happen? They would make sure that each buy was a good one. They would do lots and lots of research before they made the buy. You don't have to have many 4X growth opportunities to get rich. You don't need to do too much, but the environment makes you feel like you need to do something all the time.*[18]

Here is a checklist for evaluating a potential investment in a General: (1) Orient: What tools or special knowledge is required to understand the situation? Do I have them? (2) Analyze: What are the economics inherent to the business and the industry? How do they relate to my long-term expectations for earnings and cash flows? (3) Invert: What are the likely ways I'll be wrong? If I'm wrong, how much can I lose? (4) What is the current intrinsic value of the business? How fast is it growing or shrinking? And finally, (5) Compare: does the discount to intrinsic value, properly weighted for both the downside risk and upside reward, compare favorably to all the other options available to me?

If you find yourself unable to make it all the way through the checklist, then write down in a single paragraph the merits of the investment. If you get caught up along the way, either do more work or simply forget the idea as "too hard" and move on to something else.

While Buffett has made many investments over his long career, only a small handful have accounted for the vast majority of the wealth he's been able to create. Recognizing this, Buffett encourages investors to make a punch card, then only use it when you find yourself inside your own circle of competence. Consider this as you read the following case study of Buffett's early General, the Commonwealth Trust Company of Union City, New Jersey, where he put 20% of the early Partnership's assets:

|||||||||||||||||||||||||||||||||||||||||||||||||||||||||||||||||||||||||||||||||||||||||||||||||||||||||||||||||||||||||||||

BPL Case Study: Commonwealth Trust

|||||||||||||||||||||||||||||||||||||||||||||||||||||||||||||||||||||||||||||||||||||||||||||||||||||||||||||||||||||||||||||

FEBRUARY 11, 1959
Typical Situation

So that you may better understand our method of operation, I think it would be well to review a specific activity of 1958. Last year I referred to our largest holding which comprised 10% to 20% of the assets of the various partnerships. I pointed out that it was to our interest to have this stock decline or remain relatively steady, so that we could acquire an even larger position and that for this reason such a security would probably hold back our comparative performance in a bull market.

This stock was the Commonwealth Trust Co. of Union City, New Jersey. At the time we started to purchase the stock, it had an intrinsic value of $125 per share computed on a conservative basis. However, for good reasons, it paid no cash dividend at all despite earnings of about $10 per share which was largely responsible for a depressed price of about $50 per share. So here we had a very well managed bank with substantial earnings power selling at a large discount from intrinsic value. Management was friendly to us as new stockholders and risk of any ultimate loss seemed minimal.

Commonwealth was 25.5% owned by a larger bank (Commonwealth had assets of about $50 Million—about half the size of the First National in Omaha), which had desired a merger for many years. Such a merger was prevented for personal reasons, but there was evidence that this situation would not continue indefinitely. Thus we had a combination of:

- Very strong defensive characteristics;
- Good solid value building up at a satisfactory pace and;
- Evidence to the effect that eventually this value would be unlocked although it might be one year or ten years. If the latter were true, the value would presumably have been built up to a considerably larger figure, say, $250 per share.

Over a period of a year or so, we were successful in obtaining about 12% of the bank at a price averaging about $51 per share. Obviously it was definitely to our advantage to have the stock remain dormant in price. Our block of stock increased in value as its size grew, particularly after we became the second largest stockholder with sufficient voting power to warrant consultation on any merger proposal.

Commonwealth only had about 300 stockholders and probably averaged two trades or so per month, so you can understand why I say that the activity of the stock market generally had very little effect on the price movement of some of our holdings.

Unfortunately we did run into some competition on buying, which raised the price to about $65 where we were neither buyer nor seller. Very small buying orders can create price changes of this magnitude in an inactive stock, which explains the importance of not having any "Leakage" regarding our portfolio holdings.

Late in the year we were successful in finding a special situation where we could become the largest holder at an attractive price, so we sold our block of Commonwealth obtaining $80 per share although the quoted market was about 20% lower at the time.

It is obvious that we could still be sitting with $50 stock patiently buying in dribs and drabs, and I would be quite happy with such a program although our performance relative to the market last year would have looked poor. The year when a situation such as Commonwealth results in a realized profit is, to a great extent, fortuitous. Thus, our performance for any single year has serious limitations as a basis for estimating long term results. However, I believe that a program of investing in such undervalued well protected securities offers the surest means of long term profits in securities.

I might mention that the buyer of the stock at $80 can expect to do quite well over the years. However, the relative undervaluation at $80 with an intrinsic value of $135 is quite different from a price of $50 with an intrinsic value of $125, and it seemed to me that our capital could better be employed in the situation which replaced it. This new situation is somewhat larger than Commonwealth and represents about 25% of the assets of the various partnerships. While the degree of undervaluation is no greater than in many other securities we own (or even than some) we are the largest stockholder and this has substantial advantages many times in determining the length of time required to correct the undervaluation. In this particular holding we are virtually assured of a performance better than that of the Dow-Jones for the period we hold it.

The Current Situation

The higher the level of the market, the fewer the undervalued securities and I am finding some difficulty in securing an adequate number of attractive investments. I would prefer to increase the percentage of our assets in work-outs, but these are very difficult to find on the right terms.

To the extent possible, therefore, I am attempting to create my own work-outs by acquiring large positions in several undervalued securities. Such a policy should lead to the fulfillment of my earlier forecast—an above-average performance in a bear market. It is on this basis that I hope to be judged. If you have any questions, feel free to ask them.

Warren E. Buffett 2-11-59

From the Partnership Letters: The Generals

JANUARY 18, 1964

"Generals"—A category of generally undervalued stocks, determined primarily by quantitative standards, but with considerable attention also paid to the qualitative factor. There is often little or nothing to indicate immediate market improvement. The issues lack glamour or market sponsorship. Their main qualification is a bargain price; that is, an overall valuation on the enterprise substantially below what careful analysis indicates its value to a private owner to be. Again let me emphasize that while the quantitative comes first and is essential, the qualitative is important. We like good management—we like a decent industry—we like a certain amount of "ferment" in a previously dormant management or stockholder group. But we demand value. . . .

||||||||||||||||||||||||||||||||||||||||||||||||||||||||||||||||||||||||||||||||||||||||||||||||||||||||||||||||||||||||||||||||||||||||||||||||||||||||||||||||

JANUARY 24, 1962

Over the years, this has been our largest category of investment, and more money has been made here than in either of the other categories. We usually have fairly large positions (5% to 10% of our total assets) in each of five or six generals, with smaller positions in another ten or fifteen.

Sometimes these work out very fast; many times they take years. It is difficult at the time of purchase to know any specific reason why they should appreciate in price. However, because of this lack of glamour or anything pending which might create immediate favorable market action, they are available at very cheap prices. A lot of value can be obtained for the price paid. This substantial excess of value creates a comfortable margin of safety in each transaction. This individual margin of safety, coupled with a diversity of commitments creates a most attractive package of safety and appreciation potential. Over the years our timing of purchases has been considerably better than our timing of sales. We do not go into these generals with the idea of getting the last nickel, but are usually quite content selling out at some intermediate level between our purchase price and what we regard as fair value to a private owner.

The generals tend to behave market-wise very much in sympathy with the Dow. Just because something is cheap does not mean it is not going to go down. During abrupt downward movements in the market, this segment may very well go down percentage-wise just as much as the Dow. Over a period of years, I believe the generals will outperform the Dow, and during sharply advancing years like 1961, this is the section of our portfolio that turns in the best results. It is, of course, also the most vulnerable in a declining market.

––

JANUARY 18, 1963

Many times generals represent a form of "coattail riding" where we feel the dominating stockholder group has plans for the conversion of unprofitable or under-utilized assets to a better use. We have done that ourselves in Sanborn and Dempster, but everything else equal we would rather let others do the work. Obviously, not only do the values have to be ample in a case like this, but we also have to be careful whose coat we are holding.

––

JANUARY 18, 1965

Many times in this category we have the desirable "two strings to our bow" situation where we should either achieve appreciation of market prices from external factors or from the acquisition of a controlling position in a business at a bargain price. While the former happens in the overwhelming majority of cases, the latter represents an insurance policy most investment operations don't have. We have continued to enlarge the positions in the three companies described in our 1964 midyear report where we are the largest stockholder. All three companies are increasing their fundamental value at a very satisfactory rate, and we are completely passive in two situations and active only on a very minor scale in the third. It is unlikely that we will ever take a really active part in policy-making in any of these three companies, but we stand ready if needed.

––

JANUARY 20, 1966

Our largest yearend 1964 investment in this category was disposed of in 1965 pursuant to a tender offer. . . . The fundamental concept underlying the Generals–Private Owner category is demonstrated by the above case. A private owner was quite willing (and in our opinion quite wise) to pay a price for control of the business which isolated stock buyers were not willing to pay for very small fractions of the business. This has been a quite common condition in the securities markets over many years, and although purchases in this category work out satisfactorily in terms of just general stock market behavior, there is the occasional dramatic profit due to corporate action such as the one above.

‖‖‖

JANUARY 25, 1967

In the middle of 1965 we started purchasing a very attractive widely held security which was selling far below its value to a private owner. Our hope was that over a two or three year period we could get $10 million or more invested at the favorable prices prevailing. The various businesses that the company operated were understandable and we could check out competitive strengths and weaknesses thoroughly with competitors, distributors, customers, suppliers, ex-employees, etc. Market conditions peculiar to the stock gave us hope that, with patience, we could buy substantial quantities of the stock without disturbing the price.

At yearend 1965 we had invested $1,956,980 and the market value of our holding was $2,358,412 so that $401,432 was contributed to performance during 1965. We would have preferred, of course, to have seen the market below cost since our interest was in additional buying, not in selling. This would have dampened Buffett Partnerships Ltd.'s 1965 performance and perhaps reduced the euphoria experienced by limited partners (psychically, the net result to all partners would have been a standoff since the general partner would have been floating) but would have enhanced long term performance. The fact that the stock had risen somewhat above our cost had already slowed down our buying program and thereby reduced ultimate profit.

An even more dramatic example of the conflict between short term performance and the maximization of long term results occurred in 1966. Another party, previously completely unknown to me, issued a tender offer which foreclosed opportunities for future advantageous buying. I made the decision that the wisest course (it may not have been) for us to follow was to dispose of our holdings and we thus realized a total profit of $1,269,181 in February, of which $867,749 was applicable to 1966.

While any gains looked particularly good in the market environment that intimately developed in 1966, you can be sure I don't delight in going round making molehills out of mountains. The molehill, of course, was reflected in 1966 results. However, we would have been much better off from a long range standpoint if 1966 results had been five percentage points worse and we were continuing to buy substantial quantities of the stock at the depressed prices that might have been expected to prevail in this year's market environment.

If good ideas were a dime a dozen, such a premature ending would not be unpleasant. There is something to be said, of course, for a business operation where some of the failures produce moderate profits. However, you can see how hard it is to develop replacement ideas by examining our average investment in the Private Owner category—we came up with nothing during the remainder of the year despite lower stock prices, which should have been conducive to finding such opportunities.

IIIIIIIIIIIIIIIIIIIIIIIIIIIIIIIIIIIIIIIIIIIIIIIIIIIIIIIIIIIIIIIIIIIIIIIIIIIIIIIIIIIIIIIIIIIIIIIIIIIIIIIIIIIIIIIIIIIIIIIIIIIIIIIIIIIIIIIIIIIIIIIIIIIIIIIIIIIIII

JANUARY 22, 1969

Generals–Private Owner

Over the years this has been our best category, measured by average return, and has also maintained by far the best per-

centage of profitable transactions. This approach was the way
I was taught the business, and it formerly accounted for a large
proportion of all our investment ideas. Our total individual
profits in this category during the twelve year BPL history are
probably fifty times or more our total losses. The cash register
really rang on one simple industry idea (implemented in several ways) in this area in 1968. We even received a substantial
fee (included in Other Income in the audit) for some work in
this field.

||||||||||||||||||||||||||||||||||||||||||||||||||||||||||||||||||||||||||||||||||||||||||||||||||||||||||||||||||||||||||||||||||||||||||||||||||||||

JANUARY 18, 1965

In past annual letters I have always utilized three categories to
describe investment operations we conduct. I now feel that a
four-category division is more appropriate. Partially, the addition of a new section—"Generals–Relatively Undervalued"—
reflects my further consideration of essential differences that
have always existed to a small extent with our "Generals" group.
Partially, it reflects the growing importance of what once was
a very small sub-category but is now a much more significant
part of our total portfolio. This increasing importance has been
accompanied by excellent results to date justifying significant
time and effort devoted to finding additional opportunities in
this area. Finally, it partially reflects the development and implementation of a new and somewhat unique investment technique designed to improve the expectancy and consistency of
operations in this category.

||||||||||||||||||||||||||||||||||||||||||||||||||||||||||||||||||||||||||||||||||||||||||||||||||||||||||||||||||||||||||||||||||||||||||||||||||||||

JANUARY 18, 1965

"Generals–Relatively Undervalued"—this category consists of
securities selling at prices relatively cheap compared to securities of the same general quality. We demand substantial
discrepancies from current valuation standards, but (usually because of large size) do not feel value to a private owner to be a

meaningful concept. It is important in this category, of course, that apples be compared to apples—and not to oranges, and we work hard at achieving that end. In the great majority of cases we simply do not know enough about the industry or company to come to sensible judgments—in that situation we pass.

As mentioned earlier, this new category has been growing and has produced very satisfactory results. We have recently begun to implement a technique, which gives promise of very substantially reducing the risk from an overall change in valuation standards; e.g. If we buy something at 12 times earnings when comparable or poorer quality companies sell at 20 times earnings, but then a major revaluation takes place so the latter only sell at 10 times.

This risk has always bothered us enormously because of the helpless position in which we could be left compared to the "Generals–Private Owner" or "Workouts" types. With this risk diminished, we think this category has a promising future.

||||||||||||||||||||||||||||||||||||||||||||||||||||||||||||||||||||||||||||||||||||||||||||||||||||||||||||||||||||||||||||||||||||||

JANUARY 20, 1966

Our final category is "Generals–Relatively Undervalued." This category has been growing in relative importance as opportunities in the other categories become less frequent.

Frankly, operating in this field is somewhat more ethereal than operating in the other three categories, and I'm just not an ethereal sort. Therefore, I feel accomplishments here are less solid and perhaps less meaningful for future projections than in the other categories. Nevertheless, our results in 1965 were quite good in the "Relatively Undervalued" group, partly due to implementation of the technique referred to in last year's letter which serves to reduce risk and potentially augment gains. It should reduce risk in any year, and it definitely augmented the gains in 1965. It is necessary to point out that results in this category were greatly affected for the better by only two investments.

|||||||||||||||||||||||||||||||||||||||||||||||||||||||||||||||||||||||||||||||||||||||||||||||||||||||||||||||||||||||||||||||||||||||||

JANUARY 25, 1967

One final word about the Generals–Relatively Undervalued category. In this section we also had an experience which helped results in 1966 but hurt our long term prospects. We had just one really important new idea in this category in 1966. Our purchasing started in late spring but had only come to about $1.6 million (it could be bought steadily but at only a moderate pace) when outside conditions drove the stock price up to a point where it was not relatively attractive. Though our overall gain was $728,141 on an average holding period of six and a half months in 1966, it would have been much more desirable had the stock done nothing for a long period of time while we accumulated a really substantial position.

|||||||||||||||||||||||||||||||||||||||||||||||||||||||||||||||||||||||||||||||||||||||||||||||||||||||||||||||||||||||||||||||||||||||||

Compounded Wisdom

In his commentary on Generals we see Buffett departing from teaching *principles* and now teaching *methods*. While principles never change—they are timeless—methods can and often should change according to a given investing environment. We see different methods used by Buffett at various stages of the Partnership, in various stages of the market cycle, in order to best act in accordance with his principles. Through this migration of his style from value to quality, he's providing us with several methods for our own investment endeavors.

Generals-Private Owner and Generals-Relatively Undervalued are the first two tools he's given us and they can provide a wide variety of potential choices in the market. We can hunt for bargains or we can hunt for great businesses. In his discussion of Workouts and Controls, our next two chapters, we'll continue adding tools to our toolkit and see the ways in which Buffett chooses among them.

CHAPTER 7

WORKOUTS

||||||||||||||||||||||||||||||||||||||||||||||||||||||||||||||||||||||||||||||

"Give a man a fish and you feed him for a day. Teach him how to arbitrage and you feed him forever."[1]

—BERKSHIRE HATHAWAY'S 1988 ANNUAL REPORT

A s a boy, Buffett paid 25 cents for six-packs of Coke at his grandfather's store, then sold the individual cans for a nickel each, making 20% on every six-pack "arbitraged." Buffett had performed a financial trick called arbitrage—a practice that follows a straightforward formula: Something is bought at X, value is added or risk assumed, and then a sale is made at X plus a profit.

In a traditional or "risk-free" arbitrage, profits are made when two identical or near-identical items trade at different prices in different places at the same time. For instance, when a company's stock (identical in every way) trades for a lower price in New York than in London, equity arbitrageurs can buy stock in one city, sell it in the other, and capture the spread. Because this can be done in a nanosecond (electronic trading allows for the shares to be bought in London and sold in New York within a fraction of a second) the operation is generally considered risk-free. Because "riskless arb" produces free money, opportunities tend to be rare.

For example, Buffett executed an early arbitrage at the age of twenty-four for Graham that was not completely risk-free, but it was low-risk. Here is how he's described it:

> *Rockwood & Co., a Brooklyn based chocolate products company of limited profitability, had adopted LIFO inventory valuation in 1941 when cocoa was selling for 5¢ per pound. In 1954 a temporary shortage of cocoa caused the price to soar to over 60¢. Consequently Rockwood wished to unload its valuable inventory—quickly, before the price dropped. But if the cocoa had simply been sold off, the company would have owed close to a 50% tax on the proceeds.*
>
> *The 1954 Tax Code came to the rescue. It contained an arcane provision that eliminated the tax otherwise due on LIFO profits if inventory was distributed to shareholders as part of a plan reducing the scope of a corporation's business. Rockwood decided to terminate one of its businesses, the sale of cocoa butter, and said 13 million pounds of its cocoa bean inventory was attributable to that activity. Accordingly, the company offered to repurchase its stock in exchange for the cocoa beans it no longer needed, paying 80 pounds of beans for each share.*
>
> *For several weeks I busily bought shares, sold beans, and made periodic stops at Schroeder Trust to exchange stock certificates for warehouse receipts. The profits were good and my only expense was subway tokens.*

In the Rockwood arb, as long as the various prices didn't move around too much, easy profits could be made. Shares were bought at $34 and exchanged for beans worth $36, which were sold for cash and produced a $2 profit. As long as the price of cocoa held up, the $2 profit was a lock. Each transaction earned a 5.8% return on the capital employed. A $100 applied to the Rockwood arb could have earned $58 a year if he could get through the whole process 10 times (not compounded). Too bad such low-risk arbitrages don't come along that often. Arbitrageurs usually have to climb another rung of the risk ladder in order to find a sufficient number of opportunities.

Merger Arbitrage

For BPL, this meant a category of investment Buffett called "Workouts"—more commonly known now as merger arb or risk arb—which involved bets on the likelihood that an announced transaction (usually one company buying another) will actually close. When a company announces its intention to purchase another public company, the selling company's stock typically trades up to a level that's close, but not all the way up to the announced purchase price. The spread between the offer price and the stock price reflects the risk that something will happen to scuttle the deal as well as the time value of money between now and the expected closing. That's where the arbitrage opportunity lies. Buffett aimed to arbitrage transactions where the spread was sufficiently wide and the probability of the deal actually closing was high.

This can be a fantastic business, and it certainly was for Buffett. Like so many of his activities at BPL, he had learned the technique from Graham. Using the record of Graham-Newman, BPL, and Berkshire Hathaway in the sixty-five years through 1988, Buffett figured the average unleveraged return in the arbitrage business was about 20% per year. In the annual report that year he said, "give a man a fish and you feed him for a day. Teach a man to arbitrage and you feed him forever." Indeed. We know what 65 years of 20% average annual compounding does—it turns $100 into $14 million.

Results tend to be magnified in both directions because borrowed money is typically used alongside the partner's capital in order to obtain larger positions. Buffett's self-imposed limit on the use of borrowed money for arbitrage was 25% of partnership capital. Not a trivial sum. The key in this business is not being wrong very often. Because leverage was used, the actual returns for investors were even better.

However, to make money in merger arb, the deals have to close. While most go through as planned, some deals get scuttled by unfavorable antitrust law, tax rulings, shareholder disapproval, etc. This is what Buffett called "upsetting the applecart"; when this happens, the target's stock tends to quickly revert to its pre-buyout price. Buffett described the business, when it was profitable, as "getting the last nickel after the other fellow has made the first 95 cents." Being on the wrong side of a busted arb can be expensive. Not only do you fail to make the nickel, but you can also lose a meaningful chunk of the 95 cents. Buffett probably assessed most deals but was highly selective in the ones he participated in. Workouts is a business that doesn't accommodate very many mistakes.

Concentrating investing dollars was a common factor in all of Buffett's operations. While many merger arb businesses tend to spread their investments over many companies simultaneously, BPL typically focused on ten to fifteen at a time, versus a typical arbitrageur who might be in fifty or more. Because he concentrated on a few companies, Buffett's Workout mistakes were painfully obvious. Here's what Buffett said in a tough year for workouts:

> The streets were filled with upset apple carts—our apple carts—during 1967. Thus, on an average investment of $17,246,879, our overall gain was $153,273. For those of you whose slide rule does not go to such insulting depths, this represents a return of .89 of 1%. While I don't have complete figures, I doubt that we have been below 10% in any past year. As in other categories, we tend to concentrate our investments in the workout category in just a few situations per year. This technique gives more variation in yearly results than would be the case if we used an across-the-board approach. I believe our approach will result in as great (or greater) profitability on a long-term basis, but you can't prove it by 1967.[2]

Buffett outlined the four questions needed to evaluate a Workout in his 1988 letter to shareholders of Berkshire: (1) what chance does the deal have of going through, (2) how long will it take to close, (3) how likely is it that someone else will make an even better offer, and (4) what happens if the deal busts?

Performance Counterweight

Over the long term, Workouts were expected to do just as well as the Generals (10 points better than the market, or 15–17% per year on average). They not only produced solid, fairly stable returns, but their success was largely independent of the Dow and so insulated BPL's overall performance in down markets. In most years they made up 30–40% assets. The allocation served as a useful toggle to Buffett. He told partners in the very first letter to expect BPL to tilt the portfolio mix toward Generals when the market was falling and tilt toward Workouts when it was rising. A few years later, Controls would join Workouts as a market-agnostic business. Buffett referred to this as an "accidental" factor that sometimes helped performance and sometimes held it back:

> *To give an example of just how important the accident of division between these categories is, let me cite the example of the past three years. Using an entirely different method of calculation than that used to measure the performance of BPL in entirety, whereby the average monthly investment at market value by category is utilized, borrowed money and office operating expenses excluded, etc., (this gives the most accurate basis for intergroup comparisons but does not reflect overall BPL results) the generals (both present categories combined), workouts, and the Dow, shape up as follows:*

YEAR	GENERALS	WORKOUTS	DOW
1962	-1.0%	14.6%	-8.6%
1963	20.5%	30.6%	18.4%
1964	27.8%	10.3%	16.7%

Obviously the workouts (along with controls) saved the day in 1962, and if we had been light in this category that year, our final result would have been much poorer, although still quite respectable considering market conditions during the year. We could just as well have had a much smaller percentage of our portfolio in workouts that year; availability decided it, not any notion on my part as to what the market was going to do. Therefore, it is important to realize that in 1962 we were just plain lucky regarding mix of categories.

In 1963 we had one sensational workout which greatly influenced results, and generals gave a good account of themselves, resulting in a banner year. If workouts had been normal, (say, more like 1962) we would have looked much poorer compared to the Dow. Here it wasn't our mix that did much for us, but rather excellent situations.

Finally, in 1964 workouts were a big drag on performance. This would be normal in any event during a big plus year for the Dow such as 1964, but they were even a greater drag than expected because of mediocre experience. In retrospect it would have been pleasant to have been entirely in generals, but we don't play the game in retrospect.

I hope the preceding table drives home the point that results in a given year are subject to many variables—some regarding which we have little control or insight. We consider all categories to be good businesses and we are very happy we have several to rely on rather than just one. It makes for more discrimination within each category and reduces the chance we will be put completely out of operation by the elimination of opportunities in a single category.[3]

Let's Get Arb'ing

R eady to start arbitraging deals? Looking forward to making 20% average unleveraged annual returns? Tread carefully. Buffett's success in this category can make it look simpler than it actually can be—the devil is often in the details of these transactions and being on the wrong side of a merger arb situation can be costly. Like any of Buffett's three categories of investment, proceed only when you're within your circle of competence—you have to understand what you're doing before you do it. Because the unleveraged, unannualized returns are modest, the confidence interval has to be extremely high to do this stuff. Unless the arbitrage opportunity is obvious, these types of transactions are probably best left alone.

As you read the example of the Texas National Petroleum case study, ask yourself how qualified you would have been to assess the likelihood that the eleemosynary status (I had to look it up, too) of the University of Southern California was not going to be a problem for the IRS and that the ABC financing structure would be allowed in this case.

BPL Case Study:
Texas National Petroleum,
1963 Year-End Letter

JANUARY 18, 1964

This situation was a run-of-the-mill workout arising from the number one source of workouts in recent years—the sellouts of oil and gas producing companies.

TNP was a relatively small producer with which I had been vaguely familiar for years.

Early in 1962 I heard rumors regarding a sellout to Union Oil of California. I never act on such information, but in this case it was correct and substantially more money would have been made if we had gone in at the rumor stage rather than the announced stage. However, that's somebody else's business, not mine.

In early April, 1962, the general terms of the deal were announced. TNP had three classes of securities outstanding:

1. 6.5% debentures callable at 104.25 which would bear interest until the sale transpired and at that time would be called. There were $6.5 million outstanding of which we purchased $264,000 principal amount before the sale closed.

2. About 3.7 million shares of common stock of which the officers and directors owned about 40%. The proxy statement estimated the proceeds from the liquidation would produce $7.42 per share. We purchased 64,035 shares during the six months or so between announcement and closing.

3. 650,000 warrants to purchase common stock at $3.50 share. Using the proxy statement estimate of 7.42 for the workout on the common resulted in $3.92 as a workout on the warrants. We were able to buy 83,200 warrants or about 13% of the entire issue in six months.

The risk of stockholder disapproval was nil. The deal was negotiated by the controlling stockholders, and the price was a good one. Any transaction such as this is subject to title searches, legal opinions, etc., but this risk could also be appraised at virtually nil. There were no anti-trust problems. This absence of legal or anti-trust problems is not always the case, by any means.

The only fly in the ointment was the obtaining of the necessary tax ruling. Union Oil was using a standard ABC production payment method of financing. The University of Southern California was the production payment holder and there was some delay because of their eleemosynary status.

This posed a new problem for the Internal Revenue Service, but we understood USC was willing to waive this status which still left them with a satisfactory profit after they borrowed all the money from a bank. While getting this ironed out created delay, it did not threaten the deal.

When we talked with the company on April 23rd and 24th, their estimate was that the closing would take place in August or September. The proxy material was mailed May 9th and stated the sale "will be consummated during the summer of 1962 and that within a few months thereafter the greater part of the proceeds will be distributed to stockholders in liquidation." As mentioned earlier, the estimate was $7.42 per share. Bill Scott attended the stockholders meeting in Houston on May 29th where it was stated they still expected to close on September 1st.

The following are excerpts from some of the telephone conversations we had with company officials in ensuing months:

On June 18th the secretary stated, "Union has been told a favorable IRS ruling has been formulated but must be passed on by additional IRS people. Still hoping for ruling in July."

On July 24th the president said that he expected the IRS ruling "early next week."

On August 13th the treasurer informed us that the TNP, Union Oil, and USC people were all in Washington attempting to thrash out a ruling.

On September 18th the treasurer informed us "No news, although the IRS says the ruling could be ready by next week."

The estimate on payout was still $7.42.

The ruling was received in late September, and the sale closed October 31st. Our bonds were called November 13th. We converted our warrants to common stock shortly thereafter and received payments on the common of $3.50 December 14, 1962, $3.90 February 4, 1963, and 15 cent on April 24,

1963. We will probably get another 4 cent in a year or two. On 147,235 shares (after exercise of warrants) even 4 cent per share is meaningful.

This illustrates the usual pattern: (1) the deals take longer than originally projected; and (2) the payouts tend to average a little better than estimates. With TNP it took a couple of extra months, and we received a couple of extra percent.

The financial results of TNP were as follows:

1. On the bonds we invested $260,773 and had an average holding period of slightly under five months. We received 6.5% interest on our money and realized a capital gain of $14,446. This works out to an overall rate of return of approximately 20% per annum.
2. On the stock and warrants we have realized capital gain of $89,304, and we have stubs presently valued at $2,946. From an investment of $146,000 in April, our holdings ran to $731,000 in October. Based on the time the money was employed, the rate of return was about 22% per annum.

In both cases, the return is computed on an all equity investment. I definitely feel some borrowed money is warranted against a portfolio of workouts, but feel it is a very dangerous practice against generals.

We are not presenting TNP as any earth-shaking triumph. We have had workouts which were much better and some which were poorer. It is typical of our bread-and-butter type of operation. We attempt to obtain all facts possible, continue to keep abreast of developments and evaluate all of this in terms of our experience. We certainly don't go into all the deals that come along—there is considerable variation in their attractiveness. When a workout falls through, the resulting market value shrink is substantial. Therefore, you cannot afford many errors, although we fully realize we are going to have them occasionally.

Lessons from the Partnership Letters: Workouts

JANUARY 24, 1962

Our second category consists of "work-outs." These are securities whose financial results depend on corporate action rather than supply and demand factors created by buyers and sellers of securities. In other words, they are securities with a timetable where we can predict, within reasonable error limits, when we will get how much and what might upset the applecart. Corporate events such as mergers, liquidations, reorganizations, spin-offs, etc., lead to work-outs. An important source in recent years has been sell-outs by oil producers to major integrated oil companies.

This category will produce reasonably stable earnings from year to year, to a large extent irrespective of the course of the Dow. Obviously, if we operate throughout a year with a large portion of our portfolio in workouts, we will look extremely good if it turns out to be a declining year for the Dow or quite bad if it is a strongly advancing year. Over the years, work-outs have provided our second largest category. At any given time, we may be in ten to fifteen of these; some just beginning and others in the late stage of their development. I believe in using borrowed money to offset a portion of our work-out portfolio since there is a high degree of safety in this category in terms of both eventual results and intermediate market behavior. Results, excluding the benefits derived from the use of borrowed money, usually fall in the 10% to 20% range. My self-imposed limit regarding borrowing is 25% of partnership net worth. Oftentimes we owe no money and when we do borrow, it is only as an offset against work-outs.

II

JANUARY 18, 1965

On a long-term basis, I expect the workouts to achieve the same sort of margin over the Dow attained by generals.

IIIIIIIIIIIIIIIIIIIIIIIIIIIIIIIIIIIIIIIIIIIIIIIIIIIIIIIIIIIIIIIIIIIIIIIIIIIIIIIIIIIIIIIIIIIIIIIIIIIIIIIIIIIIIIIIIIIIIIIIIIIIIIIIIIIIIIIIII

JANUARY 24, 1968

As in other categories, we tend to concentrate our invest-ments in the workout category in just a few situations per year. This technique gives more variation in yearly results than would be the case if we used an across-the-board approach. I believe our approach will result in as great (or greater) profitability on a long-term basis, but you can't prove it by 1967.

IIIIIIIIIIIIIIIIIIIIIIIIIIIIIIIIIIIIIIIIIIIIIIIIIIIIIIIIIIIIIIIIIIIIIIIIIIIIIIIIIIIIIIIIIIIIIIIIIIIIIIIIIIIIIIIIIIIIIIIIIIIIIIIIIIIIIIIIII

JANUARY 18, 1964

. . . In this category we are not talking about rumors or "inside information" pertaining to such developments, but to publicly announced activities of this sort. We wait until we can read it in the paper. The risk pertains not primarily to general market behavior (although that is sometimes tied in to a degree), but instead to something upsetting the applecart so that the ex-pected development does not materialize.

. . . The gross profits in many workouts appear quite small. A friend refers to this as getting the last nickel after the other fellow has made the first ninety-five cents. However, the pre-dictability coupled with a short holding period produces quite decent annual rates of return. This category produces more steady absolute profits from year to year than generals do. In years of market decline, it piles up a big edge for us; during bull markets, it is a drag on performance. On a long term basis, I expect it to achieve the same sort of margin over the Dow attained by generals.

As I have mentioned in the past, the division of our port-folio among the three categories is largely determined by the accident or availability. Therefore, in a minus year for the Dow, whether we are primarily in generals or workouts is largely a matter of luck, but it will have a great deal to do with our per-formance relative to the Dow. This is one of many reasons why a single year's performance is of minor importance and, good or bad, should never be taken too seriously.

If there is any trend as our assets grow, I would expect it to be toward controls which heretofore have been our small-est category. I may be wrong in this expectation—a great deal depends, of course, on the future behavior of the market on which your guess is as good as mine (I have none). At this writ-ing, we have a majority of our capital in generals, workouts rank second, and controls are third.

Compounded Wisdom

Workouts and other forms of arbitrage can be a highly attrac-tive area for profits in their own right and have the added benefit of diversifying the sources of annual gains in a way that pro-tects overall results in down markets. They provided Buffett with an outlet for his energies when the overall market was high—doing nothing when there is "nothing to do" can be a challenge for vig-orous investors. Charlie Munger would say when he signed off on Workouts in future years, "Okay, at least it will keep you out of bars."[4] For Buffett this has meant 20% a year average return. When stock prices rose, Workouts comprised a larger amount of the capi-tal. When opportunities to invest in Generals abounded, the percent in Workouts would shrink.

Everyone can benefit from the diversification Workouts offer, but Workouts aren't something everyone is going to be comfort-able doing. For the latter group, other outlets exist for investing that can produce high returns and are also not tightly correlated to the overall market direction from day to day. If you don't think Workouts are right for you, privately owned businesses might do the trick. We'll learn more about a form of those, called Controls, in the chapter that follows.

CHAPTER 8

CONTROLS

||||||||||||||||||||||||||||||||||||||||||||||||||||||||||||||||||||||||||||||||||||||

"We do not want to get active merely for the sake of being active. Everything else being equal, I would much rather let others do the work. However, when an active role is necessary to optimize the employment of capital, you can be sure we will not be standing in the wings."[1]

—JANUARY 20, 1966

Picture a group of stodgy old men serving as members of a small, public company's board of directors back in the late 1950s. This group had been getting together for a *discussion* and *review* of the business (a generous description of their activities) followed by fine cigars for many years. They found it all rather enjoyable—it was a simple-to-manage, easy-to-understand business and no one asked too many questions or created too much extra work. Plus, they paid themselves generously. Shareholder value was low on the list of priorities, if it was on the list at all. Then, everything changed when they learned that someone whom they'd never heard of had acquired 20% of the outstanding stock and now had effective control over another 20% of the company. Who was this guy? With control over enough stock to have a material say in its operations going forward, what was he up to?

This is how I like to picture the beginning of the Sanborn Map saga, the Partnership's first Control investment. Just imagine the directors' expressions when Buffett turned up in 1959 for the first time. They must have been shocked *at least* twice: once when they saw Buffett, as he was still in his late twenties, then again when he demanded a distribution of Sanborn's huge securities portfolio, alone worth $65 a share (net), $20 more than the market value of the entire company. There is little doubt that the folks at Sanborn had no clue what they were up against with Buffett . . . at first. They would soon find out.

Here's the full story from Buffett's letter dated January 30, 1961. Two things to keep in mind as you read it: First, this was a tiny company. Book equity was only $4.3 million, or $35 million in 2015 dollars. Second, Buffett had more than a third of the Partnership invested in this stock.

BPL Case Study: Sanborn Map Company

JANUARY 30, 1961

Last year mention was made of an investment which accounted for a very high and unusual proportion (35%) of our net assets along with the comment that I had some hope this investment would be concluded in 1960. This hope materialized. The history of an investment of this magnitude may be of interest to you.

Sanborn Map Co. is engaged in the publication and continuous revision of extremely detailed maps of all cities of the United States. For example, the volumes mapping Omaha would weigh perhaps fifty pounds and provide minute details on each structure. The map would be revised by the paste-over method showing new construction, changed occupancy, new fire protection facilities, changed structural materials, etc. These revisions would be done approximately annually and a new map would be published every twenty or thirty years when further pasteovers became impractical. The cost of keeping the map revised to an Omaha customer would run around $100 per year.

This detailed information showing diameter of water mains underlying streets, location of fire hydrants, composition of roof, etc., was primarily of use to fire insurance companies. Their underwriting departments, located in a central office, could evaluate business by agents nationally. The theory was that a picture was worth a thousand words and such evaluation would decide whether the risk was properly rated, the degree of conflagration exposure in an area, advisable reinsurance procedure, etc. The bulk of Sanborn's business was done with about thirty insurance companies although maps were also sold to customers outside the insurance industry such as public utilities, mortgage companies, and taxing authorities.

For seventy-five years the business operated in a more or less monopolistic manner, with profits realized in every year accompanied by almost complete immunity to recession and lack of need for any sales effort. In the earlier years of the business, the insurance industry became fearful that Sanborn's profits would become too great and placed a number of prominent insurance men on Sanborn's board of directors to act in a watchdog capacity.

In the early 1950's a competitive method of underwriting known as "carding" made inroads on Sanborn's business and after-tax profits of the map business fell from an average annual level of over $500,000 in the late 1930's to under $100,000 in 1958 and 1959. Considering the upward bias in the economy during this period, this amounted to an almost complete elimination of what had been sizable, stable earning power.

However, during the early 1930's Sanborn had begun to accumulate an investment portfolio. There were no capital requirements to the business so that any retained earnings could be devoted to this project. Over a period of time, about $2.5 million was invested, roughly half in bonds and half in stocks. Thus, in the last decade particularly, the investment portfolio blossomed while the operating map business wilted.

Let me give you some idea of the extreme divergence of these two factors. In 1938 when the Dow-Jones Industrial Average was in the 100–120 range, Sanborn sold at $110 per share. In 1958 with the Average in the 550 area, Sanborn sold at $45 per share. Yet during that same period the value of the Sanborn investment portfolio increased from about $20 per share to $65 per share. This means, in effect, that the buyer of Sanborn stock in 1938 was placing a positive valuation of $90 per share on the map business ($110 less the $20 value of the investments unrelated to the map business) in a year of depressed business and stock market conditions. In the tremendously more vigorous climate of 1958 the same map business was evaluated at a minus $20 with the buyer of the stock unwilling to pay more than 70 cents on the dollar for the investment portfolio with the map business thrown in for nothing.

How could this come about? Sanborn in 1958 as well as 1938 possessed a wealth of information of substantial value to the insurance industry. To reproduce the detailed information they had gathered over the years would have cost tens of millions of dollars. Despite "carding" over $500 million of fire premiums were underwritten by "mapping" companies. However, the means of selling and packaging Sanborn's product information had remained unchanged throughout the year and finally this inertia was reflected in the earnings.

The very fact that the investment portfolio had done so well served to minimize in the eyes of most directors the need for rejuvenation of the map business. Sanborn had a sales volume of about $2 million per year and owned about $7 million worth of marketable securities. The income from the investment portfolio was substantial, the business had no possible financial worries, the insurance companies were satisfied with the price paid for maps, and the stockholders still received dividends. However, these dividends were cut five times in eight years although I could never find any record of suggestions pertaining to cutting salaries or director's and committee fees.

Prior to my entry on the Board, of the fourteen directors, nine were prominent men from the insurance industry who combined held 46 shares of stock out of 105,000 shares outstanding. Despite their top positions with very large companies which would suggest the financial wherewithal to make at least a modest commitment, the largest holding in this group was ten shares. In several cases, the insurance companies these men ran owned small blocks of stock but these were token investments in relation to the portfolios in which they were held. For the past decade the insurance companies had been only sellers in any transactions involving Sanborn stock.

The tenth director was the company attorney, who held ten shares. The eleventh was a banker with ten shares who recognized the problems of the company, actively pointed them out, and later added to his holdings. The next two directors were the top officers of Sanborn who owned about 300 shares combined. The officers were capable, aware of the problems of the business, but kept in a subservient role by the Board of Directors. The final member of our cast was a son of a deceased president of Sanborn. The widow owned about 15,000 shares of stock.

In late 1958, the son, unhappy with the trend of the business, demanded the top position in the company, was turned down, and submitted his resignation, which was accepted. Shortly thereafter we made a bid to his mother for her block of stock, which was accepted. At the time there were two other large holdings, one of about 10,000 shares (dispersed among customers of a brokerage firm) and one of about 8,000. These people were quite unhappy with the situation and desired a separation of the investment portfolio from the map business, as did we.

Subsequently our holdings (including associates) were increased through open market purchases to about 24,000 shares and the total represented by the three groups increased to 46,000 shares. We hoped to separate the two businesses, realize the fair value of the investment portfolio and work to re-establish the earning power of the map business. There appeared to be a real opportunity to multiply map profits through utilization of Sanborn's wealth of raw material in conjunction with electronic means of converting this data to the most usable form for the customer.

There was considerable opposition on the Board to change of any type, particularly when initiated by an outsider, although management was in complete accord with our plan and a similar plan had been recommended by Booz, Allen & Hamilton (Management Experts). To avoid a proxy fight (which very probably would not have been forthcoming and which we would have been certain of winning) and to avoid time delay with a large portion of Sanborn's money tied up in blue-chip stocks which I didn't care for at current prices, a plan was evolved taking out all stockholders at fair value who wanted out. The SEC ruled favorably on the fairness of the plan. About 72% of the Sanborn stock, involving 50% of the 1,600 stockholders, was exchanged for portfolio securities at fair value. The map business was left with over $1.25 million in government and municipal bonds as a reserve fund, and a potential corporate capital gains tax of over $1 million was eliminated. The remaining stockholders were left with a slightly improved asset value, substantially higher earnings per share, and an increased dividend rate.

Necessarily, the above little melodrama is a very abbreviated description of this investment operation. However, it does point up the necessity for secrecy regarding our portfolio operations as well as the futility of measuring our results over a short span of time such as a year. Such control situations may occur very infrequently. Our bread-and-butter business is buying undervalued securities and selling when the undervaluation is corrected along with investment in special situations where the profit is dependent on corporate rather than market action. To the extent that partnership funds continue to grow, it is possible that more opportunities will be available in "control situations."

Lessons from Controls

After Sanborn, Buffett continued executing Control transactions throughout the rest of the Partnership era and discussed two others, Dempster Mill and Berkshire Hathaway, in detail. Each case offers key insights for today's investor; each had its own way of illuminating the linkage between a security's value and a business's value in a way that helps parse out true economic value from the accounting figures.

You may have heard others claim the term *value investing* is redundant because all investing is value based—no one sets out to intentionally overpay for stocks. This is somewhat similar to the idea of "investing" in a business, as opposed to being in that business. Stocks are simply a conduit through which we own a company's assets. When we invest our capital into a company's stock, we enter into its particular business. In 1960, one-third of the Partnership was in Sanborn's stock, meaning one-third of the Partnership was in the business of selling insurance maps and managing a securities portfolio. In his discussions on Controls, Buffett is teaching us to not think about "investing in a stock" but instead to think about "being in a business."

Whether you are running a business or evaluating one, a singular question remains paramount: *what is its value*, both in terms of the assets involved and the earnings produced, then, how can it be maximized? The skill in answering the questions determines the success of investors and business managers alike. Buffett's lessons, taught through the lens of his Controls commentary, shine a bright light on the subject. Graham was first to say it and Buffett often repeats it—*Investment is most intelligent when it is most businesslike and business is most intelligent when it's most investment-like.*

Let's look at this wisdom in action—in the birth of a Control. You'll recall from our look at the Generals that these were often stocks bought at a discount to their private market value with the idea that they would be held until they appreciated, at such a time that they would then be sold. As he said, "We do not go into these generals with the idea of getting the last nickel, but are usually quite content selling out at some intermediate level between our purchase price and what we regard as fair value to a private owner." However, in certain cases, a General would languish in price long enough that BPL would come to own the majority of the company's outstanding shares, typically through buying over many years. When this happens, these can become Controls.

Buffett had no problem becoming the majority holder and saw it as a logical extension of his approach, grounded in what a reasonable private owner would pay for the entire business. Potentially becoming that private owner simply increased his degrees of freedom. This was, after all, the "two strings to his bow" advantage that made the category of Generals-Private Owner so attractive in the first place and helped make the Partnership unique. While the price paid for the General offered an attractive margin of safety in its own right, the riskiness of the investment was further reduced by the potential for control.

Oftentimes, as we've discussed, Controls required Buffett to roll up his sleeves and become confrontational, similar in some ways to what we see activist investors doing today. Perhaps this is why he eventually stopped doing it (his activist period was limited to his time running BPL). For example, he had to threaten Sanborn Map's board with a proxy fight (legal battle) to get them to act. Interacting with a board not focused on shareholder value made Buffett's blood boil.[2] At Dempster Mill, we'll see that he had to fire the CEO and bring in his own man, Harry Bottle. Together they liquidated large parts of the business to restore the economics of the company. Buffett was vilified in the local newspaper for doing so.[3]

While he saw himself as saving the business by excising the rotten parts, critics only saw the lost jobs. Early at Berkshire, he had to fire the CEO and hit the brakes on capital expenditures in textiles before redirecting the company's focus to insurance and banking. It was never easy and was often stressful, but when action was needed, action was taken. As he said, "Everything else being equal, I would much rather let others do the work. However, when an active role is necessary to optimize the employment of capital, you can be sure we will not be standing in the wings."[4]

Not only was Buffett willing to get active by exercising his ability to control a company, but he was also ready to concentrate heavily in them. With a say in how the company was being managed, the downside was limited. The value of the securities alone virtually guaranteed he would make money. When Buffett saw a highly favorable situation like Sanborn, where the upside was significant and the risk of loss was tiny, he was not afraid to load up and bet huge. By 1959 this position accounted for 35% of the Partnership. The value was clearly there. All he had to do was get it out.

In Sanborn, Buffett was by far the largest shareholder, but he was not the *majority* holder—other shareholders collectively still owned more than half the company. In other cases, however, the Partnership did have a majority, which meant full control. Here Buffett could not be overruled. We see this first with Dempster Mill, a farm implements company that was purchased over a five-year span and moved from Generals to Controls in 1961. When Buffett controlled 70% of the outstanding stock, he was quick to point out that his "own actions in such a market could drastically affect the quoted price." The same was true when he came to own a majority of Berkshire. With a market as thin as it was in these two stocks, even a minor amount of buying or selling could have dramatic impact on the quoted price. Diversified Retailing Company (DRC) was a privately owned business acquired late in the Partnership that never had a publicly traded stock. The value had to be estimated in all three.

"When a controlling interest is held, we own a business rather than a stock, and a business valuation is appropriate."[5] In the absence of a reliable market value to account for the Control company's year-end worth, Buffett had no other choice but to perform his own valuation. This could be a major positive in down markets because it insulated the carrying value of the position (and BPL) from the vagaries of the market; in sharply up markets, the valuation approach would hold back results. Either way, Mr. Market was no longer in charge—the value of each Control was dictated solely by an ongoing appraisal of the private market value of the business, performed by Buffett and confirmed by the auditors annually.

Year-end valuations were a current, conservative appraisal, not what he thought the Controls were *going* to be worth in the future. As he told partners, "The estimated value should not be what we hope it would be worth, or what it might be worth to an eager buyer, etc., but what I would estimate our interest would bring if sold under current conditions in a reasonably short period of time."[6]

Remember that partners could only add or withdraw their capital once a year, so this valuation, particularly when it accounted for a third or more of Partnership assets, was a big deal. Because the market determined the year-end valuation of the Partnership's position in the Generals and the Workouts, it was simple and straightforward to know what these were worth. Valuing Controls, on the other hand, required an estimated value, a very different kind of thing than a market value. Control valuations are subject to interpretation and dispute; no exact correct answer exists. If Buffett overvalued a Control it would inflate his performance (and his performance fee), which would be harmful to all his partners. Those who left the Partnership in a year where the estimated value was too high would also benefit at the expense of the remaining partners. On the flip side, if Buffett was too conservative in his valuation, partners adding capital would benefit at the expense of those leaving or not adding a proportionate amount of funds to the Partnership themselves. Buffett was very careful to ensure his valuations were fair to both adding and withdrawing partners, and the results were audited by the accounting firm that would later become KPMG.

The November 1966 letter gave the most detailed account of the mechanics of his appraisals:

> *The dominant factors affecting control valuations are earnings power (past and prospective) and asset values. The nature of our controlled businesses, the quality of the assets involved, and the fact that the Federal Income Tax basis applicable to the net assets substantially exceeds our valuations, cause us to place considerably more weight on the asset factor than is typical in most business valuations. . . . The Partnership Agreement charges me with the responsibility for establishing fair value for controlling interests, and this means fair to both adding and withdrawing partners at a specific point in time. Wide changes in the market valuations accorded stocks at some point obviously find reflection in the valuation of businesses, although this factor is of much less importance when asset factors (particularly when current assets are significant) overshadow earnings power considerations in the valuation process. . . .[7]*

Notice here that Buffett says that the nature of BPL's Controls caused him to *"place considerably more weight on the asset factor than is typical in most business valuation"*? Sanborn, Dempster, and Berkshire were all asset plays. The value of their assets, less all liabilities, far exceeded the market price of the stocks. These were not good businesses, didn't earn adequate or better returns on the assets they employed, and were not readily valued on current earnings. If they were, a reasonable study of the past and prospective earnings of the business would play a more dominant role.

Valuing a Business on Assets

Many of Buffett's Controls earned little or were losing money. These early "cigar butts" required Buffett to employ Graham's method for adjusting the carrying values of the assets as reported on the companies' balance sheets to uncover their true worth. While it was mostly statistically based, the adjustment still required a little art to go along with the science.

Chapter 43 of *Securities Analysis* set up the basis for this method perfectly. According to Graham, "a company's balance sheet does not convey exact information as to its value in liquidation, but it does supply clues or hints which may prove useful. The first rule in calculating liquidating value is that the liabilities are real but the value of the assets must be questioned. This means that all true liabilities shown on the books must be deducted at their face amount. The value to be ascribed to the assets, however, will vary according to their character."[8] For the liquidation plays, Graham advised, as a general rule of thumb, ascribing 100 cents on the dollar to cash, 80 cents on the dollar to receivables, 67 cents on the dollar for inventory (with a wide range depending on the business), and 15 cents on the dollar for fixed assets.

As we dive into Buffett's detailed accounts of Sanborn Map, and later Dempster Mill and Berkshire Hathaway, we'll explore how Buffett went about ascribing values to the assets of each company. Sanborn had a "hidden asset" in its portfolio of securities that was worth far more than the balance sheet suggested (convention at the time was to carry securities at cost, not market price, so the value had to be "marked up"). Dempster Mill's assets, net of all liabilities, were carried on the balance sheet at values that were significantly higher than the total value of the stock in the market. The accounting values were plain as day. The question Buffett encountered was what were the assets *really* worth? With Berkshire, the question was how could the capital in the business be redeployed to better use?

The "art" for Buffett, as it is for all investors, is to evaluate the "character" of the assets properly, thinking it through and making the appropriate adjustments when these differ from accounting values—values that only reflect facts around what the business itself had paid for the assets and the wear and tear (depreciation) since they were acquired.

Adjusting Asset Values: Up or Down?

A simplified example may help to illuminate how the process works. Imagine a ticket broker who has purchased five World Series tickets for $1,000 ($200 each) that are valid only at Yankee Stadium. If the Yankees make it to the Series, the tickets will be worth a lot. If they don't, the tickets will be worthless. In terms of the accounting, our ticket broker follows convention and records each ticket as an asset on the balance sheet at its cost. Now, let's say this entire business comes up for sale with a month left to go in the baseball season. What would you say it's worth? To make it easier, let's assume the five tickets are the only assets in the business and that it has borrowed $300 to help acquire them. Whatever you think the assets are worth, less the debt, will be your valuation for the company.

As Professor Greenblatt likes to tell his students at Columbia Business School (which remains the intellectual center of value investing), "If you do good valuation work and you are right, Mr. Market will pay you back."[9] The process you take when valuing the ticket broker, or any business, will determine the quality of your investment results and lies at the heart of the value investing process.

The initial question is always the same: Are you capable of estimating what *these* assets are worth? Or, as Buffett would put it, are you within your circle of competence? If the answer is no, forget it and move on to valuing something else. There is nothing wrong with that; in fact, you should take pride in knowing what you are and are not capable of valuing. This self-knowledge is what distinguishes the great investors and avoiding mistakes is just as important as doing a good job picking winners. Buffett puts the majority of potential investments into the "too hard to value" pile and simply moves on.

What do we see in the financials of our ticket broker? We know the liabilities are fixed—that's always the easy part—we have $300 in debt. We also know the tickets were bought for $1,000 and so we'll see them as assets recorded at cost on the balance sheet. One thousand dollars in assets less $300 in debt leaves a balance of $700 of "owners' equity," or "book value."

Just because the assets were purchased at $1,000 doesn't mean that's what they're worth now. Circumstances may have changed. All the balance sheet shows is what has happened in the past. When you do your valuation work, the assets (tickets in our example) are always worth what they can be sold for and the liabilities are always assumed to be due in full. That's the difference between accounting value and economic, or true *intrinsic* value.

In some cases, particularly when the business is of a poor quality, assets will be worth less than their carrying value. Recall, Graham advised ascribing 100 cents on the dollar to cash, 80 cents on the dollar to receivables, 67 cents on the dollar for inventory (with a wide range depending on the business), and 15 cents on the dollar for fixed assets. That's just a rough rule; you need to make your own logical assessment.

You wouldn't logically pay a penny more than $200 for the broker business if the Yankees were way out of the running with ten games to go and StubHub showed similar tickets selling for $100 each, making the broker's five worth $500 in total. With Dempster Mill, Buffett encountered just such a situation. In 1961, its book equity was $76, making the stock look ridiculously cheap at $28, at least on paper. Watching Buffett skillfully mark down Dempster's assets is a good chance to watch him in action as he conservatively assesses true market values line by line. Here, even after his markdowns, Buffett found the stock was still exceedingly cheap.

In other cases, often when the business is a good one, the balance sheet figures significantly understate the economic value of the assets. Getting back to our ticket broker example, what if the Yankees were a lock for the Series and StubHub was listing similar tickets at $500 each ($2,500 total)? While the book value will always be $700 in either case, the true liquidation value in this instance would be $2,200. This is what Buffett saw at Sanborn Map, who had acquired a portfolio of securities that were being carried on the books at their cost (not at their market value). Because the securities had appreciated, they were worth a lot more than the amount reflected on the balance sheet. Through Sanborn, we get a chance to see Buffett recast the financials up, demonstrating how he found a stock where he could pay 70 cents on the dollar for a securities portfolio, with the rest of the business coming for free.

Businesses' Activity Ties Directly to Value

Estimating the economic or true value of assets, as opposed to relying on the accounting values, the market price, or the opinions of others, is the art of investing in Generals and Controls. The process is the same whether you are valuing a slice of a business (stock) or the whole thing. However, when you are a minority holder, you're at the mercy of the existing management and the board of directors. While it's their job to act in the best interest of shareholders, they don't always live up to their responsibilities. This is the potential agency cost you bear when you don't have control and the reason why an evaluation of management can be a very important part of your investment decision.

With control comes the added ability to take charge, which is a real advantage when change is needed. By turning Generals into Controls, Buffett was able to change the behavior of companies. He stopped the value-destructive activities at Dempster and Berkshire; he fixed the lopsided capital structure of Sanborn Map. Through the Controls, we not only get to see how Buffett came to recognize undervalued securities but also how he made businesses more valuable by improving the returns on the capital (assets) they employed. In an optimally run business, the value of control to a financial buyer is zero. The right to force change is valuable only when something needs fixing. All three Controls offered significant opportunities for improvement.

Coattailing

Some of the best situations arise when you find a General where you can make a significant investment of your own but some other investor is doing the work to improve management's decision making. Today activists are still agitating managements to improve their operations. In fact, it's become a very popular strategy that has gained a lot of attention; the funds dedicated to this activity have attracted a lot of assets. Carl Icahn, Nelson Peltz, Dan Loeb, and Bill Ackman, among others, have garnered quasi-rock-star status as investors. However, not all activists are worth following, and Buffett spoke disparagingly about the activists of today at the 2015 Berkshire meeting, saying that most of what he sees nowadays is "really reaching," meaning he sees their demands as not necessarily in the interest of the long-term shareholders.[10]

In the Partnership era, Buffett was at times clearly more influential than today's activists because he controlled a much larger amount of stock. The companies he was involved with were also smaller and far cheaper. Today many activists take much smaller stakes in much larger companies and advocate for change through open letters to management and in other highly visible ways, hoping to gain support from shareholders at large.

Then and now, though, the key issue is what the *potential* is for more value in a security than what's being ascribed by the market and then doing something to close the gap. Just like we saw with the Partnership's investments, these situations can often get hostile. Today, one only needs to look at activist investors such as Nelson Peltz and his firm Trian's epic battle with DuPont. These two groups are in a very public, high-stakes slugfest. Trian's capital, and probably the DuPont CEO's job, are on the line. Trian wants major cost savings initiatives and potentially a breakup of the company. DuPont's CEO wants to keep the current strategy in place. Investors have to decide for themselves who is right. Here Graham would say, "The public must learn to judge such controversies on their merits, as developed by statements of fact and by reasoned argument. It must not allow itself to be swayed by mere accusation or by irrelevant personalities."[11]

Investors today can undertake a careful study of the modern activists and their track records. Then, when you see an activist make a move, judge the merits of his argument on your own. If you agree, going along for the ride can be a great strategy. By coattailing an activist, value can often be unlocked at a much more rapid rate that would otherwise be the case if the status quo were preserved. In the case of DuPont, for example, the company quickly "discovered" a huge amount of cost savings, found on their own (so they said) immediately after Trian went public with their campaign. The mere presence of an activist is sometimes enough to spur value-creating changes from a management team. The activists who work in the best long-term interest of all shareholders play an important role in reducing the agency costs that naturally arise from non-owner management teams. We should be glad that someone is willing to take on this role. All else being equal, Buffett would rather let others do the work. But, as he said, "just be careful whose coattail you're riding."

Buffett never did a hostile deal after the Partnership. Conventional wisdom is that his funds had grown too big or that he found a better, higher-return strategy. I think there was more to it than that. His funds didn't grow beyond the largest of today's activist funds (in constant dollars) until many years after BPL closed. He has also said that the methods he used during the BPL era would still work well today, and we have evidence to support that claim through the current returns seen by the activists.

While there is no doubt that Buffett came to prefer owning a whole business as opposed to slices of them (who wouldn't?), his writing suggests he gave up the cigar-butt controls more because he didn't like doing it than because he found some higher return for his investing dollars. In fact, giving them up probably shaved a few points off his annual returns in the early years, a choice he seemed more than comfortable with. Why trade even a little bit of misery for an extra point or two of return when you're already rich? I think you can see this in the comments he made late into the Partnership, not long before he decided to close BPL:

The satisfying nature of our activity in controlled companies is a minor reason for the moderated investment objectives discussed in the October 9th letter. When I am dealing with people I like, in businesses I find stimulating (what business isn't?), and achieving worthwhile overall returns on capital employed (say, 10–12%), it seems foolish to rush from situation to situation to earn a few more percentage points. It also does not seem sensible to me to trade known pleasant personal relationships with high grade people, at a decent rate of return, for possible irritation, aggravation or worse at potentially higher returns.[12]

There is nothing wrong with activist investing, to use a Munger phrase, "if you can stand shaving." If done properly, it seems to yield "a few more percentage points" of annual return for activists today as it did for Buffett when he was doing it. Spotting the right activist who is making a sound argument in a situation in need of their focus can be a wonderful investment strategy. Just be sure to think it through for yourself. Don't follow blindly. Again, be careful whose coattails you are riding.

‖‖

Lessons from the Partnership Letters: Controls

‖‖

JANUARY 24, 1962

The final category is "control" situations where we either control the company or take a very large position and attempt to influence policies of the company. Such operations should definitely be measured on the basis of several years. In a given year, they may produce nothing as it is usually to our advantage to have the stock be stagnant market-wise for a long period while we are acquiring it. These situations, too, have relatively little in common with the behavior of the Dow. Sometimes, of course, we buy into a general with the thought in mind that it might develop into a control situation. If the price remains low enough for a long period, this might very well happen. If it moves up before we have a substantial percentage of the company's stock, we sell at higher levels and complete a successful general operation. We are presently acquiring stock in what may turn out to be control situations several years hence.

|||||||||||||||||||||||||||||||||||||||||||||||||||||||||||||||||||||||||||||||||||||||||||||||||||||||||||||||||||||||||||||||||||||||||||||||||||||||||||||||

JANUARY 18, 1964

Unless we start off with the purchase of a sizable block of stock, controls develop from the general category. They result from situations where a cheap security does nothing price-wise for such an extended period of time that we are able to buy a significant percentage of the company's stock. At that point we are probably in a position to assume some degree of, or perhaps complete, control of the company's activities; whether we become active or remain relatively passive at this point depends upon our assessment of the company's future and the management's capabilities. The general we have been buying the most aggressively in recent months possesses ex-cellent management following policies that appear to make very good sense to us. If our continued buying puts us in a controlling position at some point in the future, we will prob-ably remain very passive regarding the operation of this busi-ness. We do not want to get active merely for the sake of being active. Everything else being equal I would much rather let others do the work. However, when an active role is necessary to optimize the employment of capital you can be sure we will not be standing in the wings.

Active or passive, in a control situation there should be a built-in profit. The sine qua non of this operation is an attractive purchase price. Once control is achieved, the value of our investment is determined by the value of the enterprise, not the oftentimes irrationalities of the marketplace.

Our willingness and financial ability to assume a controlling position gives us two-way stretch on many purchases in our group of generals. If the market changes its opinion for the better, the security will advance in price. If it doesn't, we will continue to acquire stock until we can look to the business itself rather than the market for vindication of our judgment.

Investment results in the control category have to be measured on the basis of at least several years. Proper buying takes time. If needed, strengthening management, re-directing the utilization of capital, perhaps effecting a satisfactory sale or merger, etc., are also all factors that make this a business to be measured in years rather than months. For this reason, in controls, we are looking for wide margins of profit—if it looks at all close, we pass.

Controls in the buying stage move largely in sympathy with the Dow. In the later stages their behavior is geared more to that of workouts.

llllllllllllllllllllllllllllllllllllllllllllllllllllllllllllllllllllllllllllllllllllllllllllllllllllllllllllllllllllllllllllllllll

JANUARY 18, 1964

If there is any trend as our assets grow, I would expect it to be toward controls which heretofore have been our smallest category. I may be wrong in this expectation—a great deal depends, of course, on the future behavior of the market on which your guess is as good as mine (I have none). At this writing, we have a majority of our capital in generals, workouts rank second, and controls are third.

llllllllllllllllllllllllllllllllllllllllllllllllllllllllllllllllllllllllllllllllllllllllllllllllllllllllllllllllllllllllllllllllll

JANUARY 18, 1965

An investment operation that depends on the ultimate buyer making a bum deal (in Wall Street they call this the "Bigger

Fool Theory") is tenuous indeed. How much more satisfactory it is to buy at really bargain prices so that only an average disposition brings pleasant results.

||||||||||||||||||||||||||||||||||||||||||||||||||||||||||||||||||||||||||||||||||||||||||||||||||||||||||||||||||||||||||||||||

JANUARY 20, 1966

The "Control" section of our business received a transfer member from our "Private Owner" category. Shares in Berkshire Hathaway had been acquired since November 1962 on much the same line of reasoning as prevailed in the security mentioned above. In the case of Berkshire, however, we ended up purchasing enough stock to assume a controlling position ourselves rather than the more usual case of either selling our stock in the market or to another single buyer.

Our purchases of Berkshire started at a price of $7.60 per share in 1962. This price partially reflected large losses incurred by the prior management in closing some of the mills made obsolete by changing conditions within the textile business (which the old management had been quite slow to recognize). In the postwar period the company had slid downhill a considerable distance, having hit a peak in 1948 when about $29.5 million was earned before tax and about 11,000 workers were employed. This reflected output from 11 mills.

At the time we acquired control in spring of 1965, Berkshire was down to two mills and about 2,300 employees. It was a very pleasant surprise to find that the remaining units had excellent management personnel, and we have not had to bring a single man from the outside into the operation. In relation to our beginning acquisition cost of $7.60 per share (the average cost, however, was $14.86 per share, reflecting very heavy purchases in early 1965), the company on December 31, 1965, had net working capital alone (before placing any value on the plants and equipment) of about $19 per share.

Berkshire is a delight to own. There is no question that the state of the textile industry is the dominant factor in determining the earning power of the business, but we are most fortunate to have Ken Chace running the business in a first-class manner, and we also have several of the best sales people in the business heading up this end of their respective divisions.

While a Berkshire is hardly going to be as profitable as a Xerox, Fairchild Camera or National Video in a hypertensed market, it is a very comfortable sort of thing to own. As my West Coast philosopher says, "It is well to have a diet consisting of oatmeal as well as cream puffs."

Because of our controlling interest, our investment in Berkshire is valued for our audit as a business, not as a marketable security. If Berkshire advances $5 per share in the market, it does BPL no good—our holdings are not going to be sold. Similarly, if it goes down $5 per share, it is not meaningful to us. The value of our holding is determined directly by the value of the business. I received no divine inspiration in that valuation of our holdings. (Maybe the owners of the three wonder stocks mentioned above do receive such a message in respect to their holdings—I feel I would need something at least that reliable to sleep well at present prices.) I attempt to apply a conservative valuation based upon my knowledge of assets, earning power, industry conditions, competitive position, etc. We would not be a seller of our holdings at such a figure, but neither would we be a seller of the other items in our portfolio at yearend valuations—otherwise, we would already have sold them.

||||||||||||||||||||||||||||||||||||||||||||||||||||||||||||||||||||||||||||||||||||||||||||||||||||||||||||||||||||||||||||||||||||||||||||||||

JANUARY 25, 1967

There were three main sources of gain during 1966 in respect to controlled companies. These arose through: (1) retained business earnings applicable to our holdings in 1966; (2) open market purchases of additional stock below our controlling interest valuation and; (3) unrealized appreciation in marketable securities held by the controlled companies. The total of all positive items came to $2,600,838 in 1966.

However, due to factors mentioned in my November 1, 1966 letter, specific industry conditions, and other relevant valuation items, this gain was reduced by $1,034,780 in arriving at our fair valuation applicable to controlling interests as of December 31, 1966. Thus the overall gain in the control category was reduced to $1,566,058 for the year.

We were undoubtedly fortunate that we had a relatively high percentage of net assets invested in businesses and not stocks during 1966. The same money in general market holdings would probably have produced a loss, perhaps substantial, during the year. This was not planned and if the stock market had advanced substantially during the year, this category would have been an important drag on overall performance. The same situation will prevail during 1967.

||||||||||||||||||||||||||||||||||||||||||||||||||||||||||||||||||||||||||||||||||||||||||||||||||||||||||||||||||||||||

JANUARY 22, 1969

Overall, the controlled companies turned in a decent performance during 1968. Diversified Retailing Company Inc. (80% owned) and Berkshire Hathaway Inc. (70% owned) had combined after-tax earnings of over $5 million.

Particularly outstanding performances were turned in by Associated Cotton Shops, a subsidiary of DRC run by Ben Rosner, and National Indemnity Company, a subsidiary of B-H run by Jack Ringwalt. Both of these companies earned about 20% on capital employed in their businesses. Among Fortune's "500" (the largest manufacturing entities in the country, starting with General Motors), only 37 companies achieved this figure in 1967, and our boys outshone such mildly better-known (but not better appreciated) companies as IBM, General Electric, General Motors, Procter & Gamble, DuPont, Control Data, Hewlett-Packard, etc.

I still sometimes get comments from partners like: "Say, Berkshire is up four points—that's great!" or "What's happening to us, Berkshire was down three last week?" Market price is irrelevant to us in the valuation of our controlling interests. We valued B-H at 25 at yearend 1967 when the market was about 20 and 31 at yearend 1968 when the market was about 37. We would have done the same thing if the markets had been 15 and 50 respectively. ("Price is what you pay. Value is what you get.") We will prosper or suffer in controlled investments in relation to the operating performances of our businesses— we will not attempt to profit by playing various games in the securities markets.

Whether you run a business, own a business, or are in a business through a partial claim (stock), Buffett's commentary on Controls helps you learn to think like an owner; it also helps you do asset-based valuation work along the same lines, as if you're buying the entire thing. Next, we will look at Dempster Mill, which is the Control that Buffett spent the most time discussing in the letters. It's a perfect case study that delves deeper into these ideas. We can see how assets are first evaluated, then redeployed to enhance the returns of the business and unlock significant shareholder value.

CHAPTER 9

DEMPSTER DIVING: THE ASSET CONVERSION PLAY

||||||||||||||||||||||||||||||||||||||||||||||||||||||||||||||||||||||||||||

"We are looking for wide margins of profit—if it looks at all close, we pass."[1]

—JANUARY 18, 1964

Much of the fun in investing comes from the hunting process itself. Finding a net-net situation as cheap as Dempster Mill is akin to the art dealer who finds a Renoir underneath a painting of "dogs on velvet" selling for $25 at an estate sale. It's an exceedingly rare event, requires a little work to see the real value, and at that price, it's sure to produce a huge profit.

Picture the pulse-quickening moment in 1956 when Buffett, thumbing through the Moody's Manual, came across a tiny, obscure manufacturing company whose stock had fallen 75% in the previous year. Realizing that it was now available for a fraction of its net working capital and an even smaller fraction of its book value, he started buying the stock as low as $17 a share. He got out at $80.

Buffett's commentary on the saga of Dempster Mill was the most complete account of any investment he made for the Partnership. It perfectly captures his early investing process and illuminates how he implemented Graham's quantitative style of investment. Dempster was a concentrated investment, it was cheap even on conservative assumptions, it required Buffett's active involvement, it was an asset conversion play, and it was executed in a tax-advantaged way. For those who remain in the quantitative, Generals-Private Owner school of investing, a close look at Dempster serves as a template for valuing businesses using the asset value method in the undervalued cigar-butt plays of today.

Windmill Wind-Down

Buffett started buying stock soon after he formed the very first partnership. The Moody's Manual that year described Dempster as a "manufacturer of windmills, pumps, cylinders, water systems, centrifugal pumps, steel tanks, water supply equipment, fertilizer equipment and farm implements." It was a micro-cap, family-owned company in Beatrice, Nebraska, generating de minimis profits. The equity, however, would have caught the discriminating eye of any Graham disciple—it was trading at a momentous discount.

Not long after his first purchase, Buffett joined the company's board of directors, and he kept buying the stock for the next five years. Then a large block from the Dempster family came up for sale in 1961. Control was acquired in August of that year—he owned 70% and a few "associates" owned another 10%. All in, his average price was $1.2 million ($28/share), which was roughly a 50% discount to working capital and 66% discount to book. For the purposes of the Partnership, he placed a $35/share liquidation value on the company, a process that was of "particular importance since, in effect, new partners are buying in based upon this price, and old partners are selling a portion of their interest based upon the same price."[2] Dempster accounted for roughly 20% of BPL's total assets at year-end.

This was yet another big commitment for Buffett and a tricky situation at first. Inventories were way too high and rising fast. Buffett tried to work with existing management but finally had to throw them out as inventories continued to build. The company's bank was worried and threatening to seize the collateral backing its loan. They began talking about shutting Dempster down and Buffett had to act fast.[3] If a business tying up 20% of his capital went under, the Partnership would be in serious trouble. Thankfully, on the recommendation of Munger, Buffett met an "operating man" named Harry Bottle and hired him on the spot.

Harry was a turnaround specialist and quickly got to work. Here he recalled handling the excess inventory problem: "[I]n desperation I simply hired a painter and with his help we painted a six-inch white line ten feet above the floor around the inside wall of our largest warehouse and I called in the plant supervisor and informed him that if I ever walked into the building and could not see the line above the pile of boxes I would lay off everyone, except the shipping department, until the line was exposed. I gradually moved that line down until I arrived at a satisfactory inventory turn."[4]

Harry did such an outstanding job whipping the company into shape that Buffett, in the next year's letter, named him "man of the year." Not only did he reduce inventories from $4 million to $1 million, alleviating the concerns of the bank (whose loan was quickly repaid), he also cut administrative and selling expenses in half and closed five unprofitable branches. With the help of Buffett and Munger, Dempster also raised prices on their used equipment up to 500% with little impact to sales volume or resistance from customers,[5] all of which worked in combination to restore a healthy economic return in the business.

Flexible Thinking

There is an added twist to Dempster that distinguished Buffett from the vast majority of his contemporaries and demonstrates the flexibility of his thought process: He understood his job as a business owner and his job as an investor to be one and the same. Most people think of themselves in one role or the other; it clicked with Buffett early that the roles are one and the same in that both are capital allocators.

Too often, managers of poor-return businesses feel they have no other choice but to reinvest profits back into their business. Then they judge their success relative to industry peers. This can often lead the "healthiest person in hospice" syndrome, where good money is reinvested at low incremental rates of return and serves only to perpetuate a continuation of poor returns.

Buffett was wired differently, and he achieves better results in part because he invests using an absolute scale. With Dempster he wasn't at all bogged down with all the emotional baggage of being a veteran of the windmill business. He was in it to produce the highest rate of return on the capital he had tied up in the assets of the business. This absolute scale allowed him to see that the fix for Dempster would come by not reinvesting back into windmills. He immediately stopped the company from putting more capital in and started taking the capital out.

With profits and proceeds raised from converting inventory and other assets to cash, Buffett started buying stocks he liked. In essence, he was converting capital that was previously utilized in a bad (low-return) business, windmills, to capital that could be utilized in a good (high-return) business, securities. The longer it went on, the less Dempster looked like a manufacturing company and the more it looked like the investment partnership. The willingness and ability to see investment capital as completely fungible, whether it is capital tied up in the assets of a businesses or capital that's invested in securities, is an exceedingly rare trait.

With Buffett at the helm, he saw to it that assets that could be redeployed were redeployed. Then he had the company borrow $20 a share, which was used to buy even more of the stocks he liked. The initial $35 valuation in 1961 was all Dempster; by year-end 1962, Buffett's valuation, now $51/share, comprised securities at market worth $35 and the manufacturing operations at $16. Dempster's securities portfolio had become as large as the rest of the Partnership's.[6]

Buffett gave fair warning of the natural consequences of this change:

> *It should be pointed out that Dempster last year was 100% an asset conversion problem and therefore, completely unaffected by the stock market and tremendously affected by our success with the assets. In 1963, the manufacturing assets will still be important, but from a valuation standpoint it will behave considerably more like a general since we will have a large portion of its money invested in generals pretty much identical with those in Buffett Partnership, Ltd.*

Dempster was Buffett's first experience jumping into the management of a Control with both feet, and Bottle gave him a firsthand view of the difference a high-quality, trustworthy CEO could make. Harry Bottle was showered with praise in the letters. Here we see the origins of what later became Buffett's signature style, borrowed from Dale Carnegie: Praise by name, criticize by category.

Buffett and Bottle continued to work down the assets of Dempster until all that was left was earning a satisfactory return. Then, the story ended in 1963. Dempster's remaining manufacturing assets as well as the Dempster name were sold.

One final facet of the story demonstrates Buffett's acumen for maximizing after-tax profits. Because all the manufacturing assets were gone, only securities remained. Buffett was able to avoid Dempster's corporate capital gains tax bill in a move that effectively doubled BPL's return, allowing BPL to realize a $45 per share gain.

While the Dempster investment was very profitable, Buffett never did another one like it. He was vilified in the local press as a liqui-dator.[7] Later, when faced with the question of whether to liquidate Berkshire's textiles business in 1969, he said,

> *I don't want to liquidate a business employing 1,100 people when the Management has worked hard to improve their rela-tive industry position, with reasonable results, and as long as the business does not require substantial additional capital in-vestment. I have no desire to trade severe human dislocations for a few percentage points additional return per annum.*[8]

Dempster-Diving Contemporaries

Watching Buffett put his investing knowledge to work through Dempster is instructive for today's investors on several levels. First, it reveals a false assumption many harbor about Controls being a field limited to big investors. Dempster's market value was $1.6 million in 1961, or approximately $13.3 million in today's dol-lars. Second, the ability to play in the smaller sandboxes was as big an advantage for him in the early years as it remains for anyone working with smaller sums today. The "two string to the bow" ad-vantage of the Generals-Private Owner stocks allows for activism as well as control. Even those working with smaller sums can exercise this advantage in the micro-cap companies.

Buffett was not the only investment legend to make his start in deeply undervalued securities: David Einhorn, who founded the now-colossal hedge fund Greenlight Capital in 1996 with less than $1 million, identified a micro-cap net-net company by the name of C. R. Anthony trading at 50% of net working capital. Einhorn put 15% of his assets into it and ended up making a 500% return that year when the company was acquired.[9] Now that he's a billionaire, those types of opportunities are unlikely to become available to him again. Industry experts point out how difficult it would be to put more than $1 million to work in a diversified net-net strategy in 2014.[10] If you're not too wealthy for it already, happy hunting.

Value:
Accounting Value Versus Intrinsic Value

Today, plenty of free Internet tools exist to screen for stocks trading below their accounting book value or their net working capital. Buying an equal-weighted basket of these types of properly selected stocks and holding them for a year or two (one of Tobias Carlisle's strategies) has proven to be very effective historically. But, if you want to make more concentrated bets like Buffett did, you're going to have to do some analysis, and that starts with understanding the actual economic value (realizable liquidation value) of a company's assets.

The Dempster-related letters are rich with specific detail about the actual process Buffett used to value the assets of these kinds of troubled companies; it remains the same process deep value investors are using today. The Dempster description was unique because we not only see his initial appraisal of value on a line-by-line basis; we also can see how those values changed as events unfolded.

Importantly, when it comes to an asset as opposed to an earnings valuation, we are talking about conservatively calculated liquidation value. "The estimated value should not be what we hope it would be worth, or what it might be worth to an eager buyer, etc., but what I would estimate our interest would bring if sold under current conditions in a reasonably short period of time." The process comes straight from Graham.

As can be seen in Appendix D, Buffett works progressively down the list of balance sheet items, which are listed according to their liquidity. Cash is so liquid it doesn't need a haircut. Accounts receivable (money owed by Dempster's customers but not yet collected) are valued at 85 cents on the dollar; inventory, which is carried on "the books" at cost, is marked down to 65 cents. Prepaid expenses and "other" are assumed to be worth only 25 cents on the dollar. When the adjusted figures are summed, you can see that Buffett is assuming a real-world value of $3.6 million for the current (most liquid) assets despite the fact they are on the books at $5.5 million.

Next, he values the long-term assets, which are typically less liquid, using estimated auction values. For Dempster, these would be the manufacturing facilities and equipment (officially listed as Property, Plant & Equipment). Notice the $800,000 valuation compared to $1.4 million of accounting value? Remember, Buffett's after what this stuff is worth in the event of a prompt sale—accounting values tell you only what price was paid *by* the company to acquire this stuff. He was after the price that would be paid *to* the company if sold. The process is intentionally conservative so as to leave room for a margin of error in the assumptions.

Some companies will require more conservatism than others. For example, a retailer with an inventory of mostly out-of-fashion T-shirts needs a much bigger discount than would be required for inventory of a manufacturer made up of unfinished commodities (steel plating, for example). You can do a little research to help find more accurate adjustment factors by industry. *Securities Analysis* dives deeply into the intricacies of asset valuation. For our purposes, it's sufficient if you grasp the basics of how the process works and the importance of erring on the side of caution in your estimates. That means, once you do the work, the value should be obvious. As Buffett said in the letters, "we are looking for wide margins of profit—if it looks at all close, we pass."[11]

As evident in the table in the appendix, adjusted assets totaled $4.4 million. When liabilities of $2.3 million were subtracted (always at face value), $2.2 million was left as the adjusted business value. With 60,000 shares, this works out to the initial $35 per share valuation. Buffett's average price of $28 was equal to 80% of his conservatively calculated adjusted liquidation value. In other words, while it was a ridiculously low price relative to its accounting value, more important, it was still meaningfully cheap relative to the adjusted, or intrinsic, value.

A Living Valuation

In the six months that Harry Bottle was on the job he was able to make significant progress turning around the company and again we can see in the table in the appendix how his progress made Dempster a more valuable company. Buffett delighted in reporting, "The successful conversion of substantial portions of the assets of Dempster to cash, at virtually 100 cents on the dollar, has been the high point of 1962. For example, inventory of $4.2 million at last yearend will probably be about $1.9 million this yearend, reducing the discount on this item by about $920,000 (40% of $2.3 million reduction)." Using the same adjustment factors on each item reveals exactly how this activity "produced" another $15 a share in value.

Buffett walked partners through the figures:

Three facts stand out: (1) Although net worth has been reduced somewhat by the housecleaning and write downs ($550,000 was written out of inventory; fixed assets overall brought more than book value), we have converted assets to cash at a rate far superior to that implied in our year-earlier valuation. (2) To some extent, we have converted the assets from the manufacturing business (which has been a poor business) to a business which we think is a good business—securities. (3) By buying assets at a bargain price, we don't need to pull any rabbits out of a hat to get extremely good percentage gains. This is the cornerstone of our investment philosophy: "Never count on making a good sale. Have the purchase price be so attractive that even a mediocre sale gives good results. The better sales will be the frosting on the cake."

Never Forget the Balance Sheet

Buffett teaches investors to think of stocks as a conduit through which they can own their share of the assets that make up a business. The value of that business will be determined by one of two methods: (1) what the assets are worth if sold, or (2) the level of profits in relation to the value of assets required in producing them. This is true for each and every business and they are interrelated. Buffett commented, "Harry has continued this year to turn underutilized assets into cash, but in addition, he has made the remaining needed assets productive."

Operationally, a business can be improved in only three ways: (1) increase the level of sales; (2) reduce costs as a percent of sales; (3) reduce assets as a percentage of sales. The other factors, (4) increase leverage or (5) lower the tax rate, are the financial drivers of business value. These are the only ways a business can make itself more valuable.

Buffett "pulled all the levers" at Dempster. Raising prices on replacement parts and reducing operating costs pulled lever #1 and #2. Lever #3 was pulled as inventories (assets) were reduced. Lever #4 was pulled when Buffett borrowed money to buy more stocks. Lever #5 was pulled when he avoided a big tax bill by selling all the operating assets of the company.

When profitability goes up and the capital required to produce it goes down, the returns and the value of the business go straight up. Buffett understood this intrinsically and Dempster is a powerful example for today's investors who obsess over (1) and (2) at the expense of (3). Pulling underutilized assets out of a company not only produces cash to be used elsewhere, it makes the business better and more valuable. It is a wonderful reminder to individual and professional investors alike to focus their attention first on the balance sheet (there is a reason it comes first in the set of financial statements). Never lose sight of the fact that without tangible assets, there would be no earnings in the first place.

Lessons from the Partnership Letters: Dempster Mill

We have also begun open market acquisition of a potentially major commitment which I, of course, hope does nothing marketwise for at least a year. Such a commitment may be a deterrent to short range performance, but it gives strong promise of superior results over a several year period combined with substantial defensive characteristics.

JANUARY 24, 1962

Dempster Mill Manufacturing Company

We are presently involved in the control of Dempster Mill Manufacturing Company of Beatrice, Nebraska. Our first stock was purchased as a generally undervalued security five years ago. A block later became available, and I went on the Board about four years ago. In August 1961, we obtained majority control, which is indicative of the fact that many of our operations are not exactly of the "overnight" variety.

Presently we own 70% of the stock of Dempster with another 10% held by a few associates. With only 150 or so other stockholders, a market on the stock is virtually non-existent, and in any case, would have no meaning for a controlling block. Our own actions in such a market could drastically affect the quoted price.

Therefore, it is necessary for me to estimate the value at yearend of our controlling interest. This is of particular importance since, in effect, new partners are buying in based upon this price, and old partners are selling a portion of their interest based upon the same price. The estimated value should not be what we hope it would be worth, or what it might be worth to an eager buyer, etc., but what I would estimate our interest would bring if sold under current conditions in a reasonably short period of time. Our efforts will be devoted toward increasing this value, and we feel there are decent prospects of doing this.

Dempster is a manufacturer of farm implements and water systems with sales in 1961 of about $9 million. Operations have produced only nominal profits in relation to invested capital during recent years. This reflected a poor management situation, along with a fairly tough industry situation. Presently, consolidated net worth (book value) is about $4.5 million, or $75 per share, consolidated working capital about $50 per share, and at yearend we valued our interest at $35 per share. While I claim no oracular vision in a matter such as this, I feel this is a fair valuation to both new and old partners. Certainly, if even moderate earning power can be restored, a higher valuation will be justified, and even if it cannot, Dempster should work out at a higher figure. Our controlling interest was acquired at an average price of about $28, and this holding currently represents 21% of partnership net assets based on the $35 value.

Of course, this section of our portfolio is not going to be worth more money merely because General Motors, U.S. Steel, etc., sell higher. In a raging bull market, operations in control situations will seem like a very difficult way to make money, compared to just buying the general market. However, I am more conscious of the dangers presented at current market levels than the opportunities. Control situations, along with work-outs, provide a means of insulating a portion of our portfolio from these dangers.

NOVEMBER 1, 1962

We intend to use the same method for valuing our controlling interest in Dempster Mill Manufacturing at this yearend that we did at the end of last year. This involved applying various discounts to the balance sheet items to reflect my opinion as to what could be realized on a very prompt sale. Last year this involved a 40% discount on inventories, a 15% discount on receivables, estimated auction value of fixed assets, etc., which led to an approximate value of $35.00 per share.

The successful conversion of substantial portions of the assets of Dempster to cash, at virtually 100 cents on the dollar, has been the high point of 1962. For example, inventory of $4.2 million at last yearend will probably be about $1.9 million this yearend, reducing the discount on this item by about $920,000 (40% of $2.3 million reduction). I will give this story my full journalistic treatment in my annual letter. Suffice to say at this point that applying the same discounts described above will probably result in a yearend value of at least $50.00 per share. The extent of the asset conversion job can perhaps best be illustrated in a sentence by pointing out that whereas we had $166,000 of cash and $2,315,000 of liabilities at November 30, 1961 (Dempster fiscal yearend), we expect this year to have about $1 million in cash and investments (of the type the Partnership buys) against total liabilities of $250,000. Prospects for further improvement in this situation in 1963 appear good, and we expect a substantially expanded investment portfolio in Dempster next year.

Valuing Dempster at $50 per share, our overall gain (before any payments to partners) to October 31st for the Partnership has been 5.5%. This 22.3 percentage-points advantage over the Dow, if maintained until the end of the year, will be among the largest we have ever had. About 60% of this advantage was accomplished by the portfolio other than Dempster, and 40% was the result of increased value at Dempster.

||||||||||||||||||||||||||||||||||||||||||||||||||||||||||||||||||||||||||||||||||||||||||||||||||||||||||||||||||||||||||||||||||

JANUARY 18, 1963
Dempster Mill Manufacturing Company

The high point of 1962 from a performance standpoint was our present control situation—73% owned Dempster Mill. Dempster has been primarily in farm implements (mostly items retailing for $1,000 or under), water systems, water well supplies and jobbed plumbing lines.

The operations for the past decade have been characterized by static sales, low inventory turnover and virtually no profits in relation to invested capital.

We obtained control in August, 1961 at an average price of about $28 per share, having bought some stock as low as $16 in earlier years, but the vast majority in an offer of $30.25 in August. When control of a company is obtained, obviously what then becomes all-important is the value of assets, not the market quotation for a piece of paper (stock certificate). Last year, our Dempster holding was valued by applying what I felt were appropriate discounts to the various assets. These valuations were based on their status as non-earning assets and were not assessed on the basis of potential, but on the basis of what I thought a prompt sale would produce at that date. Our job was to compound these values at a decent rate. The consolidated balance sheet last year and the calculation of fair value are shown below. *[Appendix D]*

Dempster's fiscal year ends November 30th, and because the audit was unavailable in complete form, I approximated some of the figures and rounded to $35 per share last year.

Initially, we worked with the old management toward more effective utilization of capital, better operating margins, reduction of overhead, etc. These efforts were completely fruitless. After spinning our wheels for about six months, it became obvious that while lip service was being given to our objective, either through inability or unwillingness, nothing was being accomplished. A change was necessary.

A good friend, whose inclination is not toward enthusiastic descriptions, highly recommended Harry Bottle for our type of problem. On April 17, 1962 I met Harry in Los Angeles, presented a deal which provided for rewards to him based upon our objectives being met, and on April 23rd he was sitting in the president's chair in Beatrice. Harry is unquestionably the man of the year. Every goal we have set for Harry has been met, and all the surprises have been on the pleasant side. He has accomplished one thing after another that has been labeled as impossible, and has always taken the tough things first. Our breakeven point has been cut virtually in half, slowmoving or dead merchandise has been sold or written off, marketing procedures have been revamped, and unprofitable facilities have been sold.

The results of this program are partially shown in the balance sheet below, *[Appendix D]*, which, since it still represents nonearning assets, is valued on the same basis as last year.

On January 2, 1963, Dempster received an unsecured term loan of $1,250,000. These funds, together with the funds already "freed-up" will enable us to have a security portfolio of about $35 per share at Dempster, or considerably more than we paid for the whole company. Thus our present valuation will involve a net of about $16 per share in the manufacturing operation and $35 in a security operation comparable to that of Buffett Partnership, Ltd.

We, of course, are devoted to compounding the $16 in manufacturing at an attractive rate and believe we have some good ideas as to how to accomplish this. While this will be easy if the business as presently conducted earns money, we have some promising ideas even if it shouldn't.

It should be pointed out that Dempster last year was 100% an asset conversion problem and therefore, completely unaffected by the stock market and tremendously affected by our success with the assets. In 1963, the manufacturing assets will still be important, but from a valuation standpoint it will behave considerably more like a general since we will have a large portion of its money invested in generals pretty much identical with those in Buffett Partnership, Ltd. For tax reasons, we will probably not put workouts in Dempster. Therefore, if the Dow should drop substantially, it would have a significant effect on the Dempster valuation. Likewise, Dempster would benefit this year from an advancing Dow which would not have been the case most of last year.

There is one final point of real significance for Buffett Partnership, Ltd. We now have a relationship with an operating man which could be of great benefit in future control situations. Harry had never thought of running an implement company six days before he took over. He is mobile, hardworking and carries out policies once they are set. He likes to get paid well for doing well, and I like dealing with someone who is not trying to figure how to get the fixtures in the executive washroom gold-plated.

Harry and I like each other, and his relationship with Buffett Partnership, Ltd. should be profitable for all of us.

IIIIIIIIIIIIIIIIIIIIIIIIIIIIIIIIIIIIIIIIIIIIIIIIIIIIIIIIIIIIIIIIIIIIIIIIIIIIIIIIIIIIIIIIIIIIIIIIIIIIIIIIIIIIIIIIIIIIIIIIIIIIIIIIIII

JULY 10, 1963

In our most recent annual letter, I described Harry Bottle as the "man of the year." This was an understatement. Last year Harry did an extraordinary job of converting unproductive assets into cash which we then, of course, began to invest in undervalued securities. Harry has continued this year to turn under-utilized assets into cash, but in addition, he has made the remaining needed assets productive. Thus we have had the following transformation in balance sheets during the last nineteen months *[Appendix D]*.

I have included above the conversion factors we have previously used in valuing Dempster for B.P.L. purposes to reflect estimated immediate sale values of non-earning assets.

As can be seen, Harry has converted the assets at a much more favorable basis than was implied by my valuations. This largely reflects Harry's expertise and, perhaps, to a minor degree my own conservatism in valuation.

As can also be seen, Dempster earned a very satisfactory operating profit in the first half (as well as a substantial unrealized gain in securities) and there is little question that the operating business, as now conducted, has at least moderate earning power on the vastly reduced assets needed to conduct it. Because of a very important seasonal factor and also the presence of a tax carry forward, however, the earning power is not nearly what might be inferred simply by a comparison of the 11/30/62 and 6/30/63 balance sheets. Partly because of this seasonality, but more importantly, because of possible developments in Dempster before 1963 yearend, we have left our Dempster holdings at the same $51.26 valuation used at yearend 1962 in our figures for B.P.L.'s first half. However, I would be very surprised if it does not work out higher than this figure at yearend.

One sidelight for the fundamentalists in our group: B.P.L. owns 71.7% of Dempster acquired at a cost of $1,262,577.27. On June 30, 1963 Dempster had a small safe deposit box at the Omaha National Bank containing securities worth $2,028,415.25. Our 71.7% share of $2,028,415.25 amounts to $1,454,373.70. Thus, everything above ground (and part of it underground) is profit. My security analyst friends may find this a rather primitive method of accounting, but I must confess that I find a bit more substance in this fingers and toes method than in any prayerful reliance that someone will pay me 35 times next year's earnings.

A Letter to the Stockholders of Dempster Mill (Not Included in the Partnership Letters)[12]

JULY 20, 1963

Enclosed is the notice of a special meeting of the stockholders, to be held in Beatrice on Wed, July 31, 1963, at 7 P.M. This letter is written so that you will be in a position to give advance consideration to the matters that will be voted on at this meeting.

Attached are financial statements showing the unaudited earnings for the first seven months of the fiscal year as well as a balance sheet showing the financial condition of the company on June 30, 1963. It is apparent that the fine job Harry Bottle started as president last year has been continued this year. There is a very substantial seasonal element to our business, so that operations at about break-even are expected during the balance of the year. Nevertheless, it appears that operations for the full year will result in one of the best years in recent history.

This dramatic improvement in operating results has been produced by eliminating unprofitable lines, closing unprofitable branch locations, eliminating unneeded overhead, adjusting prices where warranted, etc. In addition to restoring the Company to profitable operations, these actions have substantially reduced the capital needs of the business. Accordingly, on June 30, we owned $1,772,000 of marketable securities with a market value on that date of $2,028,000. It appears that the company will soon be in a position where only about 60% of its asset will be utilized in the manufacturing business. This over-capitalization presents important problems to the management in its efforts to produce a satisfactory return on the total capital committed to the corporation.

The management has given consideration to many alternative methods of employing this capital in the business as well as explored possibilities whereby these excess funds might be made directly available to shareholders without the imposition of very substantial ordinary income taxes. It appears to be impossible to make any prorate distribution without such a distribution being taxable as an ordinary dividend. Our legal advisors have recommended that the most effective way to placing this capital in the hands of Dempster stockholders would be through sale of the operating assets of the Company as a going concern, to be followed by the liquidation of the corporation. This does not mean a liquidation of the operating business, for it will have been previously sold as a going concern. Then all funds may be distributed pro rata to stockholders subject only to a capital gains tax on the excess amount received over each stockholder's tax basis of his stock. It is particularly recommended that this action be taken promptly since the Company has about exhausted the tax carry-forward as computed by our auditors and henceforth our operating profits will be subject to 52% Federal income taxes.

As it is now conducted, the Board of Directors unanimously believes the business of Dempster Mill has a value as a going business in excess of the mere liquidation value of its assets. Therefore, we believe it to be to the best interests of the stockholders, employees and customers that it be sold as a going concern. Harry Bottle will be available as manager for any purchaser. He has been instructed to conduct operations during the intervening period before sale in a manner consistent with our plan of operation during the past year. Material will be purchased, production planned, etc., based on the same pattern as prevailed regarding products and distribution last year.

Very recently, there have been negotiations between the Executive Committee and representatives of several possible purchasers looking toward such a sale as a going business. These have not led to a contract, although in two cases differences seemed relatively minor. Currently, the operations are being studied by an interested party whose intentions have been stated to us to involve substantial expansion of the Beatrice operation.

Because of the seasonal nature of our business, it is necessary for any purchaser to take over operations in early fall to intelligently prepare for the big spring selling season. Therefore, your Board feels something concrete should be done in the relatively near future.

The enclosed Notice of a Special Meeting describes the procedure to be followed:

Through Sept. 13th, our efforts will be continued to sell the business as a going concern on a negotiated basis.

The intent to sell will be widely advertised immediately after the stockholders' meeting. It is intended that major companies in the pump, implement and fertilizer field will be contacted. We will reserve the right to sell on a negotiated basis until Sept. 13th. During this period it will be possible to tailor a contract to the desires of a purchasing party.

Failing a negotiated sale by Sept. 13th, a Public Sale on Sept. 30th will be held with a standard Contract of Sale which we will provide and to which all bidders must conform. Such a sale will be for cash. BPL, owner of 44,557 Dempster shares, presently intends to bid if this sale should take place and would arrange to enter into a partnership or joint venture with any other stockholder or group of stockholders in a bid, if they wanted to do so. Any stockholders of Dempster, of course, will be able to bid individually.

We wish to emphasize Dempster will be sold as an operating business and the buyer will purchase the right to use the Dempster name in operation. After the sale, it is the present intention of the Board to proceed with the orderly distribution of proceeds from the sale and from the disposition of other assets except for those assets which may be conveniently distributed in kind.

While it is obviously impossible to estimate what the final realization to stockholders may be, it would appear certain to be substantially higher than current or past quotations on Dempster stock. Therefore, it would appear advisable for stockholders to retain their shares, at least until further word as to how sales efforts have proceeded.

We hope all stockholders can attend the special meeting so that all questions may be answered. If you cannot attend, any written questions will be answered promptly.

Yours very truly,

WEB, Chairman of the Board.

||||||||||||||||||||||||||||||||||||||||||||||||||||||||||||||||||||||||||||||||||||||||||||||||||||||||||||||||||||||||||||||||||||||||||||||||||||||||||||

NOVEMBER 6, 1963

In 1963, the heavy corporate taxes we were facing (Harry surprised me by the speed with which he had earned up our tax loss carry-forward) coupled with excess liquid funds within the corporation compelled us to either in some way de-incorporate or to sell the business.

We set out to do either one or the other before the end of 1963. De-incorporating had many problems but would have, in effect, doubled earnings for our partners and also eliminated the problem of corporate capital gain tax on Dempster securities.

At virtually the last minute, after several earlier deals had fallen through at reasonably advanced stages, a sale of assets was made. Although there were a good many wrinkles to the sale, the net effect was to bring approximately book value. This, coupled with the gain we have in our portfolio of marketable securities, gives us a realization of about $80 per share. Dempster (now named First Beatrice Corp.—we sold the name to the new Co.) is down to almost entirely cash and marketable securities now. On BPL's yearend audit, our First Beatrice holdings were valued at asset value (with securities at market) less a $200,000 reserve for various contingencies.

I might mention that we think the buyers will do very well with Dempster. They impress us as people of ability and they have sound plans to expand the business and its profitability. We would have been quite happy to operate Dempster on an unincorporated basis, but we are also quite happy to sell it for a reasonable price. Our business is making excellent purchases—not making extraordinary sales.

Harry works the same way I do—he likes big carrots. He is presently a limited partner of BPL, and the next belt-tightening operation we have, he's our man.

The Dempster saga points up several morals:

1. Our business is one requiring patience. It has little in common with a portfolio of high-flying glamour stocks and during periods of popularity for the latter, we may appear quite stodgy.

2. It is to our advantage to have securities do nothing price wise for months, or perhaps years, why we are buying them. This points up the need to measure our results over an adequate period of time. We suggest three years as a minimum.

3. We cannot talk about our current investment operations. Such an open-mouth policy could never improve our results and in some situations could seriously hurt us. For this reason, should anyone, including partners, ask us whether we are interested in any security, we must plead the "5th Amendment."

Compounded Wisdom

Looking back on Dempster much later, Buffett has said that "hiring Harry may have been the most important management decision I ever made. Dempster was in big trouble under the two previous managers, and the banks were treating us as a potential bankrupt. If Dempster had gone down, my life and fortunes would have been a lot different from that time forward."[13]

Not only is it an exciting story, but it's great to have the opportunity to peer over Buffett's shoulder and see how the investment evolves from year to year. The basic Graham techniques for valuing net-nets are found within the story, and then we see how Buffett pulled the five fundamental levers of business value to improve the company and make it worth more.

In the next several chapters, attention will turn to the Partnership's lessons on how to avoid some common mistakes in investing, such as confusing conventional thinking with true conservative action, overweighting taxes as a consideration, the impact of size on performance, and the importance of maintaining your investment marbles while those around you are losing theirs.

Part III

CHAPTER 10

CONSERVATIVE VERSUS CONVENTIONAL

||||||||||||||||||||||||||||||||||||||||||||||||||||||||||||||||||||||||||||||

"A public opinion poll is no substitute for thought."[1]

—JANUARY 18, 1965

Following the crowd can be a remarkably effective strategy in most situations. When you're at an unfamiliar school to watch the big game, following the mob before kickoff is usually a good way to find the stadium. Similarly, if you see people running panicked out of a movie theater, it's a pretty good sign you shouldn't go in. The next time you see a gathering of people all looking intently in the same direction, see if you can keep yourself from looking, too. I'll bet you can't. This instinct, which is programmed into our human condition, is called *social proof*, and it tends to be very helpful in most situations.

Social proof also happens to be the muse of the investing underworld. It lures you in with the comfort that comes with being part of the crowd and then kills your chances for outperformance because, by definition, being part of the herd means your investment views will lack sufficient variance. It is very hard for the majority to do better than average.

Successful investing requires you to do your own thinking and train yourself to be comfortable going against the crowd. You could say that good results come primarily from a properly calibrated balance of hubris and humility—hubris enough to think you can have insights that are superior to the collective wisdom of the market, humility enough to know the limits of your abilities and to be willing to change course when errors are recognized.

You'll have to evaluate facts and circumstances, apply logic and reason to form a hypothesis, and then act when the facts line up, irrespective of whether the crowd agrees or disagrees with your conclusions. Investing well goes against the grain of social proof; it goes against the instincts that have been genetically programmed into our human nature. That's part of what makes it so hard.

Howard Marks, a Buffett contemporary who also has a literary bent, challenges his readers to "dare to be great" in order to dare to be better investors. As he tells his readers, "the real question is whether you dare to do the things that are necessary in order to be great. Are you willing to be different, and are you willing to be wrong? In order to have a chance at great results, you have to be open to being both."[2] Throughout his career, Buffett has found success by daring to be different and rarely being wrong.

The letters provide insight about the two key ideas behind his staunchly independent approach. First, conservatism in investing is based on correct facts and sound reasoning alone—while it can be conventional, it's often unorthodox. An investment has to make sense to you; the crowd's preferences should not sway your own. In fact, the last one to "join the crowd" is likely to be the one paying the highest price. The best purchases are made at the very opposite moment in time, when your thinking puts you in opposition to the conventional wisdom or sweeping trends.

Second, a concentrated portfolio can actually be more conservative than a diversified one when the right conditions are met. Conventional, academic thinking often is at odds with this idea; it's lured away from the better "less-is-more" conclusion by elegant math that gets it wrong because it's based on a faulty premise, the idea that the *beta* of a stock (how much it wiggles around) is an appropriate measure of its riskiness (the chance of a permanent loss). This faulty linkage is then extrapolated to mean that a lower-beta portfolio is the less risky one. Because mathematically, the addition of another stock does lower a portfolio's overall beta, incremental diversification is seen as incrementally lowering overall riskiness. If A=B and B=C then A=C, right? The idea that beta=risk has caused (and continues to cause) a lot of fuzzy investment thinking. Munger and Buffett would tell you it's such a common mistake because the math is so elegant. Practitioners using the tools of engineering and calculus have the ability to come to erroneous conclusions that carry several figures to the right of a decimal point; such precision leads to a false sense of security. Better to be roughly right than precisely wrong, as Keynes liked to say.

Buffett concentrated heavily and felt his actions were highly conservative. Why buy your tenth-best idea (not to mention your hundredth-best idea) when you can still buy more of your favorite at attractive prices? There is a lot to learn from Buffett on managing risk and the opportunity costs of the marginal investment dollar, in his commentary on the true meaning of conservatism.

Thinking for Yourself

To Buffett, if it's rational, it's conservative. Period. Sometimes this approach ends up being conventional and sometimes it doesn't. As he said, "you will be right, over the course of many transactions, if your hypotheses are correct, your facts are correct, and your reasoning is correct. True conservatism is only possible through knowledge and reason." In investing, the herd typically gets it wrong. The best time to be a buyer of securities is when the mob is most fearful. When even the taxi drivers are talking about their stock portfolios, it's prudent to be cautious.

There is an old saying on Wall Street, "What is a good idea in the beginning is often a bad idea in the end." Buffett claimed no comfort when large numbers of people agreed with him; he didn't care what those in positions of influence and authority thought. He recognized that conventionally, something met the test of conservatism when a lot of people were in agreement, including the "experts." He makes a strong point to distinguish his view of what makes something conservative from the conventional view.

The Partnership lessons teach investors that there is only one set of circumstances where you or anyone else should make an investment—when the important facts in a situation are fully understood and when the course of action is as plain as day. Otherwise, pass. For instance, in Sanborn, when Buffett realized he was virtually assured to make money in the stock given he was buying the securities portfolio at 70 cents on the dollar with the map company coming for free, he invested heavily. When he saw Dempster was selling below the value of its excess inventory alone, he loaded up. In each case, when he was within his circle of competence and he understood the factors dominating the likely outcomes, he took action: "When we really sit back with a smile on our face is when we run into a situation we can understand, where the facts are ascertainable and clear, and the course of action obvious. In that case—whether other conventional or unconventional—whether others agree or disagree—we feel—we are progressing in a conservative manner."

Loading Up

As Buffett told partners, *of course* it would be ideal if he could find fifty different opportunities with equally strong probabilities of a 15% gains versus the Dow. That way, even if he turned out to be wrong on a couple, results would still be incredible. But as he said, "It doesn't work that way . . . we have to work extremely hard to find just a very few attractive investment situations."

The benefits of incremental diversification largely run their course after the first 6–8 uncorrelated businesses (stocks) are added to a portfolio. Here we're talking about diversifying the drivers of each individual company's profits, not the covariance of their stock prices or anything technical like that. You can neutralize a lot of unintended bets with just a few ideas. For example, if you own Exxon Mobil (integrated oil company) and Sherwin-Williams (architectural coatings company) you'll be rather indifferent to the direction of the price of oil. Rising prices are generally good for Exxon's profits but bad for Sherwin's because oil and oil-based derivatives comprise the lion's share of Exxon's revenues but also the lion's share of Sherwin's manufacturing costs. Presumably you've invested in these two businesses for a reason aside from your view on where oil is going (no idea), and so it's better to have it neutralized as a factor potentially affecting your portfolio, all else being equal. If you can find 6–8 diverse ideas, you can neutralize the bulk of these unintended consequences.

However, after this first handful, adding additional stocks reduces risk by an ever-decreasing amount. The benefits quickly become outweighed by the reduction to the portfolio's expected return. The fact of the matter is that good ideas—low-risk, high-return potential investment opportunities—just don't come around that often. Most times, the expected return from #7 will be far below your #1 idea.

Buffett grew increasingly convinced of the benefits of loading up when the conditions were right. In 1965, he amended the Ground Rules to include a provision that allowed up to 40% of BPL's net worth to be in a single security under conditions "coupling an extremely high probability that our facts and reasoning are correct with a very low probability that anything could drastically change the underlying value of the investment." In other words, when the facts are ascertainable and clear, the course of action obvious, and the chance of loss minimal, you load up.

He gave a group of students the following advice in the late 1990s:

If you can identify six wonderful businesses, that is all the diversification you need. And you will make a lot of money. And I can guarantee that going into a seventh one instead of putting more money into your first one is gotta be a terrible mistake. Very few people have gotten rich on their seventh best idea. But a lot of people have gotten rich with their best idea. So I would say for anyone working with normal capital who really knows the businesses they have gone into, six is plenty, and I [would] probably have half of [it in] what I like best.[3]

There are still plenty of active managers running 100-plus stock portfolios, just as there were in the Partnership era. Buffett comments derisively about this group in the letters:

Anyone owning such numbers of securities after presumably studying their investment merit (and I don't care how prestigious their labels) is following what I call the Noah School of Investing—two of everything. Such investors should be piloting arks. While Noah may have been acting in accord with certain time-tested biological principles, the investors have left the track regarding mathematical principles. (I only made it through plane geometry, but with one exception, I have carefully screened out the mathematicians from our Partnership.)

Testing Conservatism

Buffett was quick to acknowledge that his ideas were highly subjective and offered a quantifiable way to approach the question: "one rational way to evaluate the conservativeness of past policies is to study performance in declining markets." He then set out his evidence, showing how BPL consistently did better in down years. This remains a good exercise to test the past conservatism of any investor.

From BPL's start through 1965, the Dow had three down years.

When those three years were combined, the cumulative performance of the Partnership was +45%, while the Dow was –20% and
the other managers he regularly compared himself to were down
between –9% and –24% on like for like basis.

While he admitted that the comparison was not "all important,"
he did say the "evaluation of the conservatism of any investment
program or management (including self-management) should be
based upon rational objective standards, and I suggest performance
in declining markets to be at least one meaningful test."

The fact that Buffett never had a down year during the Partnership era is truly remarkable. Stanley Druckenmiller, who had
previously made billions with George Soros, never had a down year
at his hedge fund, Duquesne, where he managed money for twenty
years. Joel Greenblatt, another famous investor who averaged 50%
returns per year at Gotham, never had a down year in the ten years
from 1985 to 1994. The ability to perform well in down markets is
a hallmark shared by all three of these great investors.

Your Best Idea Defines Your Next Choice

When considering the merits of adding a new idea to the investments you already have, compare it to the best of what
you already have. Understanding your ideas in this framework will
keep you from owning too many stocks and diluting your expected
returns.

If you have never heard of the "equity cost of capital" or the
"capital asset pricing model," you are much better off. These are
somewhat complicated tools created by the mathematically oriented
crowd to answer what is otherwise a pretty simple question: Given
the investment choices available any given time, what is the minimum expected return needed from a new idea to make it a worthy
addition to your portfolio? Those who derive this number with a
calculator or a spreadsheet are again mistakenly commingling beta
and risk and often producing mathematically elegant but not very

helpful tools. Forget all that stuff. When a new idea comes along, only buy it when it's more attractive than buying more of what you already own.

Buffett's version of "true" conservatism stands in stark contrast to conventional definitions. At its root, his version is based on the power of thinking for yourself and applying sound reason. Facts determine an action's conservatism, not popularity. This allows him to go against the crowd and concentrate heavily in his best ideas.

‖‖‖

Lessons from the Partnership Letters: Conventional Versus Conservative

‖‖‖

JANUARY 24, 1962

The Question of Conservatism

The . . . description of our various areas of operation may provide some clues as to how conservatively our portfolio is invested. Many people some years back thought they were behaving in the most conservative manner by purchasing medium or long-term municipal or government bonds. This policy has produced substantial market depreciation in many cases, and most certainly has failed to maintain or increase real buying power.

Conscious, perhaps overly conscious, of inflation, many people now feel that they are behaving in a conservative manner by buying blue chip securities almost regardless of price-earnings ratios, dividend yields, etc. Without the benefit of hindsight as in the bond example, I feel this course of action is fraught with danger. There is nothing at all conservative, in my opinion, about speculating as to just how high a multiplier a greedy and capricious public will put on earnings.

You will not be right simply because a large number of people momentarily agree with you. You will not be right simply because important people agree with you. In many quarters the simultaneous occurrence of the two above factors is enough to make a course of action meet the test of conservatism. You will be right, over the course of many transactions, if your hypotheses are correct, your facts are correct, and your reasoning is correct. True conservatism is only possible through knowledge and reason.

I might add that in no way does the fact that our portfolio is not conventional prove that we are more conservative or less conservative than standard methods of investing. This can only be determined by examining the methods or examining the results.

I feel the most objective test as to just how conservative our manner of investing is arises through evaluation of performance in down markets. Preferably these should involve a substantial decline in the Dow. Our performance in the rather mild declines of 1957 and 1960 would confirm my hypothesis that we invest in an extremely conservative manner. I would welcome any partner's suggesting objective tests as to conservatism to see how we stack up. We have never suffered a realized loss of more than 0.5% of 1% of total net assets, and our ratio of total dollars of realized gains to total realized losses is something like 100 to 1. Of course, this reflects the fact that on balance we have been operating in an up market. However, there have been many opportunities for loss transactions even in markets such as these (you may have found out about a few of these yourselves) so I think the above facts have some significance.

||||||||||||||||||||||||||||||||||||||||||||||||||||||||||||||||||||||||||||||||||||||||||||||||||||||||||||||||||||||||||||||||||||||||

JANUARY 18, 1965
The Question of Conservatism

In looking at . . . investment company performance, the question might be asked: "Yes, but aren't those companies run more conservatively than the Partnership?" If you asked that question of the investment company managements, they, in absolute honesty, would say they were more conservative. If you asked the first hundred security analysts you met, I am sure that a very large majority of them also would answer for the investment companies. I would disagree. I have over 90% of my net worth in BPL, and most of my family have percentages in that area, but of course, that only demonstrates the sincerity of my view—not the validity of it.

It is unquestionably true that the investment companies have their money more conventionally invested than we do. To many people conventionality is indistinguishable from conservatism. In my view, this represents erroneous thinking. Neither a conventional nor an unconventional approach, per se, is conservative.

Truly conservative actions arise from intelligent hypotheses, correct facts and sound reasoning. These qualities may lead to conventional acts, but there have been many times when they have led to unorthodoxy. In some corner of the world they are probably still holding regular meetings of the Flat Earth Society.

We derive no comfort because important people, vocal people, or great numbers of people agree with us. Nor do we derive comfort if they don't. A public opinion poll is no substitute for thought. When we really sit back with a smile on our face is when we run into a situation we can understand, where the facts are ascertainable and clear, and the course of action obvious. In that case—whether conventional or unconventional—whether others agree or disagree—we feel we are progressing in a conservative manner.

The above may seem highly subjective. It is. You should prefer an objective approach to the question. I do. My suggestion as to one rational way to evaluate the conservativeness of past policies is to study performance in declining markets. We have only three years of declining markets in our table and unfortunately (for purposes of this test only) they were all moderate declines. In all three of these years we achieved appreciably better investment results than any of the more conventional portfolios.

Specifically, if those three years had occurred in sequence, the cumulative results would have been:

Tri-Continental Corp.	-9.7%
Dow	-20.6%
Mass. Investors Trust	-20.9%
Lehman Corp.	-22.3%
Investors Stock Fund	-24.6%
Limited Partners	45.0%

We don't think this comparison is all important, but we do think it has some relevance. We certainly think it makes more sense than saying "We own (regardless of price) A.T.&T., General Electric, IBM and General Motors and are therefore conservative." In any event, evaluation of the conservatism of any investment program or management (including self-management) should be based upon rational objective standards, and I suggest performance in declining markets to be at least one meaningful test.

||||||||||||||||||||||||||||||||||||||||||||||||||||||||||||||||||||||||||||||||||||||||||||||||||||||||||||||||||||||||||||||||||||||||||||||||||||

JANUARY 20, 1966

Diversification

Last year in commenting on the inability of the overwhelming majority of investment managers to achieve performance superior to that of pure chance, I ascribed it primarily to the product of: "(1) group decisions—my perhaps jaundiced view is that it is close to impossible for outstanding investment management to come from a group of any size with all parties really participating in decisions; (2) a desire to conform to the policies and (to an extent) the portfolios of other large well-regarded organizations; (3) an institutional framework whereby average is 'safe' and the personal rewards for independent action are in no way commensurate with the general risk attached to such action; (4) an adherence to certain diversification practices which are irrational; and finally and importantly, (5) inertia."

This year in the material which went out in November, I specifically called your attention to a new Ground Rule reading, "7. We diversify substantially less than most investment operations. We might invest up to 40% of our net worth in a single security under conditions coupling an extremely high probability that our facts and reasoning are correct with a very low probability that anything could drastically change the underlying value of the investment."

We are obviously following a policy regarding diversification which differs markedly from that of practically all public investment operations. Frankly, there is nothing I would like better than to have 50 different investment opportunities, all of which have a mathematical expectation (this term reflects the range of all possible relative performances, including negative ones, adjusted for the probability of each (no yawning, please) of achieving performance surpassing the Dow by, say, fifteen percentage points per annum. If the fifty individual expectations were not intercorrelated (what happens to one is associated with what happens to the other) I could put 2% of our capital into each one and sit back with a very high degree of certainty that our overall results would be very close to such a fifteen percentage point advantage.

It doesn't work that way.

We have to work extremely hard to find just a very few attractive investment situations. Such a situation by definition is one where my expectation (defined as above) of performance is at least ten percentage points per annum superior to the Dow. Among the few we do find, the expectations vary substantially. The question always is, "How much do I put in number one (ranked by expectation of relative performance) and how much do I put in number eight?" This depends to a great degree on the wideness of the spread between the mathematical expectation of number one versus number eight. It also depends upon the probability that number one could turn in a really poor relative performance. Two securities could have equal mathematical expectations, but one might have .05 chance of performing fifteen percentage points or more worse than the Dow, and the second might have only .01 chance of such performance. The wider range of expectation in the first case reduces the desirability of heavy concentration in it.

The above may make the whole operation sound very precise. It isn't. Nevertheless, our business is that of ascertaining facts and then applying experience and reason to such facts to reach expectations. Imprecise and emotionally influenced as our attempts may be, that is what the business is all about. The results of many years of decision-making in securities will demonstrate how well you are doing on making such calculations—whether you consciously realize you are making the calculations or not. I believe the investor operates at a distinct advantage when he is aware of what path his thought process is following.

There is one thing of which I can assure you. If good performance of the fund is even a minor objective, any portfolio encompassing one hundred stocks (whether the manager is handling one thousand dollars or one billion dollars) is not being operated logically. The addition of the one hundredth stock simply can't reduce the potential variance in portfolio performance sufficiently to compensate for the negative effect its inclusion has on the overall portfolio expectation.

Anyone owning such numbers of securities after presumably studying their investment merit (and I don't care how prestigious their labels) is following what I call the Noah School of Investing—two of everything. Such investors should be piloting arks. While Noah may have been acting in accord with certain time-tested biological principles, the investors have left the track regarding mathematical principles. (I only made it through plane geometry, but with one exception, I have carefully screened out the mathematicians from our Partnership.)

Of course, the fact that someone else is behaving illogically in owning one hundred securities doesn't prove our case. While they may be wrong in overdiversifying, we have to affirmatively reason through a proper diversification policy in terms of our objectives.

The optimum portfolio depends on the various expectations of choices available and the degree of variance in performance which is tolerable. The greater the number of selections, the less will be the average year-to-year variation in actual versus expected results. Also, the lower will be the expected results, assuming different choices have different expectations of performance.

I am willing to give up quite a bit in terms of leveling of year-to-year results (remember when I talk of "results," I am talking of performance relative to the Dow) in order to achieve better overall long-term performance.

Simply stated, this means I am willing to concentrate quite heavily in what I believe to be the best investment opportunities recognizing very well that this may cause an occasional very sour year—one somewhat more sour, probably, than if I had diversified more. While this means our results will bounce around more, I think it also means that our long-term margin of superiority should be greater.

You have already seen some examples of this. Our margin versus the Dow has ranged from 2.4 percentage points in 1958 to 33.0 points in 1965. If you check this against the deviations of the [other investment] funds . . . you will find our variations have a much wider amplitude. I could have operated in such a manner as to reduce our amplitude, but I would also have reduced our overall performance somewhat although it still would have substantially exceeded that of the investment companies. Looking back, and continuing to think this problem through, I feel that if anything, I should have concentrated slightly more than I have in the past. Hence, the new Ground Rule and this long-winded explanation.

Again let me state that this is somewhat unconventional reasoning (this doesn't make it right or wrong—it does mean you have to do your own thinking on it), and you may well have a different opinion—if you do, the Partnership is not the place for you. We are obviously only going to go to 40% in very rare situations—this rarity, of course, is what makes it necessary that we concentrate so heavily, when we see such an opportunity.

We probably have had only five or six situations in the nine-year history of the Partnership where we have exceeded 25%. Any such situations are going to have to promise very significantly superior performance relative to the Dow compared to other opportunities available at the time. They are also going to have to possess such superior qualitative and/or quantitative factors that the chance of serious permanent loss is minimal (anything can happen on a short-term quotational basis which partially explains the greater risk of widened year-to-year variation in results). In selecting the limit to which I will go in any one investment, I attempt to reduce to a tiny figure the probability that the single investment (or group, if there is intercorrelation) can produce a result for our total portfolio that would be more than ten percentage points poorer than the Dow.

We presently have two situations in the over 25% category—one a controlled company, and the other a large company where we will never take an active part. It is worth pointing out that our performance in 1965 was overwhelmingly the product of five investment situations. The 1965 gains (in some cases there were also gains applicable to the same holding in prior years) from these situations ranged from about $800,000 to about $3.5 million. If you should take the overall performance of our five smallest general investments in 1965, the results are lackluster (I chose a very charitable adjective).

Interestingly enough, the literature of investment management is virtually devoid of material relative to deductive calculation of optimal diversification. All texts counsel "adequate" diversification, but the ones who quantify "adequate" virtually never explain how they arrive at their conclusion. Hence, for our summation on overdiversification, we turn to that eminent academician Billy Rose, who says, "You've got a harem of seventy girls; you don't get to know any of them very well."

||||||||||||||||||||||||||||||||||||||||||||||||||||||||||||||||||||||||||||||||||||||||||||||||||||||||||||||||||||||||||||||||||

JANUARY 25, 1967

Our relative performance in this category [Generals–Relatively Undervalued] was the best we have ever had—due to one holding which was our largest investment at yearend 1965 and also yearend 1966. This investment has substantially outperformed the general market for us during each year (1964, 1965, 1966) that we have held it. While any single year's performance can be quite erratic, we think the probabilities are highly favorable for superior future performance over a three or four year period. The attractiveness and relative certainty of this particular security are what caused me to introduce Ground Rule 7 in November, 1965 to allow individual holdings of up to 40% of our net assets. We spend considerable effort continuously evaluating every facet of the company and constantly testing our hypothesis that this security is superior to alternative investment choices. Such constant evaluation and comparison at shifting prices is absolutely essential to our investment operation.

It would be much more pleasant (and indicate a more favorable future) to report that our results in the Generals–Relatively Undervalued category represented fifteen securities in ten industries, practically all of which outperformed the market. We simply don't have that many good ideas. As mentioned above, new ideas are continually measured against present ideas and we will not make shifts if the effect is to downgrade expectable performance. This policy has resulted in limited activity in recent years when we have felt so strongly about the relative merits of our largest holding. Such a condition has meant that realized gains have been a much smaller portion of total performance than in earlier years when the flow of good ideas was more substantial.

The sort of concentration we have in this category is bound to produce wide swings in short term performance—some, most certainly, unpleasant. There have already been some of these applicable to shorter time spans than I use in reporting to partners. This is one reason I think frequent reporting to be foolish and potentially misleading in a long term oriented business such as ours.

Personally, within the limits expressed in last year's letter on diversification, I am willing to trade the pains (forget about the pleasures) of substantial short term variance in exchange for maximization of long term performance. However, I am not willing to incur risk of substantial permanent capital loss in seeking to better long term performance. To be perfectly clear—under our policy of concentration of holdings, partners should be completely prepared for periods of substantial underperformance (far more likely in sharply rising markets) to offset the occasional over performance such as we have experienced in 1965 and 1966, and as a price we pay for hoped-for good long term performance.

All this talk about the long pull has caused one partner to observe that "even five minutes is a long time if one's head is being held under water." This is the reason, of course, that we use borrowed money very sparingly in our operation. Average bank borrowings during 1966 were well under 10% of average net worth.

Compounded Wisdom

Buffett notes that as long as the minimum amount of diversification is achieved (6–8 stocks in different businesses), the year-to-year amplitude of performance is likely to be wider but the expected cumulative returns should be higher. He said, "Looking back, and continuing to think this problem through, I feel that if anything, I should have concentrated slightly more than I have in the past."

Stan Druckenmiller, reflecting on his unbelievable success as an investor, said that the only way to make superior returns is to concentrate heavily. He thinks "diversification and all the stuff they're teaching at business school today is probably the most misguided concept everywhere. And if you look at great investors that are as different as Warren Buffett, Carl Icahn, Ken Langone, they tend to be very, very concentrated bets. They see something, they bet it, and they bet the ranch on it. . . . [T]he mistake I'd say 98 percent of the money managers and individuals make is they feel like they got to be playing in a bunch of stuff."[4]

Buffett's views on conservatism versus conventionalism contain many core orienting concepts that are critical to successful value investing: Think independently, ignore the crowd, and trust your own convictions. The best in the field balance being sufficiently arrogant enough to stand apart from the masses with the humility required to know their limitations. When they find opportunities that just sing to them, they bet, and bet big.

Those who overly diversify think they're reducing risk, but there is a limit to the benefits of diversification and we need to remind ourselves that investing is not a mathematical exercise. While mathematical tools are widely available, they are based on faulty premises and spit out faulty conclusions.

Equally fuzzy thinking around taxes is an error of the same sort. As we'll see in the next chapter, investors will often go to great lengths to minimize their tax bills and end up risking a reduction to their after-tax rate of gain.

CHAPTER 11

TAXES

||||||||||||||||||||||||||||||||||||||||||||||||||||||||||||||||||||||||||||||||||||

"More investment sins are probably committed by otherwise quite intelligent people because of 'tax considerations'
than from any other cause."[1]

—JANUARY 18, 1965

Given two otherwise identical investment options, it's axiom-
atic that the better return will come from the one taxed at
the *lower* rate. Perhaps less obvious but equally true is that
when the tax rate is equal, the better return will come from the one
taxed *later*. While a tax liability is born the moment an investment
goes to profit, it doesn't get paid until the investment is sold.

Deferred tax liabilities (DTLs) from unrealized capital gains are
best thought of as highly attractive, interest-free loans from the government, with terms so favorable no bank would ever make them.
They charge no interest and have no specific due date. DTLs provide
a form of debt that allows you to control more assets than you otherwise would. This is how the deferment creates value:

Consider two stocks, each compounding annually at 15% for 30
years (we'll assume everyone's capital gains rate is 35% to make
our calculations easier). The investor who jumps back and forth
between the two stocks each year will also have their gains taxed

each year; the 15% pretax rate will slip down to 9.75% after-tax: [15% x (1 –tax rate) = 9.75%]; $10,000 invested today will be worth $150,000 in 30 years at this rate. Not bad. However, if the investor instead holds just one stock for all 30 years and gets taxed just once at the end, they get the same pretax rate of 15% but the after-tax rate improves to 13.3%. The same $10,000 will compound at an extra 3.55% and will ultimately produce 2.5 times as many after-tax dollars after 30 years. The deferral of taxes provides a form of financial leverage that allows the second investor to control more assets for longer. When each year's gains are taxed annually, there is no deferral, and thus no benefit from leverage. That's what makes DTLs so attractive.

Buffett appreciates but doesn't obsess over these benefits and is deliberate in pointing out the degree to which bad decisions are made based on fuzzy tax considerations. While there's no doubt, as we've just seen, that tax minimization strategies can boost your results, investors can get it backward when they prioritize minimizing the tax rate ahead of the compounding rate. The allure of avoiding a check to Uncle Sam leads Buffett to make the claim italicized at the beginning of this chapter; tax considerations often lead many otherwise smart people to bad investment decisions.

Means and Ends Confused

The letters teach investors to always assess the value of their holdings as if they've already been liquidated. He would tell you your "net worth" is the market value of your holdings *less the tax payable upon sale.*[2] That's the proper way to think about it. You have to deduct the current tax liability from your gains as you go, even though they won't actually be paid until later. For example, if you put $50,000 into a handful of stocks that subsequently double, your net worth is not $100,000, even though that's the figure likely appearing at the top of your brokerage statement. Assuming the normal 35% capital gains rate applies, an unpaid tax bill of $17,500

(35% of the $50,000 gain) will come due when the stocks are sold. You have to train yourself to think of your holdings in terms of your net worth, or what you would have left if you sold everything tomorrow and paid the tax, which in this example is $82,500. This is the true value of your holdings, what Buffett would say is available to "buy groceries with"—it's what we're trying to maximize as investors. When you sell an investment at a profit, you have to pay back the deferred tax loan you incurred. Thinking about taxes in this way—repaying a loan as opposed to paying a tax—can help keep you from confusing maximizing net worth (primary goal) with minimizing taxes (secondary goal).

The knee-jerk reaction to minimize taxes can come at the expense of choosing the optimal securities to own. This can be a very expensive mistake. Buffett makes this very clear when he says that, "except in very unusual cases (I will readily admit there are some cases), the amount of the tax is of minor importance if the difference in expectable performance is significant,"[3] and "any isolation of low-basis securities merely freezes a portion of net worth at a compounding factor identical with the assets isolated. While this may work out either well or badly in individual cases, it is a nullification of investment management."[4] Clearly, holding on to a group of less attractive stocks to avoid an unavoidable tax bill is a bad strategy.

Buffett was even more explicit:

What is one really trying to do in the investment world? Not pay the least taxes, although that may be a factor to be considered in achieving the end. Means and end should not be confused, however, and the end is to come away with the largest after-tax rate of compounding. . . . It is extremely improbable that 20 stocks selected from, say, 3,000 choices are going to prove to be the optimum portfolio both now and a year from now at the entirely different prices (both for the selections and the alternatives) prevailing at that later date. If our objective is to produce the maximum after-tax compound rate, we simply have to own the most attractive securities obtainable at current prices. And, with 3,000 rather rapidly shifting variables, this must mean change (hopefully "tax-generating" change).[5]

While the presence of a DTL is going to increase your after-tax rate of compounding, all else being equal, in reality, all else is not usually equal. When the pretax returns are consistently high and the time period is long, DTLs will be additive. But if you have the chance to improve you pretax returns by optimizing your portfolio to hold the best stocks you can find, it's usually going to be wise to do so.

Let's return to our previous example of the buy-and-hold investor versus the annual trader. When returns in the two strategies were identical at 15%, the buy-and-hold investor did 2.5 times better than the one who traded yearly. Let's assume that the buy-and-hold investor who thought his stock was going to produce 15% annually ends up producing 10% instead. If he sticks with it despite the lower-than-expected returns, this works out to an 8.4% CAGR after tax. Now, let's assume investor #2, the annual trader, can maintain a 15% CAGR but still has to trade from one stock to the next each year, which you'll recall produces a 9.75% after tax. You can see from this that 15% taxed annually is still meaningfully better than 10% taxed only once. After 30 years, it amounts to investments worth 40% more. As the time period and/or the annual rates of compounding shrink, so will the advantages from the DTL. The bottom line is that if you can improve your portfolio, you should, even if it involves paying taxes.

What About Forever?

Since the 1970s, Buffett has been saying that his favorite holding period is forever. While this might raise an eyebrow in light of our tax discussions, it does in fact remain consistent with earlier commentary to partners. For the majority of the BPL years, optimal rates of compounding required him to jump from cigar butt to cigar butt, from one free puff to the next. In the early years of BPL, forever was not an option. After the free puff, Buffett was forced to move on. If he didn't, his returns would undoubtedly have suffered. These were not good businesses; they were mean reversion trades. Those who remain tilted more toward the Graham school of finding and investing in cheap stocks are likely to have a higher turnover than those who choose to go with the high-quality compounders.

Part of the allure of making the leap to investing in great businesses—BPL's large holding of American Express or the major security holdings of Berkshire today—is that they can compound at high rates for long periods of time and benefit from the leverage of deferred tax. But it's the fact that the businesses have continued to build up their values at relatively high rates, not the deferral of the taxes, that has made them great performers.

Berkshire differs from BPL in two additional ways that affect its holding period and therefore the utilization of deferred tax leverage. Typically Berkshire has excess cash, sometimes in substantial amounts, while BPL was nearly always fully invested. It doesn't make sense for Berkshire to sell one attractive investment in order to buy another when their excess cash allows them to own both. Second, given Berkshire's size, Buffett's universe of choices is limited by the number of really big companies trading at fair prices. BPL had the latitude to reach down into tiny companies to find high rates of expected compounding that simply are not usually available to larger companies. With more options usually comes more tax-generating activity.

Tax Avoidance Schemes

Ultimately the Tax Man cometh. Buffett teaches us that

there are only three ways to avoid ultimately paying the tax:
(1) die with the asset—and that's a little too ultimate for me—

even the zealots would have to view this "cure" with mixed emotions; (2) give the asset away—you certainly don't pay any taxes this way, but of course you don't pay for any groceries, rent, etc., either; and (3) lose back the gain—if your mouth waters at this tax-saver, I have to admire you—you certainly have the courage of your convictions.[6]

He provides us with a great rationale to embrace the payment of taxes as the logical result of our investment success. Many investors, however, still view paying taxes as a confiscation of wealth as opposed to a repayment of a loan. Wall Street has capitalized on the latter mindset and produced a steady supply of "innovation" in tax avoidance products in exchange for generous fees. Whatever investors want, you can be sure Wall Street will be there to meet the need. In 2004, at Berkshire's annual meeting, both Buffett and Munger commented with disgust on the tax avoidance schemes that the most prominent auditing firms were pitching. According to Munger, part of the pitch was that only the top twenty clients were being offered the product, so the regulators wouldn't notice.[7]

This innovative instinct was just as alive and well in the 1960s when "swap funds" were introduced. Buffett colorfully described them in his letters, saying that "the dominant sales argument has been the deferment (deferment, when pronounced by an enthusiastic salesman, sometimes comes very close phonetically to elimination) of capital gains taxes while trading a single security for a diversified portfolio."[8] He then went on to show the less than stellar performance of these funds, while calling out their high fees.

Buffett's comments on taxes keep us grounded and singularly focused on maintaining the highest-return portfolio possible given the choices available. "Don't sweat the taxes" has been Buffett's mantra for years. For the first couple of decades of his investing career, Buffett was producing outstanding results while paying lots of taxes; the more he had to pay, the better he'd done. In investing, look to pay the highest amount of tax you can at the lowest rate possible. If you can do that, it means you're doing splendidly.

|||||||||||||||||||||||||||||||||||||||||||||||||||||||||||||||||||||||||||||||||||||||||||||||||||||||||||||||||||||||||||||||||||||||||||||||

Lessons from the Partnership Letters: Taxes

|||||||||||||||||||||||||||||||||||||||||||||||||||||||||||||||||||||||||||||||||||||||||||||||||||||||||||||||||||||||||||||||||||||||||||||||

JULY 10, 1963

There is some possibility that we may have fairly substantial realized gains this year. Of course, this may not materialize at all and actually does not have anything to do with our investment performance this year. I am an outspoken advocate of paying large amounts of income taxes—at low rates. A tremendous number of fuzzy, confused investment decisions are rationalized through so-called "tax considerations."

My net worth is the market value of holdings less the tax payable upon sale. The liability is just as real as the asset unless the value of the asset declines (ouch), the asset is given away (no comment), or I die with it. The latter course of action would appear to at least border on a Pyrrhic victory.

Investment decisions should be made on the basis of the most probable compounding of after-tax net worth with minimum risk. Any isolation of low-basis securities merely freezes a portion of net worth at a compounding factor identical with the assets isolated. While this may work out either well or badly in individual cases, it is a nullification of investment management. The group experience holding various low basis securities will undoubtedly approximate group experience on securities as a whole, namely compounding at the compounding rate of the Dow. We do not consider this the optimum in after-tax compounding rates.

I have said before that if earnings from the partnership can potentially amount to a sizable portion of your total taxable income, the safe thing to do is to estimate this year the same tax you incurred last year. If you do this, you cannot run into penalties. In any event, tax liabilities for those who entered the partnership on 1/1/63 will be minimal because of the terms of our partnership agreement first allocating capital gains to those having an interest in unrealized appreciation.

|||||||||||||||||||||||||||||||||||||||||||||||||||||||||||||||||||||||||||||||||||||||||||||||||||||||||||||||||||||||||||||||||||||||||

JULY 8, 1964

Taxes

We entered 1964 with net unrealized gains of $2,991,090 which is all attributable to partners belonging during 1963. Through June 30th we have realized capital gains of $2,826,248.76 (of which 96% are long term) so it appears very likely that at least all the unrealized appreciation attributable to your interest and reported to you in our letter of January 25, 1964, (item 3) will be realized this year. I again want to emphasize that this has nothing to do with how we are doing. It is possible that I could have made the above statement, and the market value of your B.P.L. interest could have shrunk substantially since January 1st, so the fact that we have large realized gains is no cause for exultation. Similarly when our realized gains are very small there is not necessarily any reason to be discouraged. We do not play any games to either accelerate or defer taxes. We make investment decisions based on our evaluation of the most profitable combination of probabilities. If this means paying taxes I'm glad the rates on long-term capital gains are as low as they are.

|||||||||||||||||||||||||||||||||||||||||||||||||||||||||||||||||||||||||||||||||||||||||||||||||||||||||||||||||||||||||||||||||||||||||

JANUARY 18, 1965

Taxes

We have had a chorus of groans this year regarding partners' tax liabilities. Of course, we also might have had a few if the tax sheet had gone out blank.

More investment sins are probably committed by otherwise quite intelligent people because of "tax considerations" than from any other cause. One of my friends—a noted West Coast philosopher—maintains that a majority of life's errors are caused by forgetting what one is really trying to do. This is certainly the case when an emotionally supercharged element like taxes enters the picture (I have another friend—a noted East Coast philosopher who says it isn't the lack of representation he minds—it's the taxation).

Let's get back to the West Coast. What is one really trying to do in the investment world? Not pay the least taxes, although that may be a factor to be considered in achieving the end. Means and end should not be confused, however, and the end is to come away with the largest after-tax rate of compound. Quite obviously if two courses of action promise equal rates of pre-tax compound and one involves incurring taxes and the other doesn't the latter course is superior. However, we find this is rarely the case.

It is extremely improbable that 20 stocks selected from, say, 3,000 choices are going to prove to be the optimum portfolio both now and a year from now at the entirely different prices (both for the selections and the alternatives) prevailing at that later date. If our objective is to produce the maximum after-tax compound rate, we simply have to own the most attractive securities obtainable at current prices. And, with 3,000 rather rapidly shifting variables, this must mean change (hopefully "tax-generating" change). It is obvious that the performance of a stock last year or last month is no reason, per se, to either own it or to not own it now. It is obvious that an inability to "get even" in a security that has declined is of no importance. It is obvious that the inner warm glow that results from having held a winner last year is of no importance in making a decision as to whether it belongs in an optimum portfolio this year.

If gains are involved, changing portfolios involves paying taxes. Except in very unusual cases (I will readily admit there are some cases), the amount of the tax is of minor importance if the difference in expectable performance is significant. I have never been able to understand why the tax comes as such a body blow to many people since the rate on long-term capital gain is lower than on most lines of endeavor (tax policy indicates digging ditches is regarded as socially less desirable than shuffling stock certificates).

I have a large percentage of pragmatists in the audience so I had better get off that idealistic kick. There are only three ways to avoid ultimately paying the tax: (1) die with the asset—and that's a little too ultimate for me—even the zealots would have to view this "cure" with mixed emotions; (2) give the asset away—you certainly don't pay any taxes this way, but of course you don't pay for any groceries, rent, etc., either; and (3) lose back the gain—if your mouth waters at this tax-saver, I have to admire you—you certainly have the courage of your convictions.

So it is going to continue to be the policy of BPL to try to maximize investment gains, not minimize taxes. We will do our level best to create the maximum revenue for the Treasury—at the lowest rates the rules will allow.

An interesting sidelight on this whole business of taxes, vis-à-vis investment management, has appeared in the last few years. This has arisen through the creation of so-called "swap funds" which are investment companies created by the exchange of the investment company's shares for general market securities held by potential investors. The dominant sales argument has been the deferment (deferment, when pronounced by an enthusiastic salesman, sometimes comes very close phonetically to elimination) of capital gains taxes while trading a single security for a diversified portfolio. The tax will only finally be paid when the swap fund's shares are redeemed. For the lucky ones, it will be avoided entirely when any of those delightful alternatives mentioned two paragraphs earlier eventuates.

The reasoning implicit in the swapee's action is rather interesting. He obviously doesn't really want to hold what he is holding or he wouldn't jump at the chance to swap it (and pay a fairly healthy commission—usually up to $100,000) for a grab-bag of similar hot potatoes held by other tax-numbed investors. In all fairness, I should point out that after all offerees have submitted their securities for exchange and had a chance to review the proposed portfolio they have a chance to back out but I understand a relatively small proportion do so.

There have been twelve such funds (that I know of) established since origination of the idea in 1960, and several more are currently in the works. The idea is not without appeal since sales totaled well over $600 million. All of the funds retain an investment manager to whom they usually pay half of 1% of asset value. This investment manager faces an interesting problem; he is paid to manage the fund intelligently (in each of the five largest funds this fee currently ranges from $250,000 to $700,000 per year), but because of the low tax basis inherited from the contributors of securities, virtually his every move creates capital gains tax liabilities. And, of course, he knows that if he incurs such liabilities, he is doing so for people who are probably quite sensitive to taxes or they wouldn't own shares in the swap fund in the first place.

I am putting all of this a bit strongly, and I am sure there are some cases where a swap fund may be the best answer to an individual's combined tax and investment problems. Nevertheless, I feel they offer a very interesting test-tube to measure the ability of some of the most respected investment advisors when they are trying to manage money without paying (significant) taxes.

The three largest swap funds were all organized in 1961, and combined have assets now of about $300 million. One of these, Diversification Fund, reports on a fiscal year basis which makes extraction of relevant data quite difficult for calendar year comparisons. The other two, Federal Street Fund and

Westminster Fund (respectively first and third largest in the group) are managed by investment advisors who oversee at least $2 billion of institutional money.

Here's how they shape up for all full years of existence:

YEAR	FEDERAL STREET	WESTMINSTER	DOW
1962	-19.00%	-22.50%	-7.60%
1963	17.00%	18.70%	20.60%
1964	13.80%	12.30%	18.70%
Annual Compounded Rate	2.60%	1.10%	9.80%

This is strictly the management record. No allowance has been made for the commission in entering and any taxes paid by the fund on behalf of the shareholders have been added back to performance.

Anyone for taxes?

Compounded Wisdom

Fuzzy thinking around taxes can sometimes get in the way of what we're actually after—the highest possible rate of after-tax compounding. Usually your stock picking is going to be the major factor in determining that outcome, while taxes will play only a minor role. The size of your funds, and probably more germane, the size of the funds of an outside manager, can also play a role. The question of size is not nearly as straightforward as you might think—and it's our next topic.

CHAPTER 12

SIZE VERSUS PERFORMANCE

IIIIIIIIIIIIIIIIIIIIIIIIIIIIIIIIIIIIIIIIIIIIIIIIIIIIIIIIIIIIIIIIIIIIIIIIIIIIIIIIII

"Our idea inventory has always seemed to be 10% ahead of our bank account. If that should change, you can count on hearing from me."[1]

—JANUARY 18, 1964

As the markets marched steadily higher through the Partnership years, Buffett was continuously assessing the potential impact the rapid growth of BPL's assets might have on his future performance. For many years he courted new investors and saw the increased funds as a positive. However, once BPL's assets grew beyond what his investment ideas could absorb, Buffett stopped accepting new partners. Tracking the progression of his commentary on the issue reveals just how closely intertwined size and the market cycle really are when it comes to expected performance. The interesting question is, at what point does the incremental addition of capital flip from a positive to a negative? In general, that point will always be the moment capital outgrows ideas. In practice, the answer depends largely on where you are in the market cycle. It's not a static number—it's market dependent. In bear markets, even the largest fund managers can put huge amounts of capital to work easily; at speculative peaks, usually only the smallest will be able to find really high-return ideas.

If BPL's funds had remained below a few million dollars, Buffett would probably have remained fully invested even as the market headed toward its speculative peak. This mindset may well have prompted Buffett's comment during the tech bubble's peak when he said,

If I was running $1 million, or $10 million for that matter, I'd be fully invested. The highest rates of return I've ever achieved were in the 1950's. I killed the Dow. You ought to see the numbers. But I was investing peanuts back then. It's a huge structural advantage not to have a lot of money. I think I could make you 50% a year on $1 million. No, I know I could. I guarantee that.[2]

The idea that "the larger the funds, the harder it gets" is true only after a certain threshold is crossed. Investing a few thousand dollars or a few hundred thousand is almost never going to be more difficult, no matter what the market environment. But when you're as big as Berkshire, to use an example at the opposite extreme, size is almost always going to be a big drag on performance no matter what part of the market cycle we're in. With tens of billions in excess capital, only a small number of companies exist that are big enough to even qualify as investments, and they are well followed and typically efficiently priced.

The topic first comes up in 1962 with an essay titled "The Question of Size," which he starts in his characteristically humorous way: "Aside from the question as to what happens upon my death (which with a metaphysical twist, is a subject of keen interest to me), I am probably asked most often: 'What affect [sic] is the rapid growth of partnership funds going to have upon performance?' "[3] Partnership assets that had begun at $100,000 had grown to just over $7 million when he wrote it ($59.5 million in 2015 dollars). At this point,

Buffett still felt that bigger would be better. The key was not the absolute level of his capital or the general ferment of the market, but the intersection of the two. His ideas remained more plentiful than his capital and so more was better.

Yet even then some drawbacks existed. When dealing in smaller, more obscure securities that often had limited liquidity, having even a little more capital to invest made it harder to buy these stocks in sufficient quantity at suitable prices. As a result, Generals–Private Owner were negatively impacted early as the Partnership grew in size, especially because the number of good investment ideas was shrinking at the same time. This is yet another reminder that investing with modest amounts has its advantages. You can go places most others can't.

On the other hand, increased assets could also be an advantage. It offers the potential to participate in Controls. It was Buffett's definite belief that opportunities in Controls increased with the size of his funds as competition was lessened because a certain financial wherewithal was needed to play the game. For those who scoff at the idea of doing these themselves, remember that Buffett was investing in Controls when BPL capital was the equivalent of a couple of million in today's dollars.

Which is more important—the decreasing prospects of profitability in passive investments or the increasing prospects in control investments? I can't give a definite answer to this since to a great extent it depends on the type of market in which we are operating. My present opinion is that there is no reason to think these should not be offsetting factors; if my opinion should change, you will be told. I can say, most assuredly, that our results in 1960 and 1961 would not have been better if we had been operating with the much smaller sums of 1956 and 1957.[4]

In 1966, with the bull market in full swing and the size of BPL growing exponentially as the result of more partners and fantastic performance, Buffett was working with $43 million in capital and his mind did change. That was the point where he finally announced that he could no longer accept any new partners, in a section of his letter titled "The Sorrows of Compounding." Size had become a factor. As he explained, "As circumstances presently appear, I feel substantially greater size is more likely to harm future results than to help them. This might not be true for my own personal results, but it is likely to be true for your results."[5]

This last sentence tells us a lot about Buffett as both an investor and a human being. You'll recall that it's often not in a manager's best interest to close a fund to capital additions, even when it's in the investor's best interest. For Buffett, even if he believed that more assets would have a dampening effect on performance, with an overage of 25% on all profits above the first 6% gain, the more money he managed, the more fees he stood to earn. Here we see yet another example of how remarkably well aligned with partners he remained.

As the market continued to stay hot and funds grew even larger, Buffett took the next step of incremental caution by lowering BPL's official expected rate of return in October 1967. Still, now with roughly $65 million in capital, he made it clear that size was not the primary problem, it was the market; he thought that even if he were operating with one-tenth the capital, his performance would only be expected to be "a little better." The market environment was clearly the larger factor.

For individual investors working with average sums, however, being small is a big advantage in almost any market. It gives you a chance to hunt in areas that are off-limits to professional investors because the companies are too small for the institutional investors. When asked in 2005 if he still stood behind his comment six years earlier, that he could make 50% a year on small sums, Buffett said,

> *Yes, I would still say the same thing today. In fact, we are still earning those types of returns on some of our smaller investments. The best decade was the 1950s; I was earning*

50% plus returns with small amounts of capital. I could do the same thing today with smaller amounts. It would perhaps even be easier to make that much money in today's environment because information is easier to access. You have to turn over a lot of rocks to find those little anomalies. You have to find the companies that are off the map—way off the map. You may find local companies that have nothing wrong with them at all. A company that I found, Western Insurance Securities, was trading for $3/share when it was earning $20/ share!! I tried to buy up as much of it as possible. No one will tell you about these businesses. You have to find them.

There will always be some point, however, where the law of large numbers begins to kick in and the additional dollar begins to introduce incrementally lower returns. After the threshold has been breached, larger funds lower potential returns. If you're investing your own capital this is unlikely to be an issue, but if you're investing in a fund it can be an issue worth monitoring. It fluctuates with the market cycle; at bear market lows it will be higher (big managers can put gobs of money out at high rates of return) and at market peaks it will be lower (only the smallest will thrive). No matter where you find yourself in the market cycle, use BPL's history to get a fix on the question of size: When your ideas outweigh your capital, bigger is better, but the moment assets outnumber ideas, being bigger will lower the future rate of gains (in percent, but not necessarily in dollars).

Keep the following two points in mind, therefore, when considering an investment where size is a factor: Recognize that the record of professional investors working with small sums should naturally be better, all else being equal, and consider the impact their current size might have on their future performance. Professional managers have a financial bias toward increased size that can at times be contrary to your own interests.

||||||||||||||||||||||||||||||||||||||||||||||||||||||||||||||||||||||||||||||||||||||||||||||||||||||||||||||||||||||||||||

Lessons from the Partnership Letters: The Question of Size

||||||||||||||||||||||||||||||||||||||||||||||||||||||||||||||||||||||||||||||||||||||||||||||||||||||||||||||||||||||||||||

JANUARY 24, 1962

The Question of Size

Aside from the question as to what happens upon my death (which with a metaphysical twist, is a subject of keen interest to me), I am probably asked most often: "What affect [sic] is the rapid growth of partnership funds going to have upon performance?"

Larger funds tug in two directions. From the standpoint of "passive" investments, where we do not attempt by the size of our investment to influence corporate policies, larger sums hurt results. For the mutual fund or trust department investing in securities with very broad markets, the effect of large sums should be to penalize results only very slightly. Buying 10,000 shares of General Motors is only slightly more costly (on the basis of mathematical expectancy) than buying 1,000 or 100 shares.

In some of the securities in which we deal (but not all by any means) buying 10,000 shares is much more difficult than buying 100 and is sometimes impossible. Therefore, for a portion of our portfolio, larger sums are definitely disadvantageous. For a larger portion of the portfolio, I would say increased sums are only slightly disadvantageous. This category includes most of our work-outs and some generals.

However, in the case of control situations increased funds are a definite advantage. A "Sanborn Map" cannot be accomplished without the wherewithal. My definite belief is that the opportunities increase in this field as the funds increase. This is due to the sharp fall-off in competition as the ante mounts plus the important positive correlation that exists between increased size of company and lack of concentrated ownership of that company's stock.

Which is more important—the decreasing prospects of profitability in passive investments or the increasing prospects in control investments? I can't give a definite answer to this since to a great extent it depends on the type of market in which we are operating. My present opinion is that there is no reason to think these should not be offsetting factors; if my opinion should change, you will be told. I can say, most assuredly, that our results in 1960 and 1961 would not have been better if we had been operating with the much smaller sums of 1956 and 1957.

|||||||||||||||||||||||||||||||||||||||||||||||||||||||||||||||||||||||||||||||||||||||||||||||||||||||||||||||||||||||||||||||||||||

JANUARY 18, 1963

Partners have sometimes expressed concern as to the effect of size upon performance. This subject was reflected upon in last year's annual letter. The conclusion reached was that there were some situations where larger sums helped and some where they hindered, but on balance, I did not feel they would penalize performance. I promised to inform partners if my conclusions on this should change. At the beginning of 1957, combined limited partnership assets totaled $303,726 and grew to $7,178,500 at the beginning of 1962. To date, anyway, our margin over the Dow has indicated no tendency to narrow as funds increase.

|||||||||||||||||||||||||||||||||||||||||||||||||||||||||||||||||||||||||||||||||||||||||||||||||||||||||||||||||||||||||||||||||||||

JANUARY 18, 1964

We are starting off the year with net assets of $17,454,900. Our rapid increase in assets always raises the question of whether this will result in a dilution of future performance. To date, there is more of a positive than inverse correlation between size of the Partnership and its margin over the Dow. This should not be taken seriously however. Larger sums may be an advantage at some times and a disadvantage at others. My opinion is that our present portfolio could not be improved if our assets were $1 million or $5 million. Our idea inventory has always seemed to be 10% ahead of our bank account. If that should change, you can count on hearing from me.

|||||||||||||||||||||||||||||||||||||||||||||||||||||||||||||||||||||||||||||||||||||||||||||||||||||||||||||||||||||||||||||||||||||||||||||||||||||||||||||||

JANUARY 18, 1965

Our past policy has been to admit close relatives of present partners without a minimum capital limitation. This year a flood of children, grandchildren, etc., appeared which called this policy into question; therefore, I have decided to institute a $25,000 minimum on interests of immediate relatives of present partners.

|||||||||||||||||||||||||||||||||||||||||||||||||||||||||||||||||||||||||||||||||||||||||||||||||||||||||||||||||||||||||||||||||||||||||||||||||||||||||||||||

JANUARY 20, 1966

The Sorrows of Compounding

Usually, at this point in my letter, I have paused to modestly attempt to set straight the historical errors of the last four or five hundred years. While it might seem difficult to accomplish this in only a few paragraphs a year, I feel I have done my share to reshape world opinion on Columbus, Isabella, Francis I, Peter Minuit and the Manhattan Indians. A by-product of this endeavor has been to demonstrate the overwhelming power of compound interest. To insure reader attention I have entitled these essays "The Joys of Compounding." The sharp-eyed may notice a slight change this year.

A decent rate (better we have an indecent rate) of compound —plus the addition of substantial new money has brought our beginning capital this year to $43,645,000. Several times in the past I have raised the question whether increasing amounts of capital would harm our investment performance. Each time I have answered negatively and promised you that if my opinion changed, I would promptly report it.

I do not feel that increased capital has hurt our operation to date. As a matter of fact, I believe that we have done somewhat better during the past few years with the capital we have had in the Partnership than we would have done if we had been working with a substantially smaller amount. This was due to the partly fortuitous development of several investments that were just the right size for us—big enough to be significant and small enough to handle.

I now feel that we are much closer to the point where increased size may prove disadvantageous. I don't want to ascribe too much precision to that statement since there are many variables involved. What may be the optimum size under some market and business circumstances can be substantially more or less than optimum under other circumstances. There have been a few times in the past when on a very short-term basis I have felt it would have been advantageous to be smaller but substantially more times when the converse was true.

Nevertheless, as circumstances presently appear, I feel substantially greater size is more likely to harm future results than to help them. This might not be true for my own personal results, but it is likely to be true for your results.

Therefore, unless it appears that circumstances have changed (under some conditions added capital would improve results) or unless new partners can bring some asset to the Partnership other than simply capital, I intend to admit no additional partners to BPL.

The only way to make this effective is to apply it across-the-board and I have notified Susie that if we have any more children, it is up to her to find some other partnership for them.

Because I anticipate that withdrawals (for taxes, among other reasons) may well approach additions by present partners and also because I visualize the curve of expectable performance sloping only very mildly as capital increases, I presently see no reason why we should restrict capital additions by existing partners.

The medically oriented probably will interpret this entire section as conclusive evidence that an effective antithyroid pill has been developed.

||||||||||||||||||||||||||||||||||||||||||||||||||||||||||||||||||||||||||||||||||||||||||||||||||||||||||||||||||||||||||||||||||||||||||||||

Compounded Wisdom

There are clear advantages to investing modest amounts of capital. Tiny, obscure, and underfollowed companies tend to be least efficiently priced and offer the most fertile ground for opportunities. Sanborn Map and Dempster Mill, where Buffett had huge percentages of the Partnership invested in the early years, would be considered micro-cap companies today. Over time, opportunities of this size became too small. BPL could not put enough capital into them for even outstanding returns in the individual investments to have a meaningful impact on overall returns. Individuals who are willing to do their own work, however, can usually concentrate on these companies and find value in most market environments.

However, after funds cross a certain size threshold, the market cycle is going to have a larger impact on an investor's potential returns and ability to find sufficient quantities of suitable investment choices. Buffett stresses that it was the market environment at the time, much more than the size of the funds he was working with, that made it so hard for him to find ideas. The idea that the market will cycle between optimism and pessimism, as will the availability of good investment opportunities, is the focus of the next chapter. While Mr. Market gyrates between greed and fear, Buffett remains steadfast to his investing principles no matter what the environment and only invests when he deems it logical to do so. As we'll see, markets cycle around investing principles, never the other way around.

CHAPTER 13

GO-GO OR NO-GO

||||||||||||||||||||||||||||||||||||||||||||||||||||||||||||||||||||||||||||||||

"I would rather sustain the penalties resulting from over-conservatism than face the consequences of error, perhaps with permanent capital loss, resulting from the adoption of a 'New Era' philosophy where trees really do grow to the sky."[1]

—FEBRUARY 20, 1960

Jerry Tsai, a twenty-nine-year-old Chinese American who had been working at Fidelity for the past five years, marked the beginning of a new dawn for U.S. mutual funds in 1957. That year, his Fidelity Capital Fund ushered in a new style of investing that was distinctly different from the conventional, conservative style of preceding managers. Tsai, who quickly developed a reputation for "cat-like quickness" and an ability to call short-term market reversals,[2] broke from the traditional style of fund management by concentrating on the speculative growth companies—Xerox, Polaroid, Litton Industries, ITT, etc.—companies the old guard saw as completely unseasoned, risky, and uninvestable. At the time, his activities were considered to be closer to gambling than investing,[3] but the market's proclivity for risk was just starting to percolate after being largely dormant since the Depression era. Jerry Tsai was right there with a new kind of investment product for those with an emerging, fiercely speculative appetite. They called them *performance funds*.

If anyone can be thought of as Buffett's mirror opposite during the Partnership years, it's Jerry Tsai. Both men started their investment operations in the second half of the 1950s and both got out as the '60s came to a close, but they shared little else, especially when it came to their approach, personal results, and the results of those who invested with them. If Buffett was kissing the babies, Tsai was stealing their lollipops.

Comparing the two men provides insight into the environment BPL was operating in throughout the 1950s and '60s, showing just how special the Partnership was and highlighting some of the unique aspects of Buffett's actions and thought process.

As the 1950s were drawing to a close, an investing public that had previously been interested in buying stocks directly shifted its preference to mutual funds; the tailwind for the industry was enormous. In 1946 Fidelity was managing $13 million; by 1966 its assets had grown to $2.7 billion.[4] As the big bull run of the 1960s got under way, the era came to be known as the Go-Go years, so named because of its fast-paced, frenetic character. The timing of Jerry Tsai's new fund and the speculative style he espoused combined with the shifting preferences of the investing public to launch his fund, his career, and his reputation into the stratosphere. This was the investing backdrop against which the Buffett Partnership was attempting to operate conservatively and largely in the style of Ben Graham. At the time, conventional wisdom said that it was Jerry Tsai who was in the vanguard; Buffett was very much the unknown investor.

A Walk with BPL

As we know, Buffett's own venture got under way in May 1956. At the time, he and Tsai were looking at the same market but seeing two different things. The Dow had nearly doubled from its low ebb in the recession three years before and it was hard to call it obviously attractive. In fact, Graham himself had testified in front of the U.S. Senate's Fulbright Committee in 1955 that the market was too high. Buffett was also generally cautious but, with modest capital in those early years, there was more to choose from and his ideas remained plentiful. Over the next decade, the higher stocks went, the more fervent his warnings became.

This comes from his very first letter in 1956:

> *My view of the general market level is that it is priced above intrinsic value. This view relates to blue-chip securities. This view, if accurate, carries with it the possibility of a substantial decline in all stock prices, both undervalued and otherwise. In any event I think the probability is very slight that current market levels will be thought of as cheap five years from now.*[5]

As the years marched on, the market continued to advance and BPL's assets continued to grow. New ideas were becoming increasingly scarce and Buffett grew increasingly cautious. Throughout the late 1950s and into the mid-1960s the market was rising faster than the fundamentals of American business were improving, building in a speculative element that could not possibly last—Buffett knew a correction could occur at any time. While he never claimed to know *when* it would come, he really wanted partners to be ready for what he saw as an eventuality.

For a decade, Buffett's warnings came solely in the form of cautious rhetoric, but when 1966 brought a fresh market high, he was finally compelled to act. His first step was announcing that he was no longer accepting any new partners—it was getting hard enough putting existing partners' capital to work. Then, in the fall of 1967, he took the next step of dramatically halving the Partnership's stated performance goal of 10% relative to the Dow and warned that he was unlikely to be up more than 9% on an absolute basis in any given year. Up to that point, BPL had been compounding its gains at an average rate of 29.8% per year; now Buffett was suggesting there was little chance they would do anything close to that. In the letter announcing his reduced goals, his tone regarding the general market had become outright severe.

While he was telling partners that he understood if they had better places to invest, given his lower return expectations (and some actually withdrew), his cautionary rhetoric was not reflected in his actual performance results. The gain in 1968 alone was 58.8%—his best ever. Not only was this whopper of a year his highest-percentage-return year, but it occurred at a time when he was managing the most capital. Profits for 1968 were $40 million. In just two short years, BPL's assets had doubled once again. As good as recent performance had been, he had simply run out of suitable ideas. While partners didn't know it, the end was near. "I can't emphasize too strongly that the quality and quantity of ideas is presently at an all time low—the product of the factors mentioned in my October 9th, 1967 letter, which have largely been intensified since then."[6]

Conglomerates

One facet of the late 1960s market environment responsible for soaking up BPL's pool of new ideas was the birth and ascension of the great conglomerates—Litton, Teledyne, Textron, ITT, etc.— some of which still exist today. John Brooks's account of the period, *The Go-Go Years*, summed up the unscrupulous way they came into being: "In the sixties, as Wall Street moved rapidly through the revolution that made it the first genuinely public securities market in the world's history, the crucial new element in stock trading was the financial and accounting naiveté of the millions of new investors."[7]

Brooks was talking in part about a new phenomenon that had emerged largely in this decade, the price/earnings (PE) ratio, which was calculated by dividing the price of a company's shares by its earnings. The 1961 annual report of Sanborn Map and Berkshire

Hathaway, for instance, didn't even report earnings on a per share basis. PE's principal drawback as an investing tool is that all the assumptions used in the discounted cash flow approach are implicit as opposed to explicit, meaning the assumed growth in cash flow and the investment required to fund that growth are not clearly distinguished. Two companies could easily both trade at 10 times PE and produce vastly different results. PE is not a bad measure, per se, it's just a really blunt tool. I think of it like using a Magic Marker to take notes—why would you do that when you can use a pen?

In any event, PE had just come into vogue and the conglomerates soon figured out that they could use it to fool the market for some time. They discovered that they could acquire companies with low PE ratios and their stock would go up because it held its higher PE ratio—the additional earnings were being capitalized at a higher rate. Now, you would think that when, for example, two companies of equal size merge and one has a PE of 10 and the other 20, the combined company would trade at the combined average multiple, a PE of 15. This is what typically happens, but the market was fooled for many of these early conglomerate years into thinking otherwise.

This gets to Brooks's second set of naive actors, the accountants. Through various accounting methods used when one company buys another that are no longer permissible, as well as the use of certain types of hybrid securities that at the time did not have to be included in the measurement of the company's outstanding shares the way they need to be today, the conglomerates were able to report far larger earnings contributions from their acquisitions than would be allowable today. The rules changed later, but the accounting standards in the Go-Go years in combination with the PE trick produced an absolutely massive incentive for companies to drive their stock prices through mergers and acquisitions. They were often acquiring many of the low-PE businesses that Buffett would have otherwise been interested in. In 1968 alone, 4,500 U.S. corporations merged, three times more deals than had been seen in any year of the last decade.[8]

While simplistic valuation and bad accounting were snookering the general public, Buffett saw right through it and was appalled. In his ever-colorful style, he called it out for what it was.

The game is being played by the gullible, the self-hypnotized, and the cynical. To create the proper illusions, it frequently requires accounting distortions (one particularly progressive entrepreneur told me he believed in "bold, imaginative accounting"), tricks of capitalization and camouflage of the true nature of the operating businesses involved. The end product is popular, respectable and immensely profitable (I'll let the philosophers figure in which order those adjectives should be placed).

He went on to acknowledge that it was, perversely, albeit indirectly helping BPL performance but soaking up any decent ideas that remained at the same time.

Quite candidly, our own performance has been substantially improved on an indirect basis because of the fallout from such activities. To create an ever widening circle of chain letters requires increasing amounts of corporate raw material and this has caused many intrinsically cheap (and not so cheap) stocks to come to life. When we have been the owners of such stocks, we have reaped market rewards much more promptly than might otherwise have been the case. The appetite for such companies, however, tends to substantially diminish the number of fundamentally attractive investments which remain. . . . You should realize, however, that his "The Emperor Has No Clothes" approach is at odds (or dismissed with a "SO What?" or an "Enjoy, Enjoy") with the views of most investment banking houses and currently successful investment managers. We live in an investment world, populated not by those who must be logically persuaded to believe, but by the hopeful, credulous and greedy, grasping for an excuse to believe.[9]

In May 1969, with nearly $100 million in assets in BPL, and with many of the remaining ideas having been soaked up by the conglomerates (or dragging up what they already owned), he announced his intention to liquidate the Partnership. Nineteen sixty-nine was turning out to be a rather mediocre final year, disappointing Buffett and leading him to say,

> . . . I would continue to operate the Partnership in 1970, or even 1971, if I had some really first class ideas. Not because I want to, but simply because I would so much rather end with a good year than a poor one. However, I just don't see anything available that gives any reasonable hope of delivering such a good year and I have no desire to grope around, hoping to "get lucky" with other people's money. I am not attuned to this market environment and I don't want to spoil a decent record by trying to play a game I don't understand just so I can go out a hero."[10]

A Walk with the Capital Fund

Now let's turn back to Jerry Tsai and look at the period from his perspective as manager of the Fidelity Capital Fund, which you'll recall started in 1957 around the same time as the Partnership. Tsai saw the market in those years differently in part because his methods were so different than those of value investors. In the lexicon of Graham and Buffett, he was a speculator. As a swing trader focused on glamour names and price momentum, he bragged about being in and out of stocks at the drop of a hat. That's how he had been trained. His mentor and boss at Fidelity, Ed Johnston II, once described their methods in the following way: "We didn't want to feel that we were married to a stock when we bought it. You might say that we preferred to think of our relationship to it as 'companionate marriage.' But that doesn't go quite far enough, either. Possibly now and again we liked to have a 'liaison'—or even, very occasionally, 'a couple of nights together.' "[11] While Buffett was looking at business fundamentals for clues to their underlying intrinsic value and willing to hold them for long periods of time, Tsai was looking at stock charts and technical indicators to inform his decisions. It worked for Tsai . . . for a while.

Shrewdly moving in and out of stocks and churning his capital through his various ideas at a rate of more than 100% per year (an atypically high turnover rate at the time), Tsai managed to produce high rates of return for many years. One defining moment occurred at the beginning of 1962 when the market careened 25%, taking his portfolio of high-flying glamour stocks down with it.

The ever-competitive Buffett called him out on his performance in his midyear letter:

Particularly hard hit in the first half were the so-called "growth" funds which, almost without exception, were down considerably more than the Dow. The three large "growth" (the quotation marks are more applicable now) funds with the best record in the preceding few years, Fidelity Capital Fund, Putnam Growth Fund, and Wellington Equity Fund averaged an overall minus 32.3% for the first half. It is only fair to point out that because of their excellent records in 1959–61, their overall performance to date is still better than average, as it may well be in the future. Ironically, however, this earlier superior performance had caused such a rush of new investors to come to them that the poor performance this year was experienced by very many more holders than enjoyed the excellent performance of earlier years. This experience tends to confirm my hypothesis that investment performance must be judged over a period of time with such a period including both advancing and declining markets. There will continue to be both; a point perhaps better understood now than six months ago.[12]

Tsai held tight into the early downturn of 1962. Then he coolly put an additional $28 million to work that October. The entire fund rose a spectacular 68% into the end of the year as the market recovered. It appeared that Tsai had his finger on the pulse of the market. He had made his mark. The bull market was intact and his timing was impeccable. Nineteen sixty-five was another stellar year, in which he was up roughly 50% versus an advance of 14.2% for the Dow.[13] Performance funds as a group had become entrenched as the hot new genre and Tsai had become the headliner. It was time for him to monetize the fame.

He resigned from Fidelity to start his own management company in New York. He took up residence in a series of luxurious suites at the Regency Hotel and headquartered the company in a swank set of offices at luxurious 680 Park Avenue.[14] Tsai had become so popular with investors that when he opened his new fund to investors in 1966, he raised nearly 10 times what he expected. A good launch would have been $25 million; Tsai started the "Manhattan Fund" with $247 million, a record amount of freshly raised capital.[15]

Unfortunately, his timing, so impeccable before, was as off as it could be. The Manhattan Fund first started trading in February 1966, the very same month the Dow made its high of the decade. Unsurprisingly, Tsai's performance vaporized with the market's upward momentum. However, his popularity at the time was so great that investors continued to pour in an additional $250 million from the initial capital raised through the summer of 1968, despite the fund's lousy performance. By then, probably because it was becoming clear to him that his style was no longer suited for a market without price momentum, Tsai shrewdly decided to sell the company. That fall, with more than $500 million in total assets, the holding company that owned the Manhattan Fund was sold for $27 million and he walked away a rich man. Sadly, his investors didn't fare nearly as well. The fund went on to lose 90% of its value over the next several years.[16]

Different Outcomes

While Buffett couldn't have known the timing or extent of the losses in store for Tsai's investors, he was no less repulsed by this style of "fashion" investing. Throughout the decade, he made it clear that he felt it would very likely end badly, but didn't know when. He was trying hard to lower everyone's expectation from the start, particularly those of his own partners. He called out Tsai again, this time directly by name, in his midyear letter dated July 1968 (recall Tsai would sell his fund just a few months later). As Buffett said,

> Some of the so-called "go-go" funds have recently been re-christened "no-go" funds. For example, Gerald Tsai's Manhattan Fund, perhaps the world's best-known aggressive investment vehicle, came in at minus 6.9% for 1968. Many smaller investment entities continued to substantially out-perform the general market in 1968, but in nothing like the quantities of 1966 and 1967. . . . The investment management business, which I used to severely chastise in this section for excessive lethargy, has now swung in many quarters to acute hypertension. . . . When practiced by large and increasing numbers of highly motivated people with huge amounts of money on a limited quantity of suitable securities, the result becomes highly unpredictable. In some ways it is fascinating to watch and in other ways it is appalling.[17]

While Buffett and Tsai both came out of the 1960s nearly $30 million wealthier, Tsai's money came from the sale of his fund while Buffett simply took his share of the Partnership's capital—from the start he had plowed nearly all his performance fees back into the Partnership, where they compounded along with everyone else's. Certainly he could have made even more if he had also decided to sell the Partnership but he opted to close instead. Apparently he had offers but he turned them down.[18] In doing so, Buffett characteristically maintained the alignment with partners that he saw as all-important. He made his money *with* them, not *from* them. Closing and not selling was simply the right thing to do. If *he* didn't think *he* should be invested, why should he tell them to be?

The remarkable alignment he cherished with his partners drove him to operate and communicate honestly and transparently, as all good advisors and fiduciaries should. By talking frankly about the prospects for the Partnership and acting in the partners' best interest even when it ran counter to his financial incentives as the managing partner, Buffett once again demonstrated character that should serve as a model to the financial services industry.

Emotional IQ

A long with the lessons on integrity, there is another important takeaway from this selection of Buffett's commentary. Through a careful study of his behavior through the cycle, we can see how it's our methods, not our principles, that should be changing as the market environment ebbs and flows. As opportunities to deploy capital dried up while the bull market was maturing, "dancing just because the music's still playing" is a mistake. That's the value of our historical vantage point as modern readers. By scanning the many letters written over thirteen years (in a way similar to watching time-lapse photography), we can see how Buffett was able to stay so remarkably rational and steadfast to his own investing principles while others started believing trees actually could grow to the sky.

This is a powerful reminder of the clear benefits of maintaining discipline and being willing to think for ourselves—often against the crowd. Many find the concepts of Graham—thinking of stocks as businesses and Mr. Market—as logical in theory. However, *talking* about value investing is very different than actually *practicing* it. If it were easy, everyone would do it. The letters provide us with a road map and an example that can help turn the talk into practice. They give us *standards*: not what we hope to do, or even what we want to do, but what we know we *must* do, no matter how the investing climate unfolds. When the path is clear we proceed, and when it's uncertain we don't invest. No exceptions. Buffett, the greatest value investor of our time, had his basic principles carved in stone well before the Partnership started and the markets have simply cycled around him ever since. For an investment idea to make it past his filter he has to understand it and it has to be priced right. Otherwise, he will pass.

Buffett made sure his partners were fully aware that his standards had no chance of wavering when it came to his fundamental approach:

> . . . [W]e will not follow the frequently prevalent approach of investing in securities where an attempt to anticipate market action overrides business valuations. Such so-called "fashion" investing has frequently produced very substantial and quick profits in recent years (and currently as I write this in January). It represents an investment technique whose soundness I can neither affirm nor deny. It does not completely satisfy my intellect (or perhaps my prejudices), and most definitely does not fit my temperament. I will not invest my own money based upon such an approach hence, I will most certainly not do so with your money.[19]

At the end of the Partnership years he "passed" in a way that was admirable and true to his principles. He didn't continue the Partnership into bonds, he didn't go to cash; he simply stopped playing. He took his ball and went home. From its high at the end of 1968 to the low in 1970 the Dow fell 33%. It then roared back to a new all-time high in the first month of 1973 before falling a whopping 45% through the end of 1974. He effectively was out of the market for the collapse of the nifty fifty. The averages mask the depth of the decline—many stocks fared far worse than even the poor results of the Dow suggest. Protecting his capital from these two downturns had a major effect on his net worth.

When it comes to investing, it's critical not to "force it." Markets will cycle. There will be times when you too feel "out of step" with the market, just as Buffett did in the late 1960s. You'll find that during the late bull market mania of the Go-Go years, his standards remained firmly set, while the pressure to perform caused the standards of many of even the best around him to crumble.

It's hard not to cave your principles in at the top of the cycle when your value approach has apparently stopped working and everyone around you seems to be making money easily (that's why so many people do it). However, it's more often than not a "buy high, sell low" strategy. Buffett set his plan, established his standards, and then entered the fray, maintaining the courage of his convictions, come what may.

||||||||||||||||||||||||||||||||||||||||||||||||||||||||||||||||||||||||||||||||||||||||||||||||||||||||||||||||||||||||||||

Lessons from the Partnership Letters:
Go-Go or No-Go

||||||||||||||||||||||||||||||||||||||||||||||||||||||||||||||||||||||||||||||||||||||||||||||||||||||||||||||||||||||||||||

DECEMBER 27, 1956

My view of the general market level is that it is priced above intrinsic value. This view relates to blue-chip securities. This view, if accurate, carries with it the possibility of a substantial decline in all stock prices, both undervalued and otherwise. In any event I think the probability is very slight that current market levels will be thought of as cheap five years from now. Even a full-scale bear market, however, should not hurt the market value of our work-outs substantially.

If the general market were to return to an undervalued status our capital might be employed exclusively in general issues and perhaps some borrowed money would be used in this operation at that time. Conversely, if the market should go considerably higher our policy will be to reduce our general issues as profits present themselves and increase the work-out portfolio.

All of the above is not intended to imply that market analysis is foremost in my mind. Primary attention is given at all times to the detection of substantially undervalued securities.

IIIIIIIIIIIIIIIIIIIIIIIIIIIIIIIIIIIIIIIIIIIIIIIIIIIIIIIIIIIIIIIIIIIIIIIIIIIIIIIIIIIIIIIIIIIIIIIIIIIIIIIIIIIIIIIIIIIIIIIIIIIIIIIIIIIIIIIIIIIIIIIIII

FEBRUARY 6, 1958

The past year witnessed a moderate decline in stock prices. I stress the word "moderate" since casual reading of the press or conversing with those who have had only recent experience with stocks would tend to create an impression of a much greater decline. Actually, it appears to me that the decline in stock prices has been considerably less than the decline in corporate earning power under present business conditions. This means that the public is still very bullish on blue chip stocks and the general economic picture. I make no attempt to forecast either business or the stock market; the above is simply intended to dispel any notions that stocks have suffered any drastic decline or that the general market is at a low level. I still consider the general market to be priced on the high side based on long term investment value.

Our Activities in 1957

The market decline has created greater opportunity among undervalued situations so that, generally, our portfolio is heavier in undervalued situations relative to work-outs than it was last year. . . . At the end of 1956, we had a ratio of about 70–30 between general issues and work-outs. Now it is about 85–15.

During the past year we have taken positions in two situations which have reached a size where we may expect to take some part in corporate decisions. One of these positions accounts for between 10% and 20% of the portfolio of the various partnerships and the other accounts for about 5%. Both of these will probably take in the neighborhood of three to five years of work but they presently appear to have potential for a high average annual rate of return with a minimum of risk.

While not in the classification of work-outs, they have very little dependence on the general action of the stock market. Should the general market have a substantial rise, of course, I would expect this section of our portfolio to lag behind the action of the market.

||||||||||||||||||||||||||||||||||||||||||||||||||||||||||||||||||||||||||||||||||||||||||||||||||||||||||||||||||||||||||||||||||||||||||||

FEBRUARY 6, 1958

I can definitely say that our portfolio represents better value at the end of 1957 than it did at the end of 1956. This is due to both generally lower prices and the fact that we have had more time to acquire the more substantially undervalued securities which can only be acquired with patience. Earlier I mentioned our largest position which comprised 10% to 20% of the assets of the various partnerships. In time I plan to have this represent 20% of the assets of all partnerships but this cannot be hurried. Obviously during any acquisition period, our primary interest is to have the stock do nothing or decline rather than advance. Therefore, at any given time, a fair proportion of our portfolio may be in the sterile stage. This policy, while requiring patience, should maximize long term profits.

||||||||||||||||||||||||||||||||||||||||||||||||||||||||||||||||||||||||||||||||||||||||||||||||||||||||||||||||||||||||||||||||||||||||||||

FEBRUARY 11, 1959

A friend who runs a medium-sized investment trust recently wrote: "The mercurial temperament, characteristic of the American people, produced a major transformation in 1958 and 'exuberant' would be the proper word for the stock market, at least."

I think this summarizes the change in psychology dominating the stock market in 1958 at both the amateur and professional levels. During the past year almost any reason has been seized upon to justify "Investing" in the market. There are undoubtedly more mercurially-tempered people in the stock market now than for a good many years and the duration of their stay will be limited to how long they think profits can be made quickly and effortlessly. While it is impossible to determine how long they will continue to add numbers to their ranks and thereby stimulate rising prices, I believe it is valid to say that the longer their visit, the greater the reaction from it.

|||||||||||||||||||||||||||||||||||||||||||||||||||||||||||||||||||||||||||||||||||||||||||||||||||||||||||||||||||||||||||

FEBRUARY 20, 1960

Most of you know I have been very apprehensive about general stock market levels for several years. To date, this caution has been unnecessary. By previous standards, the present level of "blue chip" security prices contains a substantial speculative component with a corresponding risk of loss. Perhaps other standards of valuation are evolving which will permanently replace the old standard. I don't think so. I may very well be wrong; however, I would rather sustain the penalties resulting from over-conservatism than face the consequences of error, perhaps with permanent capital loss, resulting from the adoption of a "New Era" philosophy where trees really do grow to the sky.

|||||||||||||||||||||||||||||||||||||||||||||||||||||||||||||||||||||||||||||||||||||||||||||||||||||||||||||||||||||||||||

JANUARY 30, 1961

. . . [I]t is not unexpected that 1960 was a better-than-average year for us. As contrasted with an overall loss of 6.3% for the Industrial Average, we had a 22.8% gain for the seven partnerships operating throughout the year.

|||||||||||||||||||||||||||||||||||||||||||||||||||||||||||||||||||||||||||||||||||||||||||||||||||||||||||||||||||||||||||

JULY 22, 1961

The . . . point I want everyone to understand is that if we continue in a market which advances at the pace of the first half of 1961, not only do I doubt that we will continue to exceed the results of the DJIA, but it is very likely that our performance will fall behind the Average.

Our holdings, which I always believe to be on the conservative side compared to general portfolios, tend to grow more conservative as the general market level rises. At all times, I attempt to have a portion of our portfolio in securities at least partially insulated from the behavior of the market, and this portion should increase as the market rises. However appetizing results for even the amateur cook (and perhaps particularly the amateur), we find that more of our portfolio is not on the stove.

||||||||||||||||||||||||||||||||||||||||||||||||||||||||||||||||||||||||||||||||||||||||||||||||||||||||||||||||||||||||||||||||||||||||||||||||||||||||

JULY 6, 1962

Particularly hard hit in the first half were the so-called "growth" funds which, almost without exception, were down considerably more than the Dow. The three large "growth" (the quotation marks are more applicable now) funds with the best record in the preceding few years, Fidelity Capital Fund, Putnam Growth Fund, and Wellington Equity Fund averaged an overall minus 32.3% for the first half. It is only fair to point out that because of their excellent records in 1959–61, their overall performance to date is still better than average, as it may well be in the future. Ironically, however, this earlier superior performance had caused such a rush of new investors to come to them that the poor performance this year was experienced by very many more holders than enjoyed the excellent performance of earlier years. This experience tends to confirm my hypothesis that investment performance must be judged over a period of time with such a period including both advancing and declining markets. There will continue to be both; a point perhaps better understood now than six months ago.

||||||||||||||||||||||||||||||||||||||||||||||||||||||||||||||||||||||||||||||||||||||||||||||||||||||||||||||||||||||||||||||||||||||||||||||||||||||||

NOVEMBER 1, 1962

Having read this far, you are entitled to a report on how we have done to date in 1962. For the period ending October 31st, the

Dow-Jones Industrials showed an overall loss, including dividends received, of approximately 16.8%. . . . [O]ur overall gain (before any payments to partners) to October 31st for the Partnership has been 5.5%. This 22.3 percentage-points advantage over the Dow, if maintained until the end of the year, will be among the largest we have ever had. About 60% of this advantage was accomplished by the portfolio other than Dempster, and 40% was the result of increased value at Dempster.

I want all partners and prospective partners to realize the results described above are distinctly abnormal and will recur infrequently, if at all. This performance is mainly the result of having a large portion of our money in controlled assets and workout situations rather than general market situations at a time when the Dow declined substantially. If the Dow had advanced materially in 1962, we could have looked very bad on a relative basis, and our success to date in 1962 certainly does not reflect any ability on my part to guess the market (I never try), but merely reflects the fact that the high prices of generals partially forced me into other categories or investment. If the Dow had continued to soar, we would have been low man on the totem pole. We fully expect to have years when our method of operation will not even match the results of the Dow, although obviously I don't expect this on any long-term basis or I would throw in the towel and buy the Dow.

I'll cut this sermon short with the conclusion that I certainly do not want anyone to think that the pattern of the last few years is likely to be repeated; I expect future performance to reflect much smaller advantages on average over the Dow.

JANUARY 18, 1963

Because of a strong rally in the last few months, the general market as measured by the Dow really did not have such a frightening decline as many might think. From 731 at the beginning of the year, it dipped to 535 in June, but closed at

652. At the end of 1960, the Dow stood at 616, so you can see that while there has been a good deal of action the past few years, the investing public as a whole is not too far from where it was in 1959 or 1960. If one had owned the Dow last year (and I imagine there are a few people playing the high flyers of 1961 who wish they had), they would have had a shrinkage in market value of 79.04 or 10.8%. However, dividends of approximately 23.30 would have been received to bring the overall results from the Dow for the year to minus 7.6%. Our own overall record was plus 13.9%.

||||||||||||||||||||||||||||||||||||||||||||||||||||||||||||||||||||||||||||||||||||||||||||||||||||||||||||||||||||||||||||||||||||||||||||||||||||||

JANUARY 18, 1964

It appears that we have completed seven fat years. With apologies to Joseph we shall attempt to ignore the biblical script. (I've never gone overboard for Noah's ideas on diversification either.)

In a more serious vein, I would like to emphasize that, in my judgment, our 17.7 margin over the Dow shown above is unattainable over any long period of time. A ten percentage point advantage would be a very satisfactory accomplishment and even a much more modest edge would produce impressive gains as will be touched upon later. This view (and it has to be guesswork—informed or otherwise) carries with it the corollary that we must expect prolonged periods of much narrower margins over the Dow as well as at least occasional years when our record will be inferior (perhaps substantially so) to the Dow.

||||||||||||||||||||||||||||||||||||||||||||||||||||||||||||||||||||||||||||||||||||||||||||||||||||||||||||||||||||||||||||||||||||||||||||||||||||||

JANUARY 18, 1965

During our eight-year history a general revaluation of securities has produced average annual rates of overall gain from the whole common stock field which I believe unattainable in future decades. Over a span of 20 or 30 years, I would expect something more like 6%–7% overall annual gain from the Dow instead of the 11.1% during our brief history.

|||||||||||||||||||||||||||||||||||||||||||||||||||||||||||||||||||||||||||||||||||||||||||||||||||||||||||||||||||||||||||||||||||||||||||||||||||||

JANUARY 18, 1965

We do not consider it possible on an extended basis to maintain the 16.6 percentage point advantage over the Dow of the Partnership or the 11.2 percentage point edge enjoyed by the limited partners. We have had eight consecutive years in which our pool of money has out-performed the Dow, although the profit allocation arrangement left the limited partners short of Dow results in one of those years. We are certain to have years (note the plural) when the Partnership results fall short of the Dow despite considerable gnashing of teeth by the general partner (I hope not too much by the limited partners). When that happens our average margin of superiority will drop sharply. I might say that I also think we will continue to have some years of very decent margins in our favor. However, to date we have benefited by the fact that we have not had a really mediocre (or worse) year included in our average, and this obviously cannot be expected to be a permanent experience.

|||||||||||||||||||||||||||||||||||||||||||||||||||||||||||||||||||||||||||||||||||||||||||||||||||||||||||||||||||||||||||||||||||||||||||||||||||||

NOVEMBER 1, 1965

As I write this, we are orbiting in quite satisfactory fashion. Our margin over the Dow is well above average, and even those Neanderthal partners who utilize such crude yardsticks as net profit would find performance satisfactory. This is all, of course, subject to substantial change by yearend.

|||||||||||||||||||||||||||||||||||||||||||||||||||||||||||||||||||||||||||||||||||||||||||||||||||||||||||||||||||||||||||||||||||||||||||||||||||||

JANUARY 20, 1966

We achieved our widest margin over the Dow in the history of BPL with an overall gain of 47.2% compared to an overall gain (including dividends which would have been received through ownership of the Dow) of 14.2% for the Dow. Naturally, no writer likes to be publicly humiliated by such a mistake. It is unlikely to be repeated.

||||||||||||||||||||||||||||||||||||||||||||||||||||||||||||||||||||||||||||||||||||||||||||||||||||||||||||||||||||||||||||||||||||||||||||||||

JANUARY 20, 1966

After last year the question naturally arises, "What do we do for an encore?" A disadvantage of this business is that it does not possess momentum to any significant degree. If General Motors accounts for 54% of domestic new car registrations in 1965, it is a pretty safe bet that they are going to come fairly close to that figure in 1966 due to owner loyalties, dealer capabilities, productive capacity, consumer image, etc. Not so for BPL. We start from scratch each year with everything valued at market when the gun goes off. Partners in 1966, new or old, benefit to only a very limited extent from the efforts of 1964 and 1965. The success of past methods and ideas does not transfer forward to future ones.

I continue to hope, on a longer-range basis, for the sort of achievement outlined in the "Our Goal" section of last year's letter (copies still available). However, those who believe 1965 results can be achieved with any frequency are probably attending weekly meetings of the Halley's Comet Observers Club. We are going to have loss years and are going to have years inferior to the Dow—no doubt about it. But I continue to believe we can achieve average performance superior to the Dow in the future. If my expectation regarding this should change, you will hear immediately.

||||||||||||||||||||||||||||||||||||||||||||||||||||||||||||||||||||||||||||||||||||||||||||||||||||||||||||||||||||||||||||||||||||||||||||||||

JANUARY 20, 1966

Overall, we had more than our share of good breaks in 1965. We did not have a great quantity of ideas, but the quality . . . was very good and circumstances developed which accelerated the timetable in several. I do not have a great flood of good ideas as I go into 1966, although again I believe I have at least several potentially good ideas of substantial size. Much depends on whether market conditions are favorable for obtaining a larger position.

All in all, however, you should recognize that more came out of the pipeline in 1965 than went in.

||||||||||||||||||||||||||||||||||||||||||||||||||||||||||||||||||||||||||||||||||||||||||||||||||||||||||||||||||||||||||||||||||||||||||||||||||||||

JANUARY 25, 1967

The First Decade

The Partnership had its tenth anniversary during 1966. The celebration was appropriate—an all-time record (both past and future) was established for our performance margin relative to the Dow. Our advantage was 36 points which resulted from a plus 20.4% for the Partnership and a minus 15.6% for the Dow.

This pleasant but non-repeatable experience was partially due to a lackluster performance by the Dow. Virtually all investment managers outperformed it during the year. The Dow is weighted by the dollar price of the thirty stocks involved. Several of the highest priced components, which thereby carry disproportionate weight (Dupont, General Motors), were particularly poor performers in 1966. This, coupled with the general aversion to conventional blue chips, caused the Dow to suffer relative to general investment experience, particularly during the last quarter.

||||||||||||||||||||||||||||||||||||||||||||||||||||||||||||||||||||||||||||||||||||||||||||||||||||||||||||||||||||||||||||||||||||||||||||||||||||||

JANUARY 25, 1967

Trends in Our Business

A keen mind working diligently at interpreting the figures on page one could come to a lot of wrong conclusions.

The results of the first ten years have absolutely no chance of being duplicated or even remotely approximated during the next decade. They may well be achieved by some hungry twenty-five year old working with $105,100 initial partnership capital and operating during a ten year business and market environment which is frequently conducive to successful implementation of his investment philosophy.

They will not be achieved by a better fed thirty-six year old working with our $54,065,345 current partnership capital who presently finds perhaps one-fifth to one-tenth as many really good ideas as previously to implement his investment philosophy.

Buffett Associates, Ltd. (predecessor to Buffett Partnership, Ltd.) was founded on the west banks of the Missouri, May 5, 1956, by a hardy little band consisting of four family members, three close friends and $105,100. (I tried to find some brilliant flash of insight regarding our future or present conditions from my first page and a half annual letter of January, 1957 to insert as a quote here. However, someone evidently doctored my file copy so as to remove the perceptive remarks I must have made.)

At that time, and for some years subsequently, there were substantial numbers of securities selling at well below the "value to a private owner" criterion we utilized for selection of general market investments. We also experienced a flow of "workout" opportunities where the percentages were very much to our liking. The problem was always which, not what. Accordingly, we were able to own fifteen to twenty-five issues and be enthusiastic about the probabilities inherent in all holdings.

In the last few years this situation has changed dramatically. We now find very few securities that are understandable to me, available in decent size, and which offer the expectation of investment performance meeting our yardstick of ten percentage points per annum superior to the Dow. In the last three years we have come up with only two or three new ideas a year that have had such an expectancy of superior performance.

Fortunately, in some cases, we have made the most of them. However, in earlier years, a lesser effort produced literally dozens of comparable opportunities. It is difficult to be objective about the causes for such diminution of one's own productivity. Three factors that seem apparent are: (1) a somewhat changed market environment; (2) our increased size; and (3) substantially more competition.

It is obvious that a business based upon only a trickle of fine ideas has poorer prospects than one based upon a steady flow of such ideas. To date the trickle has provided as much financial nourishment as the flow. This is true because there is only so much one can digest (million dollar ideas are of no great benefit to thousand dollar bank accounts—this was impressed on me in my early days) and because a limited number of ideas causes one to utilize those available more intensively. The latter factor has definitely been operative with us in recent years. However, a trickle has considerably more chance of drying up completely than a flow.

These conditions will not cause me to attempt investment decisions outside my sphere of understanding (I don't go for the "If you can't lick 'em, join 'em" philosophy—my own leaning is toward "If you can't join 'em, lick 'em"). We will not go into businesses where technology which is way over my head is crucial to the investment decision. I know about as much about semi-conductors or integrated circuits as I do of the mating habits of the chrzaszcz. (That's a Polish May bug, students—if you have trouble pronouncing it, rhyme it with thrzaszcz.)

Furthermore, we will not follow the frequently prevalent approach of investing in securities where an attempt to anticipate market action overrides business valuations. Such so-called "fashion" investing has frequently produced very substantial and quick profits in recent years (and currently as I write this in January). It represents an investment technique whose soundness I can neither affirm nor deny. It does not completely satisfy my intellect (or perhaps my prejudices), and most definitely does not fit my temperament. I will not invest my own money based upon such an approach hence, I will most certainly not do so with your money.

Finally, we will not seek out activity in investment operations, even if offering splendid profit expectations, where major human problems appear to have a substantial chance of developing.

What I do promise you, as partners, is that I will work hard to maintain the trickle of ideas and try to get the most out of it that is possible—but if it should dry up completely, you will be informed honestly and promptly so that we may all take alternative action.

|||||||||||||||||||||||||||||||||||||||||||||||||||||||||||||||||||||||||||||||||||||||||||||||||||||||||||||||||||||||||||||||||||||

JANUARY 25, 1967

We all continue to maintain more than an academic interest in the Partnership. The employees and I, our spouses and children, have a total of over $10 million invested at January 1, 1967. In the case of my family, our Buffett Partnership, Ltd. investment represents well over 90% of our net worth.

|||||||||||||||||||||||||||||||||||||||||||||||||||||||||||||||||||||||||||||||||||||||||||||||||||||||||||||||||||||||||||||||||||||

JULY 12, 1967

First Half Performance

Again, this is being written in late June prior to the family's trip to California. To maintain the usual chronological symmetry (I try to sublimate my aesthetic urges when it comes to creating symmetry in the profit and loss statement), I will leave a few blanks and trust that the conclusions look appropriate when the figures are entered.

We began 1967 on a traumatic note with January turning out to be one of the worst months we have experienced with a plus 3.3% for BPL versus a plus 8.5% for the Dow. Despite this sour start, we finished the half about plus 21% for an edge of 9.6

percentage points over the Dow. Again, as throughout 1966, the Dow was a relatively easy competitor (it won't be every year, prevailing thinking to the contrary notwithstanding) and a large majority of investment managers outdid this yardstick.

<hr>

JULY 12, 1967

There will be a special letter (to focus your attention upon it) in October. The subject matter will not relate to change in the Partnership Agreement, but will involve some evolutionary changes in several "Ground Rules" which I want you to have ample time to contemplate before making your plans for 1968. Whereas the Partnership Agreement represents the legal understanding among us, the "Ground Rules" represent the personal understanding and in some ways is the more important document. I consider it essential that any changes be clearly set forth and explained prior to their effect on partnership activity or performance—hence, the October letter.

<hr>

OCTOBER 9, 1967

To My Partners:

Over the past eleven years, I have consistently set forth as the BPL investment goal an average advantage in our performance of ten percentage points per annum in comparison with the Dow Jones Industrial Average. Under the environment that existed during that period, I have considered such an objective difficult but obtainable.

The following conditions now make a change in yardsticks appropriate:

1. The market environment has changed progressively over the past decade, resulting in a sharp diminution in

the number of obvious quantitatively based investment
bargains available;

2. Mushrooming interest in investment performance
(which has its ironical aspects since I was among a lonely
few preaching the importance of this some years ago)
has created a hyper-reactive pattern of market behavior
against which my analytical techniques have limited value;

3. The enlargement of our capital base to about $65
million when applied against a diminishing trickle of good
investment ideas has continued to present the problems
mentioned in the January, 1967 letter; and

4. My own personal interests dictate a less compulsive
approach to superior investment results than when I was
younger and leaner.

Let's look at each of these factors in more detail.

The evaluation of securities and businesses for investment
purposes has always involved a mixture of qualitative and
quantitative factors. At the one extreme, the analyst exclusively
oriented to qualitative factors would say, "Buy the right company (with the right prospects, inherent industry conditions,
management, etc.) and the price will take care of itself." On
the other hand, the quantitative spokesman would say, "Buy at
the right price and the company (and stock) will take care of
itself." As is so often the pleasant result in the securities world,
money can be made with either approach. And, of course, any
analyst combines the two to some extent—his classification in
either school would depend on the relative weight he assigns
to the various factors and not to his consideration of one group
of factors to the exclusion of the other group.

Interestingly enough, although I consider myself to be primarily in the quantitative school (and as I write this no one has
come back from recess—I may be the only one left in the class),
the really sensational ideas I have had over the years have been
heavily weighted toward the qualitative side where I have had

a "high-probability insight." This is what causes the cash register to really sing. However, it is an infrequent occurrence, as insights usually are, and, of course, no insight is required on the quantitative side—the figures should hit you over the head with a baseball bat. So the really big money tends to be made by investors who are right on qualitative decisions but, at least in my opinion, the more sure money tends to be made on the obvious quantitative decisions.

Such statistical bargains have tended to disappear over the years. This may be due to the constant combing and recombing of investments that has occurred during the past twenty years, without an economic convulsion such as that of the '30s to create a negative bias toward equities and spawn hundreds of new bargain securities. It may be due to the new growing social acceptance, and therefore usage (or maybe it's vice versa—I'll let the behaviorists figure it out) of takeover bids which have a natural tendency to focus on bargain issues. It may be due to the exploding ranks of security analysts bringing forth an intensified scrutiny of issues far beyond what existed some years ago. Whatever the cause, the result has been the virtual disappearance of the bargain issue as determined quantitatively—and thereby of our bread and butter. There still may be a few from time to time.

There will also be the occasional security where I am really competent to make an important qualitative judgment. This will offer our best chance for large profits. Such instances will, however, be rare. Much of our good performance during the past three years has been due to a single idea of this sort.

The next point of difficulty is the intensified interest in investment performance. For years I have preached the importance of measurement. Consistently I have told partners that unless our performance was better than average, the money should go elsewhere. In recent years this idea has gained momentum throughout the investment (or more importantly, the investing) community. In the last year or two it has started to look a bit like a tidal wave. I think we are witnessing the distortion of a sound idea.

I have always cautioned partners that I considered three years a minimum in determining whether we were "performing." Naturally, as the investment public has taken the bit in its teeth, the time span of expectations has been consistently reduced to the point where investment performance by large aggregates of money is being measured yearly, quarterly, monthly, and perhaps sometimes even more frequently (leading to what is known as "instant research"). The payoff for superior short term performance has become enormous, not only in compensation for results actually achieved, but in the attraction of new money for the next round. Thus a self-generating type of activity has set in which leads to larger and larger amounts of money participating on a shorter and shorter time span. A disturbing corollary is that the vehicle for participation (the particular companies or stocks) becomes progressively less important—at times virtually incidental—as the activity accelerates.

In my opinion what is resulting is speculation on an increasing scale. This is hardly a new phenomenon; however, a dimension has been added by the growing ranks of professional (in many cases formerly quite docile) investors who feel they must "get aboard." The game is dignified, of course, by appropriate ceremonies, personages and lexicon. To date it has been highly profitable. It may also be that this is going to be the standard nature of the market in the future. Nevertheless, it is an activity at which I am sure I would not do particularly well. As I said on page five of my last annual letter,

> *Furthermore, we will not follow the frequently prevalent approach of investing in securities where an attempt to anticipate market action overrides business valuations. Such so-called "fashion" investing has frequently produced very substantial and quick profits in recent years*

(and currently as I write this in January). It represents an investment technique whose soundness I can neither affirm nor deny. It does not completely satisfy my intellect (or perhaps my prejudices), and most definitely does not fit my temperament. I will not invest my own money based upon such an approach—hence, I will most certainly not do so with your money.

Any form of hyper-activity with large amounts of money in securities markets can create problems for all participants. I make no attempt to guess the action of the stock market and haven't the foggiest notion as to whether the Dow will be at 600, 900 or 1200 a year from now. Even if there are serious consequences resulting from present and future speculative activity, experience suggests estimates of timing are meaningless. However, I do believe certain conditions that now exist are likely to make activity in markets more difficult for us for the intermediate future.

The above may simply be "old-fogeyism" (after all, I am 37). When the game is no longer being played your way, it is only human to say the new approach is all wrong, bound to lead to trouble, etc. I have been scornful of such behavior by others in the past. I have also seen the penalties incurred by those who evaluate conditions as they were—not as they are. Essentially I am out of step with present conditions. On one point, however, I am clear. I will not abandon a previous approach whose logic I understand (although I find it difficult to apply) even though it may mean foregoing large and apparently easy profits to embrace an approach which I don't fully understand, have not practiced successfully and which, possibly, could lead to substantial permanent loss of capital.

The third point of difficulty involves our much greater base of capital. For years my investment ideas were anywhere from 110% to 1,000% of our capital. It was difficult for me to conceive that a different condition could ever exist. I promised to tell partners when it did and in my January, 1967 letter had to make good on that promise. Largely because of the two conditions previously mentioned, our greater capital is now something of a drag on performance. I believe it is the least significant factor of the four mentioned, and that if we were operating with one-tenth of our present capital our performance would be little better. However, increased funds are presently a moderately negative factor.

The final, and most important, consideration concerns personal motivation. When I started the partnership I set the motor that regulated the treadmill at "ten points better than the DOW." I was younger, poorer and probably more competitive. Even without the three previously discussed external factors making for poorer performance, I would still feel that changed personal conditions make it advisable to reduce the speed of the treadmill. I have observed many cases of habit patterns in all activities of life, particularly business, continuing (and becoming accentuated as years pass) long after they ceased making sense. Bertrand Russell has related the story of two Lithuanian girls who lived at his manor subsequent to World War I. Regularly each evening after the house was dark, they would sneak out and steal vegetables from the neighbors for hoarding in their rooms; this despite the fact that food was bountiful at the Russell table. Lord Russell explained to the girls that while such behavior may have made a great deal of sense in Lithuania during the war, it was somewhat out of place in the English countryside. He received assenting nods and continued stealing. He finally contented himself with the observation that their behavior, strange as it might seem to the neighbors, was really not so different from that of the elder Rockefeller.

Elementary self-analysis tells me that I will not be capable of less than all-out effort to achieve a publicly proclaimed goal to people who have entrusted their capital to me. All-out effort makes progressively less sense. I would like to have an economic goal which allows for considerable non-economic

activity. This may mean activity outside the field of investments or it simply may mean pursuing lines within the investment field that do not promise the greatest economic reward.
An example of the latter might be the continued investment in
a satisfactory (but far from spectacular) controlled business
where I liked the people and the nature of the business even
though alternative investments offered an expectable higher
rate of return. More money would be made buying businesses
at attractive prices, then reselling them. However, it may be
more enjoyable (particularly when the personal value of incremental capital is less) to continue to own them and hopefully
improve their performance, usually in a minor way, through
some decisions involving financial strategy.

Thus, I am likely to limit myself to things which are reasonably easy, safe, profitable and pleasant. This will not make our
operation more conservative than in the past since I believe,
undoubtedly with some bias, that we have always operated
with considerable conservatism. The long-term downside risk
will not be less; the upside potential will merely be less.

Specifically, our longer term goal will be to achieve the lesser
of 9% per annum or a five percentage point advantage over the
Dow. Thus, if the Dow averages –2% over the next five years, I
would hope to average +3% but if the Dow averages +12%, I will
hope to achieve an average of only +9%. These may be limited
objectives, but I consider it no more likely that we will achieve
even these more modest results under present conditions than
I formerly did that we would achieve our previous goal of a
ten percentage point average annual edge over the Dow. Furthermore, I hope limited objectives will make for more limited
effort (I'm quite sure the converse is true).

I will incorporate this new goal into the Ground Rules to
be mailed you about November 1, along with the 1968 Commitment Letter. I wanted to get this letter off to you prior to
that mailing so you would have ample time to consider your
personal situation, and if necessary get in touch with me to

clear up some of the enclosed, before making a decision on 1968. As always, I intend to continue to leave virtually all of my capital (excluding Data Documents stock), along with that of my family, in BPL. What I consider satisfactory and achievable may well be different from what you consider so. Partners with attractive alternative investment opportunities may logically decide that their funds can be better employed elsewhere, and you can be sure I will be wholly in sympathy with such a decision.

I have always found behavior most distasteful which publicly announces one set of goals and motivations when actually an entirely different set of factors prevails. Therefore, I have always tried to be l00% candid with you about my goals and personal feelings so you aren't making important decisions pursuant to phony proclamations (I've run into a few of these in our investment experience). Obviously all the conditions enumerated in this letter haven't appeared overnight. I have been thinking about some of the points involved for a long period of time.

You can understand, I am sure, that I wanted to pick a time when past goals had been achieved to set forth a reduction in future goals. I would not want to reduce the speed of the treadmill unless I had fulfilled my objectives to this point.

Please let me know if I can be of any help in deciphering any portion of this letter.

Cordially,

Warren E. Buffett

By most standards, we had a good year in 1967. Our overall performance was plus 35.9% compared to plus 19.0% for the Dow, thus surpassing our previous objective of performance ten points superior to the Dow. Our overall gain was $19,384,250 which, even under accelerating inflation, will buy a lot of Pepsi.

And, due to the sale of some longstanding large positions in marketable securities, we had realized taxable income of $27,376,667 which has nothing to do with 1967 performance but should give all of you a feeling of vigorous participation in The Great Society on April 15th.

The minor thrills described above are tempered by any close observation of what really took place in the stock market during 1967. Probably a greater percentage of participants in the securities markets did substantially better than the Dow last year than in virtually any year in history. In 1967, for many, it rained gold and it paid to be out playing the bass tuba. I don't have a final tabulation at this time but my guess is that at least 95% of investment companies following a common stock program achieved better results than the Dow—in many cases by very substantial amounts. It was a year when profits achieved were in inverse proportion to age—and I am in the geriatric ward, philosophically.

Last year I said:

> *A few mutual funds and some private investment operations have compiled records vastly superior to the Dow and, in some cases, substantially superior to Buffett Partnership, Ltd. Their investment techniques are usually very dissimilar to ours and not within my capabilities.*

In 1967 this condition intensified. Many investment organizations performed substantially better than BPL, with gains ranging to over 100%. Because of these spectacular results, money, talent and energy are converging in a maximum effort for the achievement of large and quick stock market profits. It looks to me like greatly intensified speculation with concomitant risks—but many of the advocates insist otherwise.

My mentor, Ben Graham, used to say, "Speculation is neither illegal, immoral nor fattening (financially)." During the past year, it was possible to become fiscally flabby through a steady diet of speculative bonbons. We continue to eat oatmeal but if indigestion should set in generally, it is unrealistic to expect that we won't have some discomfort.

||||||||||||||||||||||||||||||||||||||||||||||||||||||||||||||||||||||||||||||||||||||||||||||||||||||||||||||||||||||||||||||||||||||||

JANUARY 24, 1968

Some of those who withdrew (and many who didn't) asked me, "What do you really mean?" after receiving the October 9th letter. This sort of a question is a little bruising to any author, but I assured them I meant exactly what I had said. I was also asked whether this was an initial stage in the phasing out of the partnership. The answer to this is, "Definitely, no." As long as partners want to put up their capital alongside of mine and the business is operationally pleasant (and it couldn't be better), I intend to continue to do business with those who have backed me since tennis shoes.

||||||||||||||||||||||||||||||||||||||||||||||||||||||||||||||||||||||||||||||||||||||||||||||||||||||||||||||||||||||||||||||||||||||||

JULY 11, 1968

The Present Environment

I make no effort to predict the course of general business or the stock market. Period. However, currently there are practices snowballing in the security markets and business world which, while devoid of short term predictive value, bother me as to possible long term consequences.

I know that some of you are not particularly interested (and shouldn't be) in what is taking place on the financial stage. For those who are, I am enclosing a reprint of an unusually clear and simple article which lays bare just what is occurring on a mushrooming scale. Spectacular amounts of money are being made by those participating (whether as originators, top employees, professional advisors, investment bankers, stock speculators, etc. . . .) in the chain-letter type stock-promotion vogue. The game is being played by the gullible, the self-hypnotized, and the cynical. To create the proper illusions, it frequently requires accounting distortions (one particularly progressive entrepreneur told me he believed in "bold, imaginative accounting"), tricks of capitalization and camouflage of the true nature of the operating businesses involved. The end product is popular, respectable and immensely profitable (I'll let the philosophers figure in which order those adjectives should be placed).

Quite candidly, our own performance has been substantially improved on an indirect basis because of the fallout from such activities. To create an ever widening circle of chain letters requires increasing amounts of corporate raw material and this has caused many intrinsically cheap (and not so cheap) stocks to come to life. When we have been the owners of such stocks, we have reaped market rewards much more promptly than might otherwise have been the case. The appetite for such companies, however, tends to substantially diminish the number of fundamentally attractive investments which remain.

I believe the odds are good that, when the stock market and business history of this period is being written, the phenomenon described in Mr. May's article will be regarded as of major importance, and perhaps characterized as a mania. You should realize, however, that his "The Emperor Has No Clothes" approach is at odds (or dismissed with a "SO What?" or an "Enjoy, Enjoy") with the views of most investment banking houses and currently successful investment managers. We live in an investment world, populated not by those who must be logically persuaded to believe, but by the hopeful, credulous and greedy, grasping for an excuse to believe.

Finally, for a magnificent account of the current financial scene, you should hurry out and get a copy of "The Money Game" by Adam Smith. It is loaded with insights and supreme wit. (Note: Despite my current "Support Your Local Postmaster" drive, I am not enclosing the book with this letter—it retails for $6.95.)

||||||||||||||||||||||||||||||||||||||||||||||||||||||||||||||||||||||||||||||||||||||||||||||||||||||||||||||||

JULY 11, 1968

Our Performance in 1968

Everyone makes mistakes.

At the beginning of 1968, I felt prospects for BPL performance looked poorer than at any time in our history. However, due in considerable measure to one simple but sound idea whose time had come (investment ideas, like women are often more exciting than punctual), we recorded an overall gain of $40,032,691.

Naturally, you all possess sufficient intellectual purity to dismiss the dollar result and demand an accounting of performance relative to the Dow-Jones Industrial Average. We established a new mark at plus 58.8% versus an overall plus 7.7% for the Dow, including dividends which would have been received through ownership of the Average throughout the year. This result should be treated as a freak like picking up thirteen spades in a bridge game. You bid the slam, make it look modest, pocket the money and then get back to work on the part scores. We will also have our share of hands when we go set.

||||||||||||||||||||||||||||||||||||||||||||||||||||||||||||||||||||||||||||||||||||||||||||||||||||||||||||||||

JULY 11, 1968

Some of the so-called "go-go" funds have recently been re-christened "no-go" funds. For example, Gerald Tsai's Manhattan Fund, perhaps the world's best-known aggressive investment vehicle, came in at minus 6.9% for 1968. Many smaller investment entities continued to substantially outperform the general market in 1968, but in nothing like the quantities of 1966 and 1967.

||||||||||||||||||||||||||||||||||||||||||||||||||||||||||||||||||||||||||||||||||||||||||||||||||||||||||||||||

JULY 11, 1968

I can't emphasize too strongly that the quality and quantity of ideas is presently at an all time low—the product of the factors mentioned in my October 9th, 1967 letter, which have largely been intensified since then.

Sometimes I feel we should have a plaque in our office like the one at the headquarters of Texas Instruments in Dallas which reads: "We don't believe in miracles, we rely on them." It is possible for an old, overweight ball player, whose legs and batting eye are gone, to tag a fast ball on the nose for a pinch-hit home run, but you don't change your line-up because of it.

We have a number of important negatives operating on our future and, while they shouldn't add up to futility, they certainly don't add up to more than an average of quite moderate profitability.

Compounded Wisdom

We've all heard the adage that history doesn't repeat but rather it rhymes. The stock market is the same. It goes through cycles. Great investors understand the market's history so they can see the commonality of the cycles and learn what to avoid. It's much cheaper to learn from other people's mistakes than to make them on your own. All serious investors should have an understanding of the ebbs and flows of the last hundred years or so of stock market cycles. Mr. Burke was clearly onto something when he said that those who don't know their history are destined to repeat it.

In January 1967, Buffett's year-end letter looks back on the early years, when there were substantial numbers of great ideas to work with both in Generals and Workout categories and the problem was always "which, not what" to invest in. Ten years later, the landscape had changed. What started out as a strong flow of good ideas had been reduced to a trickle, and "a trickle has considerably more chance of drying up completely than a flow." He makes sure partners understand that he has no intention of altering his investing approach; it is a behavior we would do well to emulate.

Go-Go was entering its peak state and Buffett was aware that many investment organizations did substantially better than BPL in 1967—some were up more than 100%. The market was getting really frothy and Buffett saw it. He noted that, "because of these spectacular results, money, talent and energy are converging in a maximum effort for the achievement of large and quick stock market profits. It looks to me like greatly intensified speculation with concomitant risks—but many of the advocates insist otherwise."

Buffett was clearly feeling out of step with the market. Jerry Tsai and the performance funds of his generation had taken the Dow to a level where Buffett simply could not find enough good ideas to invest in. What he saw was increasingly dangerous speculation on an increasing scale. The pressure for all money managers to "get aboard" must have been enormous. While Buffett had no idea how long it would last, or if it was simply the beginning of a new paradigm in the nature of the market, he knew that he wasn't ever going to jump in the pool just because everyone else was swimming.

Instead, he chose to close the Partnership, and we'll look at how and why he did so next.

CHAPTER 14

PARTING WISDOM

IIIIIIIIIIIIIIIIIIIIIIIIIIIIIIIIIIIIIIIIIIIIIIIIIIIIIIIIIIIIIIIIIIIIIIIIIIIIIIIII

"We live in an investment world, populated not by those who must be logically persuaded to believe, but by the hopeful, credulous and greedy, grasping for an excuse to believe."[1]

—JULY 8, 1968

Buffett's decision to hang it up went beyond the level of the market and the number of ideas he had at the time. The Partnership had served its purpose. Through it, he had built up his capital by earning, then reinvesting his incentive fees—by May 1969 his net worth had climbed to a staggering $26 million.[2] Munger has said, "If you are highly conscientious and you hate to disappoint, you will feel the pressure to live up to your incentive fee."[3] The Partnership was right for Buffett for a time, but now he was ready to move on to a better, more equitable structure. He later recalled the intense internal pressure he was feeling at the time.[4] He never took a performance fee again. At Berkshire, he takes a modest salary and is otherwise directly in alignment with his fellow shareholders.

Buffett emphasized in the fall of 1969, saying,

The October 9th, 1967 letter stated that personal consider-
ations were the most important factor among those causing
me to modify our objectives. I expressed a desire to be relieved
of the (self-imposed) necessity of focusing 100% on BPL. I
have flunked this test completely during the last eighteen
months. . . . I know I don't want to be totally occupied with
out-pacing an investment rabbit all my life. The only way to
slow down is to stop.

The way Buffett actually went about closing BPL is unique in several different ways. For starters, despite telling partners that he didn't like the prospects for stocks at 1969's prices, he recognized many would still stay in equities regardless. He hand selected Bill Ruane, who, at his request and ultimately with $20 million in capital from BPL partners, started the Sequoia Fund in 1970.[5] It was a great choice—Ruane's track record was strong over the decade (and long after). He became a legendary investor in his own right.

Recommending another manager doesn't seem like very logical behavior on the surface. Buffett acknowledged the act was "un-Buffett-like," but given many partners had nearly 100% of their net worth on the line, he knew it was the right thing to do no matter how unorthodox. Seeing how Buffett evaluated Ruane offers valuable insight into the important factors at play in choosing any professional manager.

Second, Buffett considered the prospects for the market to be quite poor at the time and described something he saw as unprecedented in his own investing lifetime. The 10-year outlook for returns in stocks looked to be on par with the yields on less risky, tax-free municipal bonds. This was a real anomaly; in most market environments, investors have to give up a significant amount of expected return from stocks in exchange for the stability and predictability they'd get from bonds. Not only did Buffett describe *how* he arrived at his conclusion about bonds, which is brilliant, but he also delivered the contents of a one-hundred-page textbook on tax-free municipal bonds in one simple, precise, and highly digestible ten-page memo. Anyone wishing to understand how bonds work, even if you're not a pro (and even if you are), will benefit from a careful study of this essay, which can be found in full in the appendix.

Then he offered to serve as a broker and advisor to partners who wished to follow his recommendations and buy munis; he selected and purchased a unique package of bonds appropriate for each partner's personal needs and circumstance and had them delivered directly to the partners' bank accounts. While all this was certainly impressive client service, it also highlights an important insight on the interchangeability of investment products—he's reminding partners one last time that the goal is the best after-tax rate of return with the minimum possible amount of risk. It doesn't matter whether this goal is achieved through stocks, bonds, Laundromats, or whatever. There is no universal preference for equities. You buy what makes sense, period.

Lastly, the way he handled the distribution of the Partnership's Controls represented the type of fair-minded and communicative style everyone should look for in an investment firm or public company. Controls such as Berkshire Hathaway, Diversified Retailing Corporation (DRC), and Blue Chip Stamps were all distributed to partners pro rata. Because Controls were on the books of BPL at a valuation that Buffett alone had determined to be fair, he wanted partners to be able to choose if they wanted their pro rata share of the businesses or their carrying value in cash. Just like at a birthday party where one person cuts the cake and then the others get to choose their pieces, Buffett was leaving it up to partners to freely decide if the Control businesses or the cash was the "bigger piece." When Munger's and another law firm looked at it and realized this option was not going to be possible, he spoke incredibly openly about the prospects for each business, something he has always been reticent to do.

Let's take a closer look at all four moves in greater detail:

The Introduction of Bill Ruane

When Ben Graham was asked to provide his opinion of Buffett as part of a reference check for a potential posting to GEICO's board in 1971, Graham said, "I'm 100% for that idea. I have known Buffett intimately for many years, and I must say I have never met anyone else with his combination of high character and brilliant business qualities."[6]

It appears Buffett was once again channeling his inner Graham when he introduced Ruane. He also listed integrity before business acumen as the primary attribute. When selecting a manager, that's what has to be first and foremost. The description on Ruane began,

> . . . [W]e met in Ben Graham's class at Columbia University in 1951 and I have had considerable opportunity to observe his qualities of character, temperament and intellect since that time. If Susie and I were to die while our children are minors, he is one of three trustees who have carte blanche on investment matters. . . . There is no way to eliminate the possibility of error when judging humans particularly in regard to future behavior in an unknown environment. However, decisions have to be made—whether actively or passively—and I consider Bill to be an exceptionally high probability decision on character and a high probability one on investment performance.

In investments, as with most things with Buffett, integrity is what counts first. This was as true then as it remains today. You have to love how he describes the types of managers he seeks out for Berkshire: "We look for three things: intelligence, energy and integrity. If they don't have the latter, then you should hope they don't have the first two either. If someone doesn't have integrity, then you want them to be dumb and lazy."[7]

Buffett was fully aware that recommending Ruane was risky and unorthodox: "In recommending Bill, I am engaging in the sort of activity I have tried to avoid in BPL portfolio activities—a decision where there is nothing to gain (personally) and considerable to lose." If Ruane's performance was good, Buffett was unlikely to get much credit, but if Ruane did poorly, he was likely to get blamed. It was a "heads you win, tails I lose" situation. But, from a moral perspective, he felt he had little choice. Doing nothing didn't seem like a viable option. "I feel it would be totally unfair for me to assume a passive position and deliver you to the most persuasive salesman who happened to contact you early in 1970."

Buffett was careful to be highly specific about the drawbacks and potential risks in going with Ruane. First off was the question of size—an exceptional manager was apt to grow assets both through performance and capital additions that would inevitably drag down performance. Ruane closed the fund to new investors in 1982 to combat this very problem. In addition to the risk from getting too big, Ruane was operating an investment advisory firm as well as the fund and would not be exclusively focused on Sequoia; his potential distraction was a risk that Buffett was careful to point out.

The recommendation worked out but it took several years to do so. (Ruane's performance figures can be found in Appendix C.) He underperformed the S&P in each of the first four years and it wasn't until his seventh year that he finally caught up and began outperforming on a cumulative basis. It's one thing to look back on this performance within a larger historical context; it's entirely something else to live through it, but those who held on were well rewarded. For the decade, Ruane trounced the market, delivering twice the average return per annum.

If you are going to pick someone else to manage your funds, you must have a firm belief in their integrity and their ability as well as a solid understanding of their process. Ruane was a Graham disciple, a true value investor, and highly likely to underperform in the late stages of a bull market top. That way, you can make exceptions to your rules, such as a 3–5 year relative performance test, when you identify the speculative nature of the market.

Here's an interesting statistic from Joel Greenblatt, who looked at the top 25% of managers who had outperformed the market over the decade: 97% spent at least 3 years in the bottom half of performance and 47% spent at least 3 years in the bottom 10%.[8] Buffett's 3–5 year test is simply a rule of thumb. If your capital is underperforming in the hands of someone else, you think hard about the choices you've made.

Muni Bonds, Anyone?

Ruane was asked to be there for BPL partners wanting to stay in the equity market, but Buffett wanted them to consider the market from a different perspective: "For the first time in my investment lifetime, I now believe there is little choice for the average investor between professionally managed money in stocks and passive investment in bonds. If correct, this view has important implications." When it comes to general equity investments in an overextended market, Munger's rule is worth remembering: If something's not worth doing, it's certainly not worth doing well.

Buffett described the situation as he saw it for the average 1969 investor in the 40% tax bracket. Tax-free municipal bonds were yielding 6.5–7% at the time. Stocks, he thought, were unlikely to rise more than 6% per annum and pay 3% in dividends throughout. To make the tax-free bonds comparable, the 9% maximum pretax gains on stocks needed to be reduced—the 6% from price appreciation became 4.75% and the 3% dividend went to 1.75%, for a combined after-tax return of about 6.5%, the same as what was on offer from the bonds.

If Buffett was right about stocks, his muni bonds offered the same yield. The 6.5% from stocks was what he expected the index to deliver; Buffett figured 90% of the funds would underperform. He concluded that, under the "historically unusual conditions, passive investment in tax-free bonds is likely to be fully the equivalent of expectations from professionally managed money in stocks, and only modestly inferior to extremely well-managed equity money."

Buffett wrote a short treatise on the muni bond market and recommended partners read and reread it several times if they decided to enlist his help in buying these bonds. The choices they had were to buy the bonds, buy stocks, or stay in cash. Whatever they decided, he was trying to spare them the experience of a slick salesperson capable of fleecing them of the returns he had worked so hard to generate for them.

In recognition of the difficult question of asset allocation, Buffett wrapped up the October letter saying,

You will have to make your own decision as between bonds and stocks and, if the latter, who advises you on such stocks. In many cases, I think the decision should largely reflect your tangible and intangible (temperamental) needs for regularity of income and absence of large principal fluctuation, perhaps balanced against psychic needs for some excitement and the fun associated with contemplating and perhaps enjoying really juicy results. If you would like to talk over the problem with me, I will be very happy to help.

Many wise men and women have put plenty of thought and effort into asset allocation questions over the years. From Buffett we learn that there is no magic formula. You can't just take 100 minus your age and put that percentage in stocks or rely on some other trick or formula. While bonds are often less risky than stocks, it's not a universal truth. Just look at what's on offer in mid-2015—there is no yield in the bond market. Sometimes, bonds are less risky and sometimes they are not. The types of securities you choose are the means to an end; don't confuse the former with the latter. In any investment there are two key questions: What is the most likely return, and what's the risk?

Today, 10-year U.S. government bonds yield 2.4%, a level just marginally above expected inflation, meaning real yields are negligible. Stocks, typically seen as more risky, sport earnings yields of just under 6%. Despite convention, government bonds appear to be the riskier asset class today. As we've learned, just because something is conventional doesn't mean it's conservative or correct. You have to do your own thinking on it. To Buffett's eye at the beginning of 1970, the only thing that made stocks more attractive than munis was the potential excitement they offered.

Control Issues

In December 1969 he gave an account of the firm's two Controls, then focused on answering questions from partners in response. This represents one of the most detailed accounts he has given on the prospects for a single security, as close to an investment recommendation as we have ever seen him make.

> *My personal opinion is that the intrinsic value of DRC and B-H will grow substantially over the years. While no one knows the future, I would be disappointed if such growth wasn't at a rate of approximately 10% per annum. . . . I think both securities should be very decent long-term holdings and I am happy to have a substantial portion of my net worth invested in them. . . . Should I continue to hold the securities, as I fully expect to do, my degree of involvement in their activities may vary depending upon my other interests. The odds are that I will take an important position on matters of policy, but I want no moral obligation to be other than a passive shareholder. . . .*

Initially, Buffett's intention was to give partners the option to either (1) receive their pro rata share of the control companies or (2) elect to take the carrying value of the Controls in cash. This was immeasurably fair since Buffett had determined the valuation; he felt partners should be able to choose whatever they felt was the more valuable of the two options. Unfortunately, the lawyers wouldn't allow it. All partners would get their share of stock and if they wished to sell, would have to do so on their own.

One interesting question that came up was why he didn't register the shares so that the stocks would be freely marketable. The idea behind the question was that the shares would be more liquid—easier to sell if Buffett had registered them. The bottom line from Buffett on this issue was that partners who wished to sell would be better off without a registration. He felt that, given the market environment at the time, there was a real likelihood that "the market for these two stocks would be little short of chaotic." And he went on to say, "It is my belief that, by confining sales to private placements, those partners who wish to sell will realize more for their stock. . . . We have had several phone calls from persons indicating that they wish to make private sales—we anticipate there will be no difficulty in effectuating such sales at prices related to our yearend valuations." Had Buffett registered the stock, there is a substantial chance that those who wanted or otherwise needed to sell stock would have gotten a lower price than they otherwise did.

Buffett made sure that all players were on a level playing field when it came to deciding what they should do with their Controls. He insisted upon not talking to partners individually about the three companies; he wanted everyone to be on equal footing, for everyone to have access to the exact same information. He took questions in writing and then included the answers so all partners would benefit.

This is how he continues to handle communications at Berkshire Hathaway. To this day, while it's extremely common for large institutional investors to gain an edge over smaller investors through regular private meetings with public company management teams, Buffett refuses to do it. All investors receive the same opportunity once a year at the shareholder meeting in Omaha to ask their questions and have them answered in front of everyone. This idea was as unique then as it remains today; it conveys management's belief that selective disclosure, even if it's of an immaterial nature, is unethical.

Given his announced plans to accumulate more stock after the Partnership, it was in his best financial interest to say very little; the less he said the more likely it was that partners would choose to sell their stock. It's amazing to think (especially with hindsight) that anyone actually sold, although many did. Buffett's already substantial stakes in all three at least doubled a year after BPL closed and all were later fully consolidated into Berkshire at different times.

Lessons from the Partnership Letters: Closing Remarks

MAY 29, 1969

To My Partners:

About eighteen months ago I wrote to you regarding changed environmental and personal factors causing me to modify our future performance objectives.

The investing environment I discussed at that time (and on which I have commented in various other letters) has generally become more negative and frustrating as time has passed. Maybe I am merely suffering from a lack of mental flexibility. (One observer commenting on security analysts over forty stated: "They know too many things that are no longer true.")

However, it seems to me that: (1) opportunities for investment that are open to the analyst who stresses quantitative factors have virtually disappeared, after rather steadily drying up over the past twenty years; (2) our $100 million of assets further eliminates a large portion of this seemingly barren investment world, since commitments of less than about $3 million cannot have a real impact on our overall performance, and this virtually rules out companies with less than about $100 million of common stock at market value; and (3) a swelling interest in investment performance has created an increasingly short-term oriented and (in my opinion) more speculative market.

The October 9th, 1967 letter stated that personal considerations were the most important factor among those causing me to modify our objectives. I expressed a desire to be relieved of the (self-imposed) necessity of focusing 100% on BPL. I have flunked this test completely during the last eighteen months. The letter said: I hope limited objectives will make for more limited effort. It hasn't worked out that way. As long as I am "on stage," publishing a regular record and assuming responsibility for management of what amounts to virtually 100% of the net worth of many partners, I will never be able to put sustained effort into any non-BPL activity. If I am going to participate publicly, I can't help being competitive. I know I don't want to be totally occupied with out-pacing an investment rabbit all my life. The only way to slow down is to stop.

Therefore, before yearend, I intend to give all limited partners the required formal notice of my intention to retire. There are, of course, a number of tax and legal problems in connection with liquidating the Partnership, but overall, I am concerned with working out a plan that attains the following objectives:

1. The most important item is that I have an alternative regarding money management to suggest to the many partners who do not want to handle this themselves. Some partners of course, have alternatives of their own in which they have confidence and find quite acceptable. To the others, however, I will not hand over their money with a "good luck." I intend to suggest an alternative money manager to whom I will entrust funds of my relatives and others for whom I have lifetime financial responsibility. This manager has integrity and ability and will probably perform as well or better than I would in the future (although nowhere close to what he or I have achieved in the past). He will be available to any partner, so that no minimum size for accounts will cause any of you a problem. I intend, in the future, to keep in general touch with what he is doing, but only on an infrequent basis with any advice on my part largely limited to a negative type.

2. I want all partners to have the option of receiving cash and possibly readily marketable securities (there will probably be only one where this will apply) where I like both the prospects and price but which partners will be able to freely convert to cash if they wish.

3. However, I also want all partners to have the option of maintaining their proportional interests in our two controlled companies (Diversified Retailing Company Inc. and Berkshire Hathaway Inc.) and one other small "restricted" holding. Because these securities will be valued unilaterally by me at fair value, I feel it is essential that, if you wish, you can maintain your proportionate interest at such valuation.

However, these securities are not freely marketable (various SEC restrictions apply to "control" stock and non-registered stock) and they will probably be both non-transferable and non-income-producing for a considerable period of time. Therefore, I want you to be able to go either way in our liquidation—either stick with the restricted securities or take cash equivalent. I strongly like all of the people running our controlled businesses (joined now by the Illinois National Bank and Trust Company of Rockford, Illinois, a $100 million plus, extremely well-run bank, purchased by Berkshire Hathaway earlier this year), and want the relationship to be life long. I certainly have no desire to sell a good controlled business run by people I like and admire, merely to obtain a fancy price. However, specific conditions may cause the sale of one operating unit at some point.

I believe we will have a liquidation program which will accomplish the above objectives. Our activities in this regard should cause no change in your tax planning for 1969.

One final objective, I would like very much to achieve (but

which just isn't going to happen) is to go out with a bang. I hate to end with a poor year, but we are going to have one in 1969. My best guess is that at yearend, allowing for a substantial increase in value of controlled companies (against which all partners except me will have the option of taking cash), we will show a breakeven result for 1969 before any monthly payments to partners. This will be true even if the market should advance substantially between now and yearend, since we will not be in any important position which will expose us to much upside potential.

Our experience in workouts this year has been atrocious—during this period I have felt like the bird that inadvertently flew into the middle of a badminton game. We are not alone in such experience, but it came at a time when we were toward the upper limit of what has been our historical range of percentage commitment in this category.

Documenting one's boners is unpleasant business. I find "selective reporting" even more distasteful. Our poor experience this year is 100% my fault. It did not reflect bad luck, but rather an improper assessment of a very fast-developing governmental trend. Paradoxically, I have long believed the government should have been doing (in terms of the problem attacked—not necessarily the means utilized) what it finally did—in other words, on an overall basis, I believe the general goal of the activity which has cost us substantial money is socially desirable and have so preached for some time. Nevertheless, I didn't think it would happen. I never believe in mixing what I think should happen (socially) with what I think will happen in making decisions—in this case, we would be some millions better off if I had.

Quite frankly, in spite of any factors set forth on the earlier pages, I would continue to operate the Partnership in 1970, or even 1971, if I had some really first class ideas. Not because I want to, but simply because I would so much rather end with a good year than a poor one. However, I just don't see anything available that gives any reasonable hope of delivering such a good year and I have no desire to grope around, hoping to "get lucky" with other people's money. I am not attuned to this market environment and I don't want to spoil a decent record by trying to play a game I don't understand just so I can go out a hero.

Therefore, we will be liquidating holdings throughout the year, working toward a residual of the controlled companies, the one "investment letter" security, the one marketable security with favorable long-term prospects, and the miscellaneous "stubs," etc. of small total value which will take several years to clean up in the Workout category.

I have written this letter a little early in lieu of the mid-year letter. Once I made a decision, I wanted you to know. I also wanted to be available in Omaha for a period after you received this letter to clear up anything that may be confusing in it. In July, I expect to be in California.

Some of you are going to ask, "What do you plan to do?" I don't have an answer to that question. I do know that when I am 60, I should be attempting to achieve different personal goals than those which had priority at age 20. Therefore, unless I now divorce myself from the activity that has consumed virtually all of my time and energies during the first eighteen years of my adult life, I am unlikely to develop activities that will be appropriate to new circumstances in subsequent years.

We will have a letter out in the fall, probably October, elaborating on the liquidation procedure, the investment advisor suggestion, etc. . . .

Cordially,

Warren E. Buffett

||||||||||||||||||||||||||||||||||||||||||||||||||||||||||||||||||||||||||||||||||||||||||||||||||||||||||||||||||||||||||||||||||||||||||||||||

OCTOBER 9, 1969

Unless there is a further substantial decline in the market, I still expect about a breakeven performance before any monthly

payments for 1969. We were lucky—if we had not been in liquidation this year, our results would have been significantly
worse. Ideas that looked potentially interesting on a "continuing" basis have on balance performed poorly to date. We have
only two items of real size left—one we are selling as I write this
and the other is a holding of limited marketability represent-
ing about 7.5% of the outstanding stock of Blue Chip Stamps
which we may sell via a registered public offering around yearend, depending upon market conditions and other factors.

|||||||||||||||||||||||||||||||||||||||||||||||||||||||||||||||||||||||||||||||||||||||||||||||||||||||||||||||||||||||||||||||||||||||||||||||||||||||

OCTOBER 9, 1969

. . . Bill Ruane—we met in Ben Graham's class at Columbia
University in 1951 and I have had considerable opportunity to
observe his qualities of character, temperament and intellect
since that time. If Susie and I were to die while our children are
minors, he is one of three trustees who have carte blanche on
investment matters—the other two are not available for continuous investment management for all partners, large or small.

There is no way to eliminate the possibility of error when
judging humans particularly in regard to future behavior in an
unknown environment. However, decisions have to be made—
whether actively or passively—and I consider Bill to be an ex-
ceptionally high probability decision on character and a high
probability one on investment performance. I also consider it
likely that Bill will continue as a money manager for many years
to come.

Bill has recently formed a New York Stock Exchange firm,
Ruane, Cunniff & Stires, Inc., 85 Broad Street, New York, N.Y.
10004, telephone number (212) 344-6700. John Harding presently plans to establish an office for the firm in Omaha about
March 1st, 1970. Bill manages accounts individually on a fee
basis and also executes brokerage for the accounts—presently
with some portion of the brokerage commissions used to
offset a portion of the investment advisory fee. His method

of operation allows monthly withdrawals on a basis similar to BPL—as a percentage of capital and unrelated to realized or unrealized gain or loss. It is possible he may form some sort of pooled account but such determinations will be made between him and those of you who elect to go with him. I, of course, will not be involved with his operation. I am making my list of partners available to him and he will be writing you fairly soon regarding a trip he plans to make before yearend to Omaha, Los Angeles and Chicago, so that those of you who wish to meet him may do so. Any of you who are going to be in New York during the next few months can contact him directly.

Bill's overall record has been very good—averaging fairly close to BPL's, but with considerably greater variation. From 1956–1961 and from 1964–1968, a composite of his individual accounts averaged over 40% per annum. However, in 1962, undoubtedly somewhat as a product of the euphoric experience of the earlier years, he was down about 50%. As he re-oriented his thinking, 1963 was about breakeven.

While two years may sound like a short time when included in a table of performance, it may feel like a long time when your net worth is down 50%. I think you run this sort of short-term risk with virtually any money manager operating in stocks and it is a factor to consider in deciding the portion of your capital to commit to equities. To date in 1969, Bill is down about 15%, which I believe to be fairly typical of most money managers.

Bill, of course, has not been in control situations or workouts, which have usually tended to moderate the swings in BPL year-to-year performance. Even excluding these factors, I believe his performance would have been somewhat more volatile (but not necessarily poorer by any means) than mine—his style is different, and while his typical portfolio (under most conditions) would tend to have a mild overlap with mine, there would always be very significant differences.

Bill has achieved his results working with an average of $5 to $10 million. I consider the three most likely negative factors in his future to be: (1) the probability of managing significantly larger sums—this is a problem you are going to have rather quickly with any successful money manager, and it will tend to moderate performance; I believe Bill's firm is now managing $20–$30 million and, of course, they will continue to add accounts; (2) the possibility of Bill's becoming too involved in the detail of his operation rather than spending all of his time simply thinking about money management. The problems of being the principal factor in a NYSE firm as well as handling many individual accounts can mean that he, like most investment advisors, will be subject to pressures to spend much of his time in activities that do nothing to lead to superior investment performance. In this connection, I have asked Bill to make his services available to all BPL partners—large or small—and he will, but I have also told him he is completely a free agent if he finds particular clients diverting him from his main job; (3) the high probability that even excellent investment management during the next decade will only produce limited advantages over passive management. I will comment on this below.

The final point regarding the negatives listed above is that they are not the sort of drawbacks leading to horrible performance, but more likely the sort of things that lead to average performance. I think this is the main risk you run with Bill—and average performance is just not that terrible a risk.

In recommending Bill, I am engaging in the sort of activity I have tried to avoid in BPL portfolio activities—a decision where there is nothing to gain (personally) and considerable to lose. Some of my friends who are not in the Partnership have suggested that I make no recommendation since, if results were excellent it would do me no good and, if something went wrong, I might well get a portion of the blame. If you and I had just had a normal commercial relationship, such reasoning might be sound. However, the degree of trust partners have extended to me and the cooperation manifested in various ways precludes such a "hands off" policy. Many of you are professional investors or close thereto and need no advice from me on managers—you may well do better yourself. For those partners who are financially inexperienced, I feel it would be totally unfair for me to assume a passive position and deliver you to the most persuasive salesman who happened to contact you early in 1970.

||||||||||||||||||||||||||||||||||||||||||||||||||||||||||||||||||||||||||||||||||||||||||||||||||||||||||||||||||||||||||||||||||

OCTOBER 9, 1969

A decade or so ago I was quite willing to set a target of ten percentage points per annum better than the Dow, with the expectation that the Dow would average about 7%. This meant an expectancy for us of around 17%, with wide variations and no guarantees, of course—but, nevertheless, an expectancy. Tax-free bonds at the time yielded about 3%. While stocks had the disadvantage of irregular performance, overall they seemed much the more desirable option. I also stressed this preference for stocks in teaching classes, participating in panel discussions, etc. . . . .

For the first time in my investment lifetime, I now believe there is little choice for the average investor between professionally managed money in stocks and passive investment in bonds. If correct, this view has important implications. Let me briefly (and in somewhat oversimplified form) set out the situation as I see it:

1. I am talking about the situation for, say, a taxpayer in a 40% Federal Income Tax bracket who also has some State Income Tax to pay. Various changes are being proposed in the tax laws, which may adversely affect net results from presently tax-exempt income, capital gains, and perhaps other types of investment income. More proposals will probably come in the future. Overall, I feel such changes over the years will not negate my relative expectations about after-tax income from presently tax-free bonds versus common stocks, and may well even mildly reinforce them.

2. I am talking about expectations over the next ten years—not the next weeks or months. I find it much easier to think about what should develop over a relatively long period of time than what is likely in any short period. As Ben Graham said: "In the long run, the market is a weighing machine—in the short run, a voting machine." I have always found it easier to evaluate weights dictated by fundamentals than votes dictated by psychology.

3. Purely passive investment in tax-free bonds will now bring about 6.5%. This yield can be achieved with excellent quality and locked up for just about any period for which the investor wishes to contract. Such conditions may not exist in March when Bill and I will be available to assist you in bond purchases, but they exist today.

4. The ten year expectation for corporate stocks as a group is probably not better than 9% overall, say 3% dividends and 6% gain in value. I would doubt that Gross National Product grows more than 6% per annum—I don't believe corporate profits are likely to grow significantly as a percentage of GNP—and if earnings multipliers don't change (and with these assumptions and present interest rates they shouldn't) the aggregate valuation of American corporate enterprise should not grow at a long-term compounded rate above 6% per annum. This typical experience in stocks might produce (for the taxpayer described earlier) 1.25% after tax from dividends and 4.75% after tax from capital gain, for a total after-tax return of about 6.5%. The pre-tax mix between dividends and capital gains might be more like 4% and 5%, giving a slightly lower after tax result. This is not far from historical experience and overall, I believe future tax rules on capital gains are likely to be stiffer than in the past.

5. Finally, probably half the money invested in stocks over the next decade will be professionally managed. Thus, by definition, virtually the total investor experience with professionally managed money will be average results (or 6.5% after tax if my assumptions above are correct).

My judgment would be that less than 10% of professionally managed money (which might imply an average of $40 billion just for this superior segment) handled consistently for the decade would average 2 points per annum over group expectancy. So-called "aggressively run" money is unlikely to do significantly better than the general run of professionally managed money. There is probably $50 billion in various gradations of this "aggressive" category now—maybe 100 times that of a decade ago—and $50 billion just can't "perform."

If you are extremely fortunate and select advisors who achieve results in the top 1% to 2% of the country (but who will be working with material sums of money because they are that good), I think it is unlikely you will do much more than 4 points per annum better than the group expectancy. I think the odds are good that Bill Ruane is in this select category. My estimate, therefore, is that over the next decade the results of really excellent management for our "typical taxpayer" after tax might be 1.75% from dividends and 7.75% from capital gain, or 9.5% overall.

6. The rather startling conclusion is that under today's historically unusual conditions, passive investment in tax-free bonds is likely to be fully the equivalent of expectations from professionally managed money in stocks, and only modestly inferior to extremely well-managed equity money.

7. A word about inflation—it has very little to do with the above calculation except that it enters into the 6% assumed growth rate in GNP and contributes to the causes producing 6.5% on tax-free bonds. If stocks should produce 8% after tax and bonds 4%, stocks are better to own than bonds, regardless of whether prices go up, down or sidewise. The converse is true if bonds produce 6.5% after tax, and stocks 6%. The simple truth, of course, is that the best expectable after-tax rate of return makes the most sense—given a rising, declining or stable dollar.

All of the above should be viewed with all the suspicion properly accorded to assessments of the future. It does seem to me to be the most realistic evaluation of what is always an uncertain future—I present it with no great feeling regarding its approximate accuracy, but only so you will know what I think at this time.

You will have to make your own decision as between bonds and stocks and, if the latter, who advises you on such stocks. In many cases, I think the decision should largely reflect your tangible and intangible (temperamental) needs for regularity of income and absence of large principal fluctuation, perhaps balanced against psychic needs for some excitement and the fun associated with contemplating and perhaps enjoying really juicy results. If you would like to talk over the problem with me, I will be very happy to help.

||||||||||||||||||||||||||||||||||||||||||||||||||||||||||||||||||||||||||||||||||||||||||||||||||||||||||||||||||||||||||||||||||||||||||||

DECEMBER 5, 1969

We have various annual reports, audits, interim reports, proxy materials prospectuses, etc. . . . applicable to our control holdings and we will be glad to supply you with any item you request. I also solicit your written questions and will send to all partners the questions and answers shortly before yearend. Don't hesitate to ask any question at all that comes to mind—if it isn't clear to you, it probably isn't clear to others—and there is no reason for any of you to be wondering about something that I might clear up.

||||||||||||||||||||||||||||||||||||||||||||||||||||||||||||||||||||||||||||||||||||||||||||||||||||||||||||||||||||||||||||||||||||||||||||||||

DECEMBER 5, 1969

My personal opinion is that the intrinsic value of DRC and B-H will grow substantially over the years. While no one knows the future, I would be disappointed if such growth wasn't at a rate of approximately 10% per annum.

Market prices for stocks fluctuate at great amplitudes around intrinsic value but, over the long term, intrinsic value is virtually always reflected at some point in market price. Thus, I think both securities should be very decent long-term holdings and I am happy to have a substantial portion of my net worth invested in them. You should be unconcerned about short-term price action when you own the securities directly, just as you were unconcerned when you owned them indirectly through BPL. I think about them as businesses, not "stocks," and if the business does all right over the long term, so will the stock.

I want to stress that I will not be in a managerial or part-nership status with you regarding your future holdings of such securities. You will be free to do what you wish with your stock in the future and so, of course, will I. I think that there is a very high probability that I will maintain my investment in DRC and B-H for a very long period, but I want no implied moral com-mitment to do so nor do I wish to advise others over an indefi-nite future period regarding their holdings. The companies, of course, will keep all shareholders advised of their activities and you will receive reports as issued by them, probably on a semi-annual basis. Should I continue to hold the securities, as I fully expect to do, my degree of involvement in their activities may vary depending upon my other interests. The odds are that I will take an important position on matters of policy, but I want no moral obligation to be other than a passive shareholder, should my interests develop elsewhere.

|||||||||||||||||||||||||||||||||||||||||||||||||||||||||||||||||||||||||||||||||||||||||||||||||||||||||||||||||||||||||||||||

DECEMBER 5, 1969

If you wish Bill and me to give you our ideas regarding bonds in March, you should purchase U.S. Treasury Bills maturing in late March with the applicable portion of the January 5th distribution. Then advise us in the last week of February of the amount you wish to invest in bonds and we will let you know our thoughts.

About the middle of January (as soon as the exact amounts are figured and shares are received from the Transfer Agent after having been registered in your name) we will distribute the DRC and B-H stock applicable to your partnership interest and subsequently advise you of your tax basis and acquisition date attributable to the stock. Such shares will be "legended" as described in the enclosed letter from Monen, Seidler & Ryan. These stock certificates are valuable and should be kept in a safe place.

|||||||||||||||||||||||||||||||||||||||||||||||||||||||||||||||||||||||||||||||||||||||||||||||||||||||||||||||||||||||||||||||

DECEMBER 5, 1969

In past letters I had expressed the hope that BPL could supply a mechanism whereby you could, if you wished, automatically convert your DRC and B-H to cash. I have had two law firms consider extensively the status of these shares in your hands following the liquidation and the accompanying letters (which should be saved and kept with the shares) give their conclusions. As you can see, it is not an area that produces simple, clear-cut guidelines. I see no prudent way to implement the alternatives I had previously been considering. Therefore, you must follow the guidelines they set forth if you wish to dispose of your shares. As you probably realize, the restrictions on subsequent sale apply more severely to Susie and me (because of my continued "insider" position) than they probably do to you. Substantial quantities of securities often are sold via the "private sale" option described in paragraph (3) of the opinion. If the rules become clearer or more simplified in the future, I will be sure to let you know.

At the time of distribution of DRC and B-H, I will advise you of the values applied to such shares at 1969 yearend. You will receive our audit and tax letter about the end of January. It presently appears that sale of our Blue Chip shares and a substantial increase in value of DRC and B-H will bring our overall gain for the year to slightly over 6%.

|||||||||||||||||||||||||||||||||||||||||||||||||||||||||||||||||||||||||||||||||||||||||||||||||||||||||||||||||||||||||||||||||||||

DECEMBER 26, 1969

Various questions have been asked pursuant to the last letter. . . .

If we are not getting a good return on the textile business of Berkshire Hathaway Inc., why do we continue to operate it?

Pretty much for the reasons outlined in my letter. I don't want to liquidate a business employing 1,100 people when the Management has worked hard to improve their relative industry position, with reasonable results, and as long as the business does not require substantial additional capital investment. I have no desire to trade severe human dislocations for a few percentage points additional return per annum. Obviously, if we faced material compulsory additional investment or sustained operating losses, the decision might have to be different, but I don't anticipate such alternatives.

|||||||||||||||||||||||||||||||||||||||||||||||||||||||||||||||||||||||||||||||||||||||||||||||||||||||||||||||||||||||||||||||||||||

DECEMBER 26, 1969

Why did you not register our Berkshire Hathaway and Diversified Retailing shares so that the stock, when received by the partners, would be freely marketable?

We considered this possibility but rejected it for both practical and legal considerations. I will just discuss the practicalities, since they would independently dictate the decision we made.

There is presently no existing market for Diversified Retailing, and our holdings of Berkshire Hathaway are probably four or five times the present floating supply of this stock. An attempt to quickly buy or sell a few thousand shares can easily move BH stock several points or more. We own 691,441 shares. Were we to distribute these stocks to you via a registration without an underwriting, and with the possibility that a substantial portion would be offered for sale by many sellers operating individually but virtually simultaneously, there is a real likelihood, particularly in a stock market environment such as we have seen recently, that the market for these two stocks would be little short of chaotic. It has not seemed to me that this was the kind of situation with which I should leave you, both from the standpoint of the price level which might prevail, as well as for the reason that different partners might well have to liquidate at widely varying price levels. The more sophisticated partners might have an important edge on the less sophisticated ones, and I believe many partners might have no chance to realize the prices I anticipate using for yearend valuation. This would rightly seem most unfair to you, since I would have received some allocation of 1969 BPL profits based upon these yearend valuations. If the markets were to become distressed, I would probably come in for criticism, whether I personally bought at lower prices or, perhaps more so, if I refrained from buying.

Were we to attempt to sponsor an underwriting in connection with a registration for those partners who might wish to sell, there would be, in my opinion, the likelihood that the result would still be far less than satisfactory. We have just been around this track with our holdings of Blue Chip Stamps, where we watched the price of our stock go from 24 to 16.5 after announcement of the underwriting, of which we originally were to be a part. I did not want this sort of result for the partners with respect to their holdings of Berkshire and Diversified.

It is my belief that, by confining sales to private placements, those partners who wish to sell will realize more for their stock (with the sophisticated partners having no marketing edge on the less knowledgeable) than would be achieved, through an underwriting at this time. Also, the stock should be more likely to find its way into the hands of long-term investment-minded holders, which should mean less volatile markets in the future. We have had several phone calls from persons indicating that they wish to make private sales—we anticipate there will be no difficulty in effectuating such sales at prices related to our yearend valuations.

||||||||||||||||||||||||||||||||||||||||||||||||||||||||||||||||||||||||||||||||||||||||||||||||||||||||||||||||||||||||||||||||||||||||

DECEMBER 26, 1969

"Should I hold my BH or DRC stock?"

I can't give you the answer on this one. All I can say is that I'm going to do so and I plan to buy more. I am very happy to have a material portion of my net worth invested in these companies on a long term basis. Obviously, I think they will be worth significantly more money five or ten years hence. Compared to most stocks, I think there is a low risk of loss. I hope their price patterns follow a rather moderate range related to business results rather than behaving in a volatile manner related to speculative enthusiasm or depression.

Obviously, I cannot control the latter phenomena, but there is no intent to "promote" the stocks a la much of the distasteful general financial market activity of recent years.

||||||||||||||||||||||||||||||||||||||||||||||||||||||||||||||||||||||||||||||||||||||||||||||||||||||||||||||||||||||||||||||||||||||||

FEBRUARY 18, 1970

My activity has not been burdened by second-guessing, discussing non sequiturs, or hand holding. You have let me play the game without telling me what club to use, how to grip it, or how much better the other players were doing. I've appreciated this, and the results you have achieved have significantly reflected your attitudes and behavior. If you don't feel this is the case, you underestimate the importance of personal encouragement and empathy in maximizing human effort and achievement.

Compounded Wisdom

The manner in which Buffett went about winding up the Partnership provides three valuable lessons. First and foremost, the integrity and the genuine care for his partners shines through. From finding a suitable equity manager, to buying bonds for those wishing to follow his advice on munis, to the near-explicit recommendation that partners hold on to their stakes in Berkshire and DRC despite his own desire to own more, he put partners first. How much better off would our whole financial services profession be if everyone acted this way.

Second, from a practical perspective, we see how he thought about picking managers, and we receive a clinic on the inner workings of the muni bond market.

Third, he advises us to think of our securities portfolio as a collection of instruments selected for their combined ability to produce the highest possible rate of tax-free compounding with the minimum amount of risk possible. Nothing illustrates this better than the comparison of what was on offer at the time from stocks in comparison to munis. When it comes to risk and reward, convention and conservatism are once again shown to be independent.

TOWARD A HIGHER FORM

||||||||||||||||||||||||||||||||||||||||||||||||||||||||||||||||||||||||||||||

"Ben would say that what I do now makes sense, but he would say that it's much harder for most people to do."[1]

—JUNE 25, 2011

The end of the Partnership was just the end of the beginning for Buffett. In 1970 he took on the title of Berkshire's chairman and CEO. By transitioning from a partnership to a corporation, he was evolving to a higher form. In it, he had gained a controlling interest in an entity with permanent capital and the ability to move that capital tax-free from one operating company to another. The Partnership mentality, however, hasn't changed a bit. If anything, it's gotten stronger.

A Corporate Partnership

As Buffett sees it, shareholders, just like BPL partners, commingle their capital with his and together they own the assets of the corporation, just as they had owned the assets in the

Partnership. Berkshire's Owners' Manual, the corporate equivalent
to the Partnership's Ground Rules, says it all rather explicitly:

> *Although our form is corporate, our attitude is partnership.*
> *Charlie Munger and I think of our shareholders as owner-*
> *partners, and of ourselves as managing partners. (Because of*
> *the size of our shareholdings we are also, for better or worse,*
> *controlling partners.) We do not view the company itself as*
> *the ultimate owner of our business assets but instead view the*
> *company as a conduit through which our shareholders own*
> *the assets.*

Not only did Buffett maintain a partnership mentality; he drew
even closer into financial alignment with fellow owners because
there is no performance fee. At BPL, he took a 25% override on all
profits beyond the first 6% for his services as the capital allocator.
Since taking the role of chairman of Berkshire, he collects a modest
salary but doesn't take a performance fee or otherwise benefit in
any way that is disproportionate to his interest as a shareholder.

Snapshots Versus Movie Reels

Bill Ruane reportedly once said that when it comes to investing,
Graham wrote the Bible and Buffett wrote the New Testament.[2]
That sums it up beautifully. It's as if Buffett began as the ultimate
Old Testament scholar and then forged his own distinct path. He has
been constantly evolving, supplementing and building upon the base
of "first principles" laid down by Graham. A good deal of this evolution occurred throughout the Partnership years, where we have seen
a willingness to concentrate his investments to greater and greater
degrees, a steady migration toward quality compounders from statistically cheap cigar butts, and the forging of his highly unique ability to break down the distinction between assets and capital in a way
that allows for their fungibility in the pursuit of higher returns.

He starts with an early focus on statistical snapshots of corporate balance sheets where he would find the very cheapest of the small and micro-cap net-nets and cigar butts available. Then, in his earliest deviation from his mentor's method, he pursued an extreme level of portfolio concentration. While Graham liked to be well diversified and never took big bets, when Buffett saw a sure thing like Sanborn Map, he loaded up to one-third of his capital into a single idea.

Buffett goes on to gain an increasing appreciation for the qualitative measures of value. Graham's methods had allowed him to see the cheapness of a company's stock in a way that was like taking a photograph—it produced a statistical snapshot of a company at a signal moment in time. The qualitative method that Buffett slowly came around to was more like taking a video.[3] He began to look beyond today's value and increasingly began to appreciate where that value was headed. The high-quality companies like the Walt Disney Company or American Express gain in intrinsic value over time because they are advantaged in some way. The quantitative cigar-butt ideas of Graham are more of a "sure thing" but typically offer a single free puff. Buffett came to increasingly appreciate the high-quality businesses that compound their value over time. Buffett gives Charlie Munger, his "West Coast Philosopher," the credit for slowly tugging him away from the cigar butts and the exhausting hunts for their free puffs.

Twenty years after the Partnership ended, the door to "just cheap" was closed permanently when he summarized his evolved view by saying, "It's better to buy a wonderful business at a fair price than a fair company at a wonderful price. Charlie understood this early; I was a slow learner. But now, when buying companies or common stocks, we look for first-class businesses accompanied by first-class managements."[4] The crossover from searching for Graham-style free puffs to paying a fair price for a very long smoke would come to define a significant portion of Buffett's contributions to his evolved approach.

While this was clearly different from what Graham had been doing, it was not incongruent. As Buffett said,

Ben felt that what I do now makes sense for my situation. It still has its founding in Graham, but it does have more of a qualitative dimension to it because, for one thing, we manage such large sums of money that you can't go around and find these relatively small price-value discrepancies anymore. Instead, we have to place larger bets, and that involves looking at more criteria, not all of them quantitative. But, Ben would say that what I do now makes sense, but he would say that it's much harder for most people to do.[5]

The shift from quantitative to qualitative was evolutionary, not revolutionary. Nothing from Graham or early Buffett has been nullified; it was simply added upon.

Seeing the Field

Graham always said that investing is done best when it's most businesslike and business is done best when it's most investment-like. Buffett not only exemplifies this idea, but he also furthers it by tearing down the distinction between the two terms. He sees equities as simply the conduit through which shareholders literally own their portion of the assets held within a corporation. The assets themselves can be bought or sold and are therefore fungible. Assets are simply a form of capital in a given state—it's the corporation's and the investor's responsibility alike to maintain the state of their capital in the highest and most productive form possible.

Buffett converted corporate assets of poor quality into capital, which in turn was converted back into assets that were more productive. At Dempster, this meant converting unproductive inventory into highly productive securities. At Berkshire, this meant converting low-returning assets tied up in textiles and redeploying them into highly productive insurance and banking assets.

Bedrock Principles Taken
to Higher Levels

The arc of the evolution of Warren Buffett's investment process continues to break new ground. His sterling reputation coupled with his investing acumen has opened up an exclusive field of investment for Berkshire over the decades. Recently, he has received unique access to securities like the high-coupon preferred shares of Bank of America, Goldman Sachs, and General Electric during the financial crisis. He not only has had a hand in designing them, but also they are made available for Berkshire alone to purchase.

Perhaps the most remarkable thing of all is the internal consistency throughout all of his letters, despite the evolution in his methods. No ideas are later nullified or in need of revision. There is really nothing about a 1957 letter, for example, that has become intellectually inconsistent with any other letter since. Instead, ideas are supplemented, nurtured, or simply left intact. With deeper insights and different circumstances (more money, fewer potential investments), the old ideas don't get replaced; they just get less useful to *him*. Meaning, of course, they can still be useful to *us*.

Buffett leaves us a road map that is invaluable for students and investors alike. It's as if he's laid down a challenge to all of us. It's as if he has written the letters, made them public, and said, "Here's how to invest, here's how I did it; this is the road I took. Now, let's see if you can follow me down the path."

ACKNOWLEDGMENTS

||||||||||||||||||||||||||||||||||||||||||||||||||||||||||||||||||||||||||||||

My entire family has been a bedrock of support and encouragement.

Eunice, my wonderful wife, you have made an otherwise impossible task possible—you gave me the gift of taking on literally everything in our household—while working full-time—so I could duck into the back and work. Olivia and David, my two beautiful young children, you gave up time with your daddy on countless nights and weekends and I'm especially grateful to you, too. This book is as much yours as it is mine.

It's hard to describe the deep sense of responsibility that hit me the day my intellectual hero and favorite teacher actually said yes to my idea for publishing his Partnership Letters. I've felt honored and terrified at the same time, pretty much continuously ever since. There is little that would make me happier than to learn Mr. Buffett remains pleased with his decision to entrust to me an important task involving his legacy.

For that reason, I viewed my role more as a steward or project manager and welcomed as much input as I could get. I was fortunately able to surround myself with some truly exceptional people who have improved the outcome of this book in very meaningful ways. Steve Troha convinced me to include the essays in between the excerpts. Bruce Wexler considerably sharpened my writing and kept the project focused. Hollis Heimbouch inspired me to stay on track and write the book she knew we were both going for.

There were of course many other important friends and colleagues who helped me materially along the way. I'd like to especially thank Zach Haberman and Marc Lovci for their early introductions into the literary world, where I was an outsider; my "Dr. Gonzo Team" of Dylan and Tanaya Mattes for their hours of careful reading of contracts and letters; Shirish Apte, Chris Blake, Omar Kara, Tom Kolefas, Tom McManus, and Daniel Roberts for their friendship and professional mentorship; Brian Konigsberg for his careful reading of the early manuscript; Eric Wellmann for enthusiastically welcoming me into his annual meeting traditions; and all my colleagues at Vertical Research Partners for their support and encouragement.

APPENDIX A:
THE RESULTS OF BUFFETT'S PARTNERSHIPS

YEAR	OVERALL RESULTS FROM DOW (1)	PARTNERSHIP RESULTS (2)	LIMITED PARTNERS' RESULTS (3)
1957	–8.4%	10.4%	9.3%
1958	38.5%	40.9%	32.2%
1959	20.0%	25.9%	20.9%
1960	–6.2%	22.8%	18.6%
1961	22.4%	45.9%	35.9%
1962	–7.6%	13.9%	11.9%
1963	20.6%	38.7%	30.5%
1964	18.7%	27.8%	22.3%
1965	14.2%	47.2%	36.9%
1966	–15.6%	20.4%	16.8%
1967	19.0%	35.9%	28.4%
1968	7.7%	58.8%	45.6%
1969	–11.6%	6.8%	6.6%

YEAR	OVERALL RESULTS FROM DOW	PARTNERSHIP RESULTS	LIMITED PARTNERS' RESULTS
1957	-8.4%	10.4%	9.3%
1957–1958	26.9%	55.6%	44.5%
1957–1959	52.3%	95.9%	74.7%
1957–1960	42.9%	140.6%	107.2%
1957–1961	74.9%	251.0%	181.6%
1957–1962	61.6%	299.8%	215.1%
1957–1963	95.1%	454.5%	311.2%
1957–1964	131.3%	608.7%	402.9%
1957–1965	164.1%	943.2%	588.5%
1957–1966	122.9%	1156.0%	704.2%
1957–1967	165.3%	1606.9%	932.6%
1957–1968	185.7%	2610.6%	1403.5%
1957–1969	152.6%	2794.9%	1502.7%
ANNUAL COMPOUNDED RATE	**7.4%**	**29.5%**	**23.8%**

(1) Based on yearly changes in the value of the Dow plus dividends that would have been received through ownership of the Dow during that year. The table includes all complete years of Partnership activity.

(2) For 1957–61 consists of combined results of all predecessor limited partnerships operating throughout the entire year after all expenses, but before distributions to partners or allocations to the general partner.

(3) For 1957–61 computed on the basis of the preceding column of Partnership results allowing for allocation to the general partner based upon the present Partnership Agreement, but before monthly withdrawals by limited partners.

Source: The Super Investors of Graham & Doddsville, Partnership Letters

APPENDIX B:
THE RESULTS OF BUFFETT'S PARTNERSHIPS VERSUS LEADING TRUST AND MUTUAL FUNDS

YEAR	MASS INV. TRUST (1)	INVESTORS STOCK (1)	LEHMAN (2)	TRI-CONT (2)	DOW	LIMITED PARTNERS
1957	-11.40%	-12.40%	-11.40%	-2.40%	-8.40%	9.30%
1958	42.70%	47.50%	40.80%	33.20%	38.50%	32.20%
1959	9.00%	10.30%	8.10%	8.40%	20.00%	20.90%
1960	-1.00%	-0.60%	2.50%	2.80%	-6.20%	18.60%
1961	25.60%	24.90%	23.60%	22.50%	22.40%	35.90%
1962	-9.80%	-13.40%	-14.40%	-10.00%	-7.60%	11.90%
1963	20.00%	16.50%	23.70%	18.30%	20.60%	30.50%
1964	15.90%	14.30%	13.60%	12.60%	18.70%	22.30%
1965	10.20%	9.80%	19.00%	10.70%	14.20%	36.90%
1966	-7.70%	-10.00%	-2.60%	-6.90%	-15.60%	16.80%
1967	20.00%	22.80%	28.00%	25.40%	19.00%	28.40%
1968	10.30%	8.10%	6.70%	6.80%	7.70%	45.60%

CUMULATIVE RESULTS

	189.30%	167.70%	225.60%	200.20%	185.70%	1403.50%

ANNUAL COMPOUNDED RATE

	9.30%	8.60%	10.30%	9.60%	9.10%	25.30%

Source: Partnership Letters

APPENDIX C:
SEQUOIA FUND PERFORMANCE

||||||||||||||||||||||||||||||||||||||||||||||||||||||||||||||||||||||||||||

Sequoia Funds First Decade Versus the S&P 500

	ANNUAL RESULTS				CUMULATIVE RESULTS (CAGR)		
	S&P 500	**SEQUIX**	**DIFF**			**S&P 500**	**SEQUIX**
1970	20.6%	12.1%	-8.5%	1970		20.6%	12.1%
1971	14.3%	13.6%	-0.7%	1970–71		37.8%	27.4%
1972	19.0%	3.6%	-15.4%	1970–72		64.0%	32.0%
1973	-14.7%	-24.8%	-10.1%	1970–73		39.9%	-0.7%
1974	-26.5%	-15.5%	11.0%	1970–74		2.8%	-16.1%
1975	37.3%	61.8%	24.5%	1970–75		41.1%	35.8%
1976	24.0%	72.4%	48.4%	1970–76		74.9%	134.0%
1977	-7.2%	19.9%	27.1%	1970–77		62.3%	180.6%
1978	6.5%	23.9%	17.4%	1970–78		72.9%	247.7%
1979	18.6%	12.1%	-6.6%	1970–79		105.1%	289.6%

		COMPOUNDED	**8.8%**	**17.4%**

Source: Sequoia Funds, Bloomberg

APPENDIX D: DEMPSTER MILL

Dempster Mill

		1961		1962		1963	
Assets	Valued @	Book Figure	Adjusted	Book Figure	Adjusted	Book Figure	Adjusted
Cash	100%	166	166	60	60	144	144
Marketable Securities	Market			758	834	1,772	2029
Accounts Receivable	85%	1,040	884	796	677	1,262	1073
Inventory	60%	4,203	2522	1,634	980	977	586
Cash Value of Life Insurance	100%	45	45	41	41	-	0
Ppd. Exp. Ect.	25%	82	21	14	4	12	3
Recoverable Income Tax	100%			170	170	-	0
Total Current Assets		5,536	3,637	3,473	2,766	4,167	3,835
Misc Investment	66%			5	5	62	62
Net PP&E	100% Est. Auction	1383	800	945	700	872	650
Total Assets		6,919	4,437	4,423	3,471	5,101	4,547
Liabilities & Shareholder's Equity							
Notes Payable		1,230	1,230	-	-	125	125
Other Liabilities		1,088	1,088	346	346	394	394
Total Liabilities		2,318	2,318	346	346	519	519
Shareholders' Equity		4,601	2,119	4,077	3,125	4,582	4,028
Total Liabilities & Shareholders' Equity		6,919	4,437	4,423	3,471	5,101	4,547
Share's Outstanding		60	60	62	62	62	62
Book Value Per Share		$76.50		$65.60		$73.73	
Adjusted Value Per Share			$35.24		$51.24		$64.81

Source: Partnership Letters, Dempster's Annual Reports

APPENDIX E:
BUFFETT'S LAST LETTER:
THE MECHANICS OF TAX-FREE
MUNICIPAL BONDS

||||||||||||||||||||||||||||||||||||||||||||||||||||||||||||||||||||||||||||||

February 25, 1970

To My Partners:

    This letter will attempt to provide a very elementary education regarding tax-exempt bonds with emphasis on the types and maturities of bonds which we expect to help partners in purchasing next month. If you expect to use our help in the purchase of bonds, it is important that you carefully read (and, if necessary, reread) this letter as it will serve as background for the specific purchases I suggest. If you disagree with me as to conclusions regarding types of bonds or maturities (and you would have been right and I would have been wrong if you had disagreed with me on the latter point either one or two years ago), you may well be correct, but we cannot be of assistance to you in the purchase of bonds outside our area. We will simply have our hands full concentrating in our recommended area, so will be unavailable to assist or advise in the purchase of convertible bonds, corporate bonds or short term issues.

    I have tried to boil this letter down as much as possible. Some of it will be a little weighty—some a little over-simplified. I apologize for the shortcomings in advance. I have a feeling I am trying to put all the meat of a 100 page book in 10 pages— and have it read like the funny papers.

II

I am sure you understand that our aid in the purchase of bonds will involve no future assistance regarding either these specific bonds or general investment decisions. I want to be available at this time to be of help because of the unusual amount of cash you have received in one distribution from us. I have no desire to be in the investment counseling business, directly or indirectly, and will not be available for discussion of financial matters after March 31st.

IIIIIIIIIIIIIIIIIIIIIIIIIIIIIIIIIIIIIIIIIIIIIIIIIIIIIIIIIIIIIIIIIIIIIIIIIIIIIIIIIIIIIIIIIIIIIIIIIIIIIIIIIIIIIIIIIIIIIIIIIIIIIIIIIIIIII

The Mechanics of Tax-Free Bonds

For those who wish our help, we will arrange the purchase of bonds directly from municipal bond dealers throughout the country and have them confirm sale of the bonds directly to you. The confirmation should be saved as a basic document for tax purposes. You should not send a check to the bond dealer since he will deliver the bonds to your bank, along with a draft which the bank will pay by charging your account with them. In the case of bonds purchased in the secondary market (issues already outstanding), this settlement date will usually be about a week after confirmation date whereas, on new issues, the settlement date may be as much as a month later. The settlement date is shown plainly on the confirmation ticket (in the case of new issues this will be the second and final ticket rather than the preliminary "when issued" ticket), and you should have the funds at your bank ready to pay for the bonds on the settlement date. If you presently own Treasury Bills, they can be sold on a couple of days notice by your bank upon your instructions, so you should experience no problems in having the money available on time. Interest begins to accrue to you on the settlement date, even if the bond dealer is late in getting them delivered to your bank.

Bonds will be delivered in negotiable form (so-called "bearer" form which makes them like currency) with coupons attached. Usually the bonds are in $5,000 denominations and frequently they can be exchanged for registered bonds (sometimes at considerable expense and sometimes free—it depends upon the terms). Bonds in registered form are nonnegotiable without assignment by you, since you are the registered owner on the Transfer Agent's books. Bonds trade almost exclusively on a bearer basis and it is virtually impossible to sell registered bonds without converting them back into bearer form. Thus, unless you are going to own great physical quantities of bonds, I recommend keeping bonds in bearer form. This means keeping them in a very safe place and clipping the coupons every six months. Such coupons, when clipped, can be deposited in your bank account just like checks. If you have $250,000 in bonds, this probably means about fifty separate pieces of paper ($5,000 denominations) and perhaps six or eight trips a year to the safe deposit section to cut and deposit coupons.

It is also possible to open a custody account with a bank where, for a fairly nominal cost, they will keep the bonds, collect the interest and preserve your records for you. For example, a bank will probably perform the custodial service for you for about $200 a year on a $250,000 portfolio. If you are interested in a custodial account, you should talk to a Trust Officer at your commercial bank as to the nature of their services and cost. Otherwise, you should have a safe deposit box.

Taxation

The interest received upon the deposit of coupons from tax-free bonds is, of course, free from Federal Income Taxes. This means if you are at a 30% top Federal Income Tax bracket, a 6% return from tax-free bonds is equivalent to about 8.5% from taxable bonds. Thus, for most of our partners, excluding minors or some retired people, tax-free bonds will be more attractive than taxable bonds. For people with little or no income from wages or dividends, but with substantial capital, it is possible that a combination of taxable bonds (to bring taxable income up to about the 25% or 30% bracket) plus tax-free bonds will bring the highest total after-tax income. Where appropriate, we will work with you to achieve such a balance.

The situation in respect to State Income Taxes is more complicated. In Nebraska, where the State Income Tax is computed as a percentage of the Federal Income Tax, the effect is that there is no state tax on interest from tax-free bonds. My understanding of both the New York and California law is that tax-free bonds of entities within the home state are not subject to State Income Tax, but tax-free bonds from other states are subject to the local State Income Tax. I also believe that the New York City Income Tax exempts tax-free bonds of entities based within the State of New York, but taxes those from other states. I am no expert on state income taxes and make no attempt to post myself on changes taking place within the various states or cities. Therefore, I defer to your local tax advisor, but simply mention these few general impressions so that you will be alert to the existence of a potential problem. In Nebraska there is no need to have any local considerations enter into the after-tax calculation. Where out-of-state issues are subject to local taxation, the effective cost of your State or Municipal Income Tax is reduced by the benefit received from deducting it on your Federal Income Tax return. This, of course, varies with the individual. Additionally, in some states there are various taxes on intangible property which may apply to all tax-free bonds or just those of out-of-state entities. There are none of these in Nebraska, but I cannot advise on the other states.

When bonds are bought at a discount from par and later are sold or mature (come due and get paid), the difference between the proceeds and cost is subject to capital gain or loss treatment. (There are minor exceptions to this statement as, unfortunately, there are to most general statements on investments and taxes but they will be pointed out to you should they affect any securities we recommend.) This reduces the net after-tax yield by a factor involving the general rate of future capital gains taxes and the specific future tax position of the individual. Later on, we will discuss the impact of such capital gains taxes in calculating the relative attractiveness of discount bonds versus "full coupon" bonds.

Finally, one most important point. Although the law is not completely clear, you should probably not contemplate owning tax-free bonds if you have, or expect to have, general purpose bank or other indebtedness. The law excludes the deductibility of interest on loans incurred or continued to purchase or carry tax-free bonds, and the interpretation of this statute will probably tend to be broadened as the years pass. For example, my impression is that you have no problem if you have a mortgage against real property (unless the debt was incurred in order to acquire municipal bonds) in deducting the mortgage interest on your Federal Tax return, even though you own tax-free bonds at the same time. However, I believe that if you have a general bank loan, even though the proceeds were directly used to purchase stocks, a handball court, etc. and the tax-free bonds are not used for security for the loan, you are asking for trouble if you deduct the interest and, at the same time, are the owner of tax-free bonds. Therefore, I would pay off bank loans before owning tax-free bonds, but I leave detailed examination of this question to you and your tax advisor. I merely mention it to make you aware of the potential problem.

Marketability

Tax-free bonds are materially different from common stocks or corporate bonds in that there are literally hundreds of thousands of issues, with the great majority having very few holders. This substantially inhibits the development of close, active markets. Whenever the City of New York or Philadelphia wants to raise money it sells perhaps twenty, thirty or forty non-identical securities, since it will offer an issue with that many different maturities. A 6% bond of New York coming due in 1980 is a different animal from a 6% bond of New York coming due in 1981. One cannot be exchanged for the other, and a seller has to find a buyer for the specific item he holds. When you consider that New York may offer bonds several times a year, it is easy to see why just this one city may have somewhere in the neighborhood of 1,000 issues outstanding. Grand Island, Nebraska, may have 75 issues outstanding. The average amount of each issue might be $100,000 and the average number of holders may be six or eight per issue. Thus, it is absolutely impossible to have quoted markets at all times for all issues and spreads between bids and offers may be very wide. You can't set forth in the morning to buy a specific Grand Island issue of your choosing. It may not be offered at any price, anywhere, and if you do find one seller, there is no reason why he has to be realistic compared to other offerings of similar quality. On the other hand, there are single issues such as those of the Ohio Turnpike, Illinois Turnpike, etc. that amount to $200 million or more and have thousands of bondholders owning a single entirely homogeneous and interchangeable issue. Obviously, here you get a high degree of marketability.

My impression is that marketability is generally a function of the following three items, in descending order of importance: (1) the size of the particular issue; (2) the size of the issuer (a $100,000 issue of the State of Ohio will be more marketable than a $100,000 issue of Podunk, Ohio); and (3) the quality of the issuer. By far the most sales effort goes into the selling of new issues of bonds. An average of over $200 million per week of new issues comes up for sale, and the machinery of bond distribution is geared to get them sold, large or small. In my opinion, there is frequently insufficient differential in yield at time of issue for the marketability differences that will exist once the initial sales push is terminated. We have frequently run into markets in bonds where the spread between bid and asked prices may get to 15%. There is no need to buy bonds with the potential for such grotesque markets (although the profit spread to the dealer who originally offers them is frequently wider than on more marketable bonds) and we will not be buying them for you. The bonds we expect to buy will usually tend to have spreads (reflecting the difference between what you would pay net for such bonds on purchase and receive net on sale at the same point in time) of from 2% to 5%. Such a spread would be devastating if you attempted to trade in such bonds, but I don't believe it should be a deterrent for a long-term investor. The real necessity is to stay away from bonds of very limited marketability—which frequently are the type local bond dealers have the greatest monetary incentive to push.

IIIIIIIIIIIIIIIIIIIIIIIIIIIIIIIIIIIIIIIIIIIIIIIIIIIIIIIIIIIIIIIIIIIIIIIIIIIIIIIIIIIIIIIIIIIIIIIIIIIIIIIIIIIIIIIIIIIIIIIIIIIIIIIIIIIIIIIIIIIIIIII

Specific Areas of Purchase

We will probably concentrate our purchases in the following general areas:

1. Large revenue-producing public entities such as toll roads, electric power districts, water districts, etc. Many of these issues possess high marketability, are subject to quantitative analysis, and sometimes have favorable sinking fund or other factors which tend not to receive full valuation in the market place.

2. Industrial Development Authority bonds which arise when a public entity holds title to property leased to a private corporation. For example, Lorain, Ohio holds title to an $80 million project for U.S. Steel Corp. The Development Authority Board issued bonds to pay for the project and has executed a net and absolute lease with U.S. Steel to cover the bond payments. The credit of the city or state is not behind the bonds and they are only as good as the company that is on the lease. Many top-grade corporations stand behind an aggregate of several billion dollars of these obligations, although new ones are being issued only in small amounts ($5 million per project or less) because of changes in the tax laws. For a period of time there was a very substantial prejudice against such issues, causing them to sell at yields considerably higher than those commensurate with their inherent credit standing. This prejudice has tended to diminish, reducing the premium yields available, but I still consider it a most attractive field. Our insurance company owns a majority of its bonds in this category.

3. Public Housing Authority Issues for those of you who wish the very highest grade of tax-free bonds. In effect, these bonds bear the guarantee of the U.S. Government, so they are all rated AAA. In states where local taxes put a premium on buying in-state issues, and I can't fill your needs from (1) and (2), my tendency would be to put you into Housing Authority issues rather than try to select from among credits that I don't understand. If you direct me to buy obligations of your home state, you should expect substantial quantities of Housing Authority issues. There is no need to diversify among such issues, as they all represent the top credit available.

4. State obligations of a direct or indirect nature.

You will notice I am not buying issues of large cities. I don't have the faintest idea how to analyze a New York City, Chicago, Philadelphia, etc. (a friend mentioned the other day when Newark was trying to sell bonds at a very fancy rate that the Mafia was getting very upset because Newark was giving them a bad name). Your analysis of a New York City—and I admit it is hard to imagine them

not paying their bills for any extended period of time—
would be as good as mine. My approach to bonds is pretty
much like my approach to stocks. If I can't understand
something, I tend to forget it. Passing an opportunity which
I don't understand—even if someone else is perceptive
enough to analyze it and get paid well for doing it—doesn't
bother me. All I want to be sure of is that I get paid well for
the things I do feel capable of handling—and that I am right
when I make affirmative decisions.

We will probably tend to purchase somewhere between
five and ten issues for most of you. However, if you wish to
limit me to your home state, it may be fewer issues—and
perhaps those will only be Housing Authorities. We will try
not to buy in smaller than $25,000 pieces and will prefer
larger amounts where appropriate. Smaller lots of bonds
are usually penalized upon resale, sometimes substantially.
The bond salesman doesn't usually explain this to you
when you buy the $10,000 of bonds from him, but it gets
explained when you later try to sell the $10,000 to him.
We may make exceptions where we are buying secondary
market issues in smaller pieces—but only if we are getting
an especially good price on the buy side because of the
small size of the offering.

||||||||||||||||||||||||||||||||||||||||||||||||||||||||||||||||||||||||||||||||||||||||||||||||||||||||||||||||||||||||||||||||||||||||||||||||||||||||||||

Callable Bonds

We will not buy bonds where the issuer of the bonds has a right
to call (retire) the bonds on a basis which substantially loads
the contract in his favor. It is amazing to me to see people buy
bonds which are due in forty years, but where the issuer has
the right to call the bonds at a tiny premium in five or ten years.
Such a contract essentially means that you have made a forty
year deal if it is advantageous to the issuer (and disadvantageous to you) and a five year deal if the initial contract turns

out to be advantageous to you (and disadvantageous to the issuer). Such contracts are really outrageous and exist because bond investors can't think through the implications of such a contract form and bond dealers don't insist on better terms for their customers. One extremely interesting fact is that bonds with very unattractive call features sell at virtually the same yield as otherwise identical bonds which are noncallable.

It should be pointed out that most Nebraska bonds carry highly unfair call provisions. Despite this severe contractual disadvantage, they do not offer higher yields than bonds with more equitable terms.

One way to avoid this problem is to buy bonds which are totally noncallable. Another way is to buy discount bonds where the right of the issuer to call the bond is at a price so far above your cost as to render the possible call inconsequential. If you buy a bond at 60 which is callable at 103, the effective cost to you of granting the issuer the right to prematurely terminate the contract (which is a right you never have) is insignificant. But to buy a bond of the Los Angeles Department of Water and Power at 100 to come due at 100 in 1999 or to come due at 104 in 1974, depending on which is to the advantage of the issuer and to your disadvantage, is the height of foolishness when comparable yields are available on similar credits without such an unfair contract. Nevertheless, just such a bond was issued in October, 1969 and similar bonds continue to be issued every day. I only write at such length about an obvious point, since it is apparent from the continual sale of such bonds that many investors haven't the faintest notion how this loads the dice against them and many bond salesmen aren't about to tell them.

||||||||||||||||||||||||||||||||||||||||||||||||||||||||||||||||||||||||||||||||||||||||||||||||||||||||||||||||||||||||||||||||||||||||||||||||||||

Maturity and the Mathematics of Bonds

Many people, in buying bonds, select maturities based on how long they think they are going to want to hold bonds, how long they are going to live, etc. While this is not a silly approach, it is not necessarily the most logical. The primary determinants in selection of maturity should probably be (1) the shape of the yield curve; (2) your expectations regarding future levels of interest rates; and (3) the degree of quotational fluctuation you are willing to endure or hope to possibly profit from. Of course, (2) is the most important but by far the most difficult upon which to comment intelligently.

Let's tackle the yield curve first. When other aspects of quality are identical, there will be a difference in interest rates paid based upon the length of the bond being offered. For example, a top grade bond being offered now might have a yield of 4.75% if it came due in six or nine months, 5.00% in two years, 5.25% in five years, 5.50% in ten years and 6.25% in twenty years. When long rates are substantially higher than short rates, the curve is said to be strongly positive. In the U.S. Government bond market, rates recently have tended to produce a negative yield curve; that is, a long term Government bond over the last year or so has consistently yielded less than a short term one. Sometimes the yield curve has been very flat, and sometimes it is positive out to a given point, such as ten years, and then flattens out. What you should understand is that it varies, often very substantially, and that on an historical basis the present slope tends to be in the high positive range. This doesn't mean that long bonds are going to be worth more but it does mean that you are being paid more to extend maturity than in many periods. If yields remained constant for several years, you would do better with longer bonds than shorter bonds, regardless of how long you intended to hold them.

The second factor in determining maturity selection is expectations regarding future rate levels. Anyone who has done much predicting in this field has tended to look very foolish very fast. I did not regard rates as unattractive one year ago, and I was proved very wrong almost immediately. I believe present rates are not unattractive and I may look foolish again. Nevertheless, a decision has to be made and you can make just as great a mistake if you buy short term securities now and rates available on reinvestment in a few years are much lower.

The final factor involves your tolerance for quotational fluctuation. This involves the mathematics of bond investment and may be a little difficult for you to understand. Nevertheless, it is important that you get a general grasp of the principles. Let's assume for the moment a perfectly flat yield curve and a non-callable bond. Further assume present rates are 5% and that you buy two bonds, one due in two years and one due in twenty years. Now assume one year later that yields on new issues have gone to 3% and that you wish to sell your bonds.

Forgetting about market spreads, commissions, etc., you will receive $1,019.60 for the original two year $1,000 bond (now with one year to run) and $1,288.10 for the nineteen year bond (originally twenty years). At these prices, a purchaser will get exactly 3% on his money after amortizing the premium he has paid and cashing the stream of 5% coupons attached to each bond. It is a matter of indifference to him whether to buy your nineteen year 5% bond at $1,288.10 or a new 3% bond (which we have assumed is the rate current—one year later) at $1,000.00. On the other hand, let's assume rates went to 7%. Again we will ignore commissions, capital gains taxes on the discount, etc. Now the buyer will only pay $981.00 for the bond with one year remaining until maturity and $791.60 for the bond with nineteen years left. Since he can get 7% on new issues, he is only willing to buy your bond at a discount sufficient so that accrual of this discount will give him the same economic benefits from your 5% coupon that a 7% coupon at $1,000.00 would give him.

The principle is simple. The wider the swings in interest rates and the longer the bond, the more the value of a bond can go up or down on an interim basis before maturity. It should be pointed out in the first example where rates went to 3%, our long term bond would only have appreciated to about $1,070.00 if it had been callable in five years at par, although it would have gone down just as much if 7% rates had occurred. This just illustrates the inherent unfairness of call provisions.

For over two decades, interest rates on tax-free bonds have almost continuously gone higher and buyers of long term bonds have continuously suffered. This does not mean it is bad now to buy long term bonds—it simply means that the illustration in the above paragraph has worked in only one direction for a long period of time and people are much more conscious of the downside risks from higher rates than the upside potential from lower ones.

If it is a 50–50 chance as to the future general level of interest rates and the yield curve is substantially positive, then the odds are better in buying long term non-callable bonds than shorter term ones. This reflects my current conclusion and, therefore, I intend to buy bonds within the ten to twenty-five year range. If you have any preferences within that range, we will try to select bonds reflecting such preferences, but if you are interested in shorter term bonds, we will not be able to help you as we are not searching out bonds in this area.

Before you decide to buy a twenty year bond, go back and read the paragraph showing how prices change based upon changes in interest rates. Of course, if you hold the bond straight through, you are going to get the contracted rate of interest, but if you sell earlier, you are going to be subject to the mathematical forces described in that paragraph, for better or for worse. Bond prices also change because of changes in quality over the years but, in the tax-free area, this has tended to be—and probably will continue to be—a relatively minor factor compared to the impact of changes in the general structure of interest rates.

‖‖‖

Discount Versus Full Coupon Bonds

You will have noticed in the above discussion that if you now wanted to buy a 7% return on a nineteen year bond, you had a choice between buying a new nineteen year bond with a 7% coupon rate or buying a bond with a 5% coupon at $791.60, which would pay you $1,000.00 in nineteen years. Either purchase would have yielded exactly 7% compounded semi-annually to you. Mathematically, they are the same. In the case of tax-free bonds the equation is complicated, however, by the fact that the $70.00 coupon is entirely tax-free to you, whereas the bond purchased at a discount gives you tax-free income of $50.00 per year but a capital gain at the end of the nineteenth year of $208.40. Under the present tax law, you would owe anything from a nominal tax, if the gain from realization of the discount was your only taxable income in the nineteenth year, up to a tax of over $70.00 if it came on top of very large amounts of capital gain at that time (the new tax law provides for capital gain rates of 35%, and even slightly higher on an in-direct basis in 1972 and thereafter for those realizing very large gains). In addition to this, you might have some state taxes to pay on the capital gain.

Obviously, under these circumstances you are not going to pay the $791.60 for the 5% coupon and feel you are equally as well off as with the 7% coupon at $1,000.00. Neither is anyone else. Therefore, identical quality securities with identical maturities sell at considerably higher gross yields when they have low coupons and are priced at discounts than if they bear current high coupons.

Interestingly enough, for most taxpayers, such higher gross yields over-compensate for the probable tax to be paid. This is due to several factors. First, no one knows what the tax law will be when the bonds mature and it is both natural and probably correct to assume the tax rate will be stiffer at that time than now. Second, even though a 5% coupon on a $1,000.00 bond purchased at $791.60 due in nineteen years is the equivalent of a 7% coupon on a $1,000.00 bond purchased at par with the same maturity, people prefer to get the higher current return in their pocket. The owner of the 5% coupon bond is only getting around 6.3% current yield on his $791.60 with the balance necessary to get him up to 7% coming from the extra $208.40 he picks up at the end. Finally, the most important factor affecting prices currently on discount bonds (and which will keep affecting them) is that banks have been taken out of the market as buyers of discount tax-free bonds by changes brought about in bank tax treatment through the 1969 Tax Reform Act. Banks have historically been the largest purchasers and owners of tax-free bonds and anything that precludes them from one segment of the market has dramatic effects on the supply-demand situation in that segment. This may tend to give some edge to individuals in the discount tax-free market, particularly those who are not likely to be in a high tax bracket when the bonds mature or are sold.

If I can get a significantly higher effective after-tax yield (allowing for sensible estimates of your particular future tax rate possibilities), I intend to purchase discount bonds for you. I know some partners prefer full coupon bonds, even though their effective yield is less, since they prefer to maximize the current cash yield and if they will so advise me, we will stick to full coupon issues (or very close thereto) in their cases.

▪▪

Procedure

I intend to be in the office solidly through March (including every Saturday except March 7th) and will be glad to see any partner or talk with him by phone. To aid in scheduling, please make an appointment with Gladys (or me).

The only request I make is that you absorb as much as possible of this letter before we talk. As you can see, it would be an enormous problem if I had to explain each item to all of you.

If you decide you want us to help you in buying bonds, you should let us know:

1. Whether you want to restrict purchases to your home state for local tax reasons;

2. Whether you want to restrict us to full coupon issues or let us use our judgment as to where you get the best value;

3. Your preference as to maturity in the ten to twenty-five year range or if you prefer to let us use our judgment in that area;

4. How much you want to invest—we may end up several per cent short of the figure you name, but we will never go over;

5. On what bank the bonds should be drafted.

We will advise you by phone or letter as we buy bonds. Bill and John will be doing much of the mechanical work. Needless to say, none of us will have any financial interest in any transaction. Should you have any questions regarding the mechanics, please direct them to John or Bill as I will probably be swamped and they will be more familiar with specific transactions. After March 31st, I don't expect to be around the office for several months. Therefore, if you want to talk things over, come in by then. The completion of all purchases may go into

April, but Bill will be taking care of this and the mechanics will all be set up.

You should realize that because of the enormous diversity of issues mentioned earlier, it is impossible to say just what will be bought. Sometimes the tax-free bond market has more similarities to real estate than to stocks. There are hundreds of thousands of items of varying comparability, some with no sellers, some with reluctant sellers and some with eager sellers. Which may be the best buy depends on the quality of what is being offered, how well it fits your needs and the eagerness of the seller. The standard of comparison is always new issues where an average of several hundred million dollars worth have to be sold each week—however, specific secondary market opportunities (issues already outstanding) may be more attractive than new issues and we can only find out how attractive they are when we are ready to make bids.

Although markets can change, it looks as if we will have no difficulty in getting in the area of 6.5% after tax (except from Housing Authority issues) on bonds in the twenty-year maturity range.

Cordially,
Warren E. Buffett

NOTES

Disclaimer

1. Lawrence Cunningham, *The Essays of Warren Buffett: Lessons for Corporate America* (Boston: Lawrence A. Cunningham, 2001), 25.

Introduction

1. Anthony Bianco, "Homespun Wisdom from the 'Oracle of Omaha,'" *BusinessWeek*, July 5, 1999.

2. Alice Schroeder, *The Snowball: Warren Buffett and the Business of Life* (New York: Bantam Dell, 2008), 202.

3. Warren Buffett, "Warren Buffett's $50 Billion Decision," *Forbes*, March 26, 2012.

4. Warren Buffett's Partnership Letter, January 18, 1963.

Chapter 1: Orientation

1. Warren Buffett's Partnership Letter, July 12, 1966.

2. Alice Schroeder, *The Snowball: Warren Buffett and the Business of Life* (New York: Bantam Dell, 2008), 126–27.

3. Warren Buffett, "The Superinvestors of Graham-and-Doddsville," *Hermes*, Columbia Business School magazine, 1984.

4. Joe Carlen, *The Einstein of Money: The Life and Timeless Financial Wisdom of Benjamin Graham* (New York: Prometheus Books, 2012), 231.

5. "Warren Buffett's $50 Billion Decision," *Forbes*, March 26, 2012.

6. Warren Buffett's Partnership Letter, July 12, 1966.

7. Ibid.

8. Warren Buffett's Partnership Letter, January 24, 1968.

9. Myles Udland, "Fidelity Reviewed Which Investors Did Best and What They Found Was Hilarious," *Business Insider*, September 4, 2014, http://www.businessinsider.com/forgetful-investors-performed-best-2014-9.

10. Benjamin Graham and David L. Dodd, *Security Analysis: The Classic 1951 Edition* ([New York]: McGraw-Hill, 2005), Chapter 8.

11. In the current edition of *Intelligent Investor*, this is now Chapter 8.

Chapter 2: Compounding

1. Warren Buffett, "Warren Buffett's $50 Billion Decision," *Forbes*, March 26, 2012.

2. While this quote is widely attributed to Einstein, there is some controversy as to whether he actually made this statement.

3. Warren Buffett's Partnership Letter, January 18, 1964.

4. Alice Schroeder, *The Snowball: Warren Buffett and the Business of Life* (New York: Bantam Dell, 2008), 249.

5. Michelle Fox, "Here's How a Janitor Amassed an $8M Fortune," CNBC, February 9, 2015, http://www.cnbc.com/2015/02/09/.

6. Warren Buffett's Partnership Letter, January 18, 1963.

7. Warren Buffett's Partnership Letter, January 18, 1964.

8. Ibid.

9. Warren Buffett's Partnership Letter, October 9, 1969.

10. Warren Buffett's Partnership Letter, January 18, 1965.

11. Sam Ro, "CHART OF THE DAY: The Average Person Is Absolutely Horrible at Investing," *Business Insider*, December 4, 2012, http://www .businessinsider.com/chart-average-investor-returns-2012-12.

12. Warren Buffett's Partnership Letter, January 18, 1965.

13. Warren Buffett's Partnership Letter, July 10, 1963.

Chapter 3: Market Indexing: The Do-Nothing Rationale

1. Warren Buffett's Partnership Letter, January 24, 1962.

2. Warren Buffett's Partnership Letter, July 6, 1962.

3. Warren Buffett's Partnership Letter, January 18, 1964.

4. Warren Buffett, Chairman's Letter to the Shareholders of Berkshire Hathaway Inc., 2013.

5. Warren Buffett's Partnership Letter, July 8, 1964.

6. Warren Buffett's Partnership Letter, January 18, 1965.

Chapter 4: Measuring Up: The Do-Nothings Versus the Do-Somethings

1. Warren Buffett's Partnership Letter, July 9, 1965.

2. Warren Buffett's Partnership Letter, January 24, 1962.

3. Warren Buffett's Partnership Letter, November 1, 1962.

4. Ibid.

5. Warren Buffett, Owner's Manual for the Shareholders of Berkshire Hathaway Inc., 1996.

6. Warren Buffett's Partnership Letter, January 30, 1961.

7. Warren Buffett's Partnership Letter, January 20, 1966.

8. Warren Buffett's Partnership Letter, July 6, 1962.

Chapter 5 : The Partnership: An Elegant Structure

1. Warren Buffett's Partnership Letter, July 2, 1961.

2. Charlie Munger, "Charlie Munger on the Psychology of Human Misjudgment," speech delivered at Harvard University, Cambridge, Mass., June 1995.

3. Ibid.

4. Warren Buffett, "Warren Buffett's $50 Billion Decision," *Forbes*, March 26, 2012.

5. Warren Buffett's Partnership Letter, January 30, 1961.

Chapter 6: The Generals

1. Warren Buffett's Partnership Letter, January 18, 1964.

2. Warren Buffett's Partnership Letter, January 24, 1962.

3. Author's interview with Thomas Graham Kahn and Andrew Kahn, New York City, July 2015.

4. Warren Buffett's Partnership Letter, January 24, 1962.

5. Ibid.

6. Warren Buffett's Partnership Letter, January 25, 1967.

7. Ben Graham, 1945 Letter to Stockholders of Graham-Newman, February 28, 1946.

8. Warren Buffett's Partnership Letter, January 18, 1965.

9. Alon Brav et al., "Hedge Fund Activism, Corporate Governance, and Firm Performance," *Journal of Finance* 63, No. 4 (August 2008).

10. The author gives thanks to the Kahn Brothers for highlighting this idea.

11. Warren Buffett's Partnership Letter, October 9, 1967.

12. Ibid.

13. "A Lesson on Elementary, Worldly Wisdom as It Relates to Investment Management and Business," speech, April 14, 1994.

14. Roger Lowenstein, *Buffett: The Making of an American Capitalist* (New York: Random House, 2008), 92.

15. Tobias Carlisle, *Deep Value: Why Activist Investors and Other Contrarians Battle for Control of Losing Corporations* (Hoboken, NJ: John Wiley & Sons, 2014), 191.

16. Author telephone interview with Tom Gayner, July 24, 2015.

17. Sham Gad, "Permanent Value: The Teachings of Warren Buffett," buffettspeaks (blog), January 28, 2007, http://buffettspeaks.blogspot .com/2007/01/permanent-value-teachings-of-warren.html.

18. Ibid.

Chapter 7: Workouts

1. Warren Buffett, Chairman's Letter to the Shareholders of Berkshire Hathaway Inc., 1988.

2. 1967 Year-end Letter, January 24, 1968.

3. Warren Buffett's Partnership Letter, January 18, 1965.

4. Warren Buffett, Chairman's Letter to the Shareholders of Berkshire Hathaway Inc., 1988.

Chapter 8: Controls

1. Warren Buffett's Partnership Letter, January 20, 1966.

2. Alice Schroeder, *The Snowball: Warren Buffett and the Business of Life* (New York: Bantam Dell, 2008), 223.

3. Ibid.

4. Warren Buffett's Partnership Letter, January 20, 1966.

5. Warren Buffett's Partnership Letter, July 9, 1965.

6. Warren Buffett's Partnership Letter, January 24, 1962.

7. Warren Buffett's Partnership Letter, November 1, 1966.

8. Benjamin Graham and David L. Dodd, *Security Analysis: The Classic 1951 Edition* ([New York]: McGraw-Hill, 2005), 560.

9. Joel Greenblatt's Special Situation Investing Class at Columbia Business School, September 7, 2005.

10. Author's notes from 2015 Annual Meeting.

11. Benjamin Graham & David L. Dodd, *Security Analysis: The Classic 1951 Edition* ([New York]: McGraw-Hill, 2005), 581.

12. Warren Buffet's Partnership Letter, January 24, 1968.

Chapter 9: Dempster Diving: The Asset Conversion Play

1. Warren Buffett's Partnership Letter, January 18, 1964.

2. Warren Buffett's Partnership Letter, January 24, 1962.

3. Alice Schroeder, *The Snowball: Warren Buffett and the Business of Life* (New York: Bantam Dell, 2008), 244.

4. Andrew Kilpatrick, *Of Permanent Value: The Story of Warren Buffett* (Birmingham, AL: AKPE, 2014), 92.

5. Ibid., 91.

6. Alice Schroeder, *The Snowball*, 245.

7. Warren Buffett's Partnership Letter, January 18, 1963.

8. Warren Buffett's Partnership Letter, December 26, 1969.

9. Tobias Carlisle, *Deep Value: Why Activist Investors and Other Contrarians Battle for Control of Losing Corporations* (Hoboken, NJ: John Wiley & Sons, 2014), 189.

10. Ibid.

11. Warren Buffett's Partnership Letter, January 18, 1964.

12. Warren Buffett, "To the Stockholders of Dempster Mill Mfg. Co.," July 20, 1963.

13. Andrew Kilpatrick, *Of Permanent Value*, 92.

Chapter 10: Conservative Versus Conventional

1. Warren Buffet's Partership Letter, January 18, 1955.

2. Howard Marks, "Dare to Be Great II," Memo to Oaktree Clients, April 8, 2014, https://www.oaktreecapital.com/memotree/Dare%20to%20Be%20 Great%20II.pdf.

3. Warren Buffett, Lecture at the University of Florida Business School, October 15, 1998.

4. Stanley Druckenmiller, speech delivered at the Lost Tree Club, North Palm Beach, Fla., January 18, 2015.

Chapter 11: Taxes

1. Warren Buffett's Partnership Letter, January 18, 1965.

2. Warren Buffett's Partnership Letter, July 10, 1963.

3. Warren Buffett's Partnership Letter, January 18, 1965.

4. Warren Buffett's Partnership Letter, July 10, 1963.

5. Warren Buffett's Partnership Letter, January 18, 1965.

6. Ibid.

7. Whitney Tilson, "Notes from 2004 Annual Meeting," http://www
.tilsonfunds.com/brkmtg04notes.doc, accessed June 11, 2015.

8. Warren Buffett's Partnership Letter, January 18, 1965.

Chapter 12: Size Versus Performance

1. Warren Buffett's Partnership Letter, January 18, 1964.

2. Anthony Bianco, "Homespun Wisdom from the 'Oracle of Omaha,'"
BusinessWeek, July 5, 1999.

3. Warren Buffett's Partnership Letter, January 24, 1962.

4. Ibid.

5. Warren Buffett's Partnership Letter, January 20, 1966.

Chapter 13: Go-Go or No-Go

1. Warren Buffett's Partnership Letter, February 20, 1960.

2. John Brooks, *The Go-Go Years: The Drama and Crashing Finale of Wall
Street's Bullish 60s* (New York: Allworth Press, 1998), 135.

3. Ibid.

4. "Fidelity timeline," https://www.fidelity.com/static/dcle/welcome/doc
uments/Timeline_fid_092709fla.swf, accessed June 11, 2015.

5. Warren Buffett's Partnership Letter, December 27, 1956.

6. Warren Buffett's Partnership Letter, July 11, 1968.

7. John Brooks, *The Go-Go Years: The Drama and Crashing Finale of Wall
Street's Bullish 60s* (New York: Allworth Press, 1998), 160.

8. Ibid., 154.

9. Warren Buffett's Partnership Letter, July 11, 1968.

10. Warren Buffett's Partnership Letter, May 29, 1969.

11. John Brooks, *The Go-Go Years: The Drama and Crashing Finale of Wall Street's Bullish 60s* (New York: Allworth Press, 1998), 131.

12. Warren Buffett's Partnership Letter, July 6, 1962.

13. John Brooks, *The Go-Go Years: The Drama and Crashing Finale of Wall Street's Bullish 60s* (New York: Allworth Press, 1998), 136.

14. Ibid., 145.

15. Ibid., 24.

16. Carrie Coolidge, "Jerry Tsai's Smart Timing," *Forbes*, January 10, 2000.

17. Warren Buffett's Partnership Letter, July 11, 1968.

18. Alice Schroeder, *The Snowball: Warren Buffett and the Business of Life* (New York: Bantam Dell, 2008), 327.

19. Warren Buffett's Partnership Letter, January 25, 1967.

Chapter 14: Parting Wisdom

1. Warren Buffett's Partnership Letter, July 8, 1968.

2. Alice Schroeder, *The Snowball: Warren Buffett and the Business of Life* (New York: Bantam Dell, 2008), 334.

3. BRK Annual Meeting 2003 Tilson Notes (Buffett FAQ).

4. BRK Annual Meeting, 1999.

5. Dr. Zen, "William J. Ruane, The Making of a Superinvestor," gurufocus, May 19, 2011, http://www.gurufocus.com/news/133912/william-j-ruane--the-making-of-a-superinvestor.

6. Joe Carlen, *The Einstein of Money: The Life and Timeless Financial Wisdom of Benjamin Graham* (New York: Prometheus Books, 2012), 285.

7. Whitney Tilson, "Notes from 2005 Annual Meeting," http://www.tilsonfunds.com/brkmtg05notes.pdf, accessed June 11, 2015.

8. Steve Forbes, "Steve Forbes Interview: Author Joel Greenblatt," *Forbes*, July 5, 2011, http://www.forbes.com/sites/steveforbes/2011/07/05/joel-greenblatt-interview-transcript/.

Epilogue: Toward a Higher Form

1. Joe Carlen, *The Einstein of Money: The Life and Timeless Financial Wisdom of Benjamin Graham* (New York: Prometheus Books, 2012), 244.

2. Dr. Zen, "William J. Ruane, The Making of a Superinvestor," gurufocus, May 19, 2011, http://www.gurufocus.com/news/133912/william-j-ruane--the-making-of-a-superinvestor.

3. Author telephone interview with Tom Gayner, July 24, 2015.

4. Warren Buffett, Chairman's Letter to the Shareholders of Berkshire Hathaway Inc., 1988.

5. Joe Carlen, *The Einstein of Money*, 244.

INDEX